UNIVERSITY COLLEGE BIRMINGHAM
COLLEGE LIBRARY, SUMMER ROW
BIRMINGHAM. B3 1JB
Tel: (0121) 243 0055

DATE OF RETURN

Please remember to return on time or pay the fine

Tourist Customer Service Satisfaction

Customer satisfaction and loyalty in the tourism sector is highly dependent upon the behaviour of frontline service providers. Service is about people, how they relate to one another, fulfill each other's needs, and ultimately care for each other. Yet, surprisingly, there are few (if any) books that focus on the detailed specifics of the social exchange and interaction between service provider and customer.

Tourist Customer Service Satisfaction fully explores this relationship by defining the specific kinds of verbal and nonverbal messages needed for successful exchanges, outlining how the service provider ought to behave and cope in a situation, as well as detailing positive approaches that enhance service providers' role performance. The book uses encounter theory to examine the customer–provider relationship, as well as drawing on current research and theories from hospitality, tourism, management, and psychology. In doing so, the book offers important insights into how employee-centric competitive advantage in this sector can be achieved in various markets.

This book is unique in its approach in focusing on the specifics of the social exchange and interaction between service provider and customer. It offers a novel synthesis of knowledge on service satisfaction in the tourism sector, which will serve as a valuable pedagogical and research reference for students and academics interested in hospitality and tourism.

Francis P. Noe PhD is retired Southeast Regional Social Scientist for the National Park Service (NPS), US Department of the Interior. His work focused on social satisfaction surveys and studies measuring the public's perceptions, attitudes, and values toward facilities, services, and programs. The results not only provided applied information for NPS management, but were relevant to the recreation and tourism industries.

Muzaffer Uysal, Professor of Tourism in the Department of Hospitality and Tourism Management at Pamplin College of Business at Virginia Polytechnic Institute and State University, has extensive experience in the travel and tourism field. He is a member of the International Academy for the Study of Tourism and the Academy of Leisure Sciences. He has received a number of awards for research, excellence in international education, and teaching excellence.

Vincent P. Magnini is an Assistant Professor of Hospitality Marketing (PhD, Old Dominion University), Department of Hospitality and Tourism Management, Virginia Polytechnic Institute and State University. He has significant expertise in the area of customer satisfaction in service settings, and he has received a number of awards for research, institutional leadership ability, and teaching excellence.

Routledge Advances in Tourism
Edited by Stephen Page,
London Metropolitan University, London

Tourist Customer Service Satisfaction

An encounter approach

Francis P. Noe, Muzaffer Uysal and Vincent P. Magnini

Routledge
Taylor & Francis Group

LONDON AND NEW YORK

First published 2010 by Routledge
2 Park Square, Milton Park, Abingdon, Oxon, OX14 4RN

Simultaneously published in the USA and Canada
by Routledge
270 Madison Avenue, New York, NY 10016

Routledge is an imprint of the Taylor & Francis Group, an informa business

Typeset in Times New Roman by Taylor & Francis Books
Printed and bound by MPG Books Group in the UK

British Library Cataloguing in Publication Data
A catalogue record for this book is available from the British Library

Library of Congress Cataloguing in Publication Data
Noe, Francis P., 1939–
    Tourist customer service satisfaction : an encounter approach / by
    Francis P. Noe, Muzaffer Uysal and Vincent P. Magnini.
        p. cm.
    Includes bibliographical references and index.
    1. Tourism–Management. 2. Hospitality industry–Management.
    3. Hospitality industry–Management. I. Uysal, Muzaffer. II. Magnini,
    Vincent P. III. Title.
    G155.A1N58 2010
    910.68'8–dc22   2010005855

ISBN: 978-0-415-57804-2 (hbk)
ISBN: 978-0-203-85236-1 (ebk)

Contents

About the authors

Francis P. Noe (MS, Michigan State University; PhD State University of New York at Buffalo) is retired from his position as the Southeast Regional Social Science Research Director for the National Park Service. During his twenty-four-year tenure, he also held adjunct professorships at Georgia State, Clemson, Virginia Polytechnic Institute & State Universities and the University of Tennessee. His research interests focus on applied issues affecting visitor use through site-specific surveys within travel and tourism. His work appears in refereed environmental, leisure–recreation and travel–tourism journals. He has co-authored books on outdoor recreation policy and one on tourist visual preferences, and authored a book on tourist service satisfaction. Contributions have included professional memberships, editorial review boards, serving on doctoral committees, and consultant to various federal agencies. In his retirement, he has maintained a professional relationship with his colleagues.

Muzaffer Uysal is a professor of tourism (PhD, Texas A&M University), Department of Hospitality and Tourism Management, Virginia Polytechnic Institute and State University (Virginia Tech). He has extensive experience in the travel and tourism field, authoring or co-authoring a significant number of articles in tourism, hospitality and recreation journals, proceedings, book chapters, and four monographs and one book relating to different aspects of tourism marketing, demand/supply interaction and international tourism. He also has conducted workshops and seminars on similar topics and field research in several countries. He is a member of the International Academy for the Study of Tourism and the Academy of Leisure Sciences, and serves as co-editor of *Tourism Analysis: An Interdisciplinary Journal*. In addition, he sits on the editorial boards of a significant number of journals, including *Journal of Travel Research*, and *Annals of Tourism Research* as resource editor. He has also received a number of awards for research, excellence in international education, and teaching excellence. His current research interests center on tourism demand/supply interaction, tourism development, quality of life research, and satisfaction in tourism.

Vincent P. Magnini is an assistant professor of hospitality marketing (PhD, Old Dominion University), Department of Hospitality and Tourism Management, Virginia Polytechnic Institute and State University (Virginia Tech). He has significant expertise in the area of customer satisfaction in service settings, authoring or co-authoring numerous articles in hospitality, marketing, and management journals on the subject. He serves on the editorial boards of the *Cornell Hospitality Quarterly* and the *Journal of Vacation Marketing*. He has also received a number of awards for research, institutional leadership ability, and teaching excellence. His current research interests focus on blending marketing and strategic management theories with the aim of identifying opportunities for sustainable competitive advantage for hospitality and tourism firms.

Introduction

Service is about people, how they relate to one another, fulfill each other's needs, and ultimately care for each other. There are literally thousands of books and articles written on the subject of service satisfaction. Yet few, if any, focus on the detailed specifics of the social exchange and interaction between service provider and customer. Socially engineering that process in a complex bureaucratic organization, to fulfill the customer's expectations via the service agent in a direct or indirect exchange of communication, requires normative guidelines acceptable to all the participants. That takes specifics, and we hope to start defining that process.

This book attempts to start defining the specific kinds of verbal and nonverbal messages needed for successful exchanges. It goes a step further by outlining how the service provider ought to behave in different situations. Few adults like to be told how to behave, but the service process is not immune from an analytic perspective detailing positive approaches that enhance a service provider's role performance. After years of observing service providers at work and being part of the system as participant observers, we offer up what works pragmatically so far, and compare these findings with recommendations by experts. This is not the "be all and end all" – role interactive performances are being refined and added to, even as this text is being written. The goal is also to serve as a reference to the most current literature that addresses the service provider–customer interaction process so that students and practitioners may build upon it.

Our emphasis evaluates coping along the frontline as a service provider. Coping is so important in the hospitality and personal services sector because customers become part of a tourist situation for a very short time. Maximizing their gain during that time is critical to customer loyalty and success. Researchers have quite successfully pointed out that the frontline is an important part of the bottom line in profit and personal customer satisfaction (Heskett *et al.*, 1997). The ultimate value an organization can communicate, according to what we have seen, is the personal touch. Tailoring the service to the customer by reaching out to them, but keeping a perspective on the reality of a mass market, is woven through many of the studies on enhancing customer satisfaction (Noe, 1999, pp. 95–96). Interpersonal techniques and strategies are proposed to enhance customer perceptions and promote employees' performance and self-esteem.

Simplifying the bottom line in this book can be summarized into two commandments of service. One: "Do unto your internal customers as you would have them do unto your external customers" (Brown, 1995, p. 11). In other words, take care of your employees, take good care of them, be concerned for their wellbeing, and invest in them. Two: "Always treat a customer as if he will remain a customer. Never treat him as though this is the last time you'll see him" (Carr, 1990, p. 169). Both commandments lead to loyalty, promoting profits, corporate growth, and longevity.

The following chapter outline details the simple and compact structure of this book. Chapters 1 and 2 define encounter theory, the theoretical model of social relationships, and situations upon which observations are premised. Chapters 3 and 4 recognize the importance of the manager's role and the market segment that is being sought. Chapters 5 and 6 describe positioning the service provider role and ways of appealing positively to both customer and provider roles through communication. Chapter 7 designs the role model for service providers – how they should react, project, and promote a positive posture or attitude when interacting with the customer. Chapter 8 goes beyond just attempting to ensure customer satisfaction, setting a higher mark of achieving a more complete state of customer loyalty. Finally, Chapter 9 presents conclusions and future directions for inquiry.

Who should be interested in this compendium? The intended readers are students and practitioners in the hospitality field, from the frontline to the back office. A sharply focused review was always our intention. Practitioners should not underestimate the recent increased competition among tourism providers (Kandampully, 2007) and the consequent need to deliver top-rate frontline service. It builds heavily on the most recent works of those in business, tourism, and social psychology. Also, it follows upon an earlier study by one of the authors on tourist service satisfaction in the hotel, transportation, and recreation segments of the travel tourism industry.

1 Defining encounter theory

Preview

This chapter introduces the attribution theory and proposes its appropriateness as a model to examine the customer–provider relationship and the interactions necessary to achieve a mutually satisfactory experience. The channels of interaction take place through the use of verbal and nonverbal (gestural) expressions of communication in real time. The process of exchange takes place not only between the actors – the customer and service provider – but also within each actor as they weigh and imagine different outcomes. This exchange is a kind of test case to be played out later in real time. Thus the relationship between persons stays in flux as information on expectations is shared. The second part of the chapter describes the importance of the social situations and identifies those observable attributes which help define the inter-subjective act.

Symbolic interaction and attribution theory

The framework

Into the early part of the twentieth century, explanations of human behavior were still based on so-called instincts. Whenever actions and behaviors flowed from our self, names were tagged onto the acts. In fact, the list of instincts grew to well over a hundred of these inner drives stimulating human actions. One was even termed "miscellaneous." Perhaps it was the length of the list, and the continuing process of adding newer instincts that the theory discredited itself as an explanation of human behavior. Into this void, a more plausible approach to understanding human action and self-awareness grew from the Chicago school of social psychology of symbolic interaction.

In an outstanding historical summary on symbolic interaction theory, Prus (1996, pp. 10, 129) points out that two developers and founders are most significant: George Herbert Mead and Herbert Blumer, who represent the Chicago School. "Symbolic interaction may be envisioned as the study of the ways in which people make sense of their life-situations and the ways in which they go about their activities, in conjunction with others, on a day-to day basis." It is cognizant of human interaction in daily relationships or exchanges taking an ethnographic perspective. George Herbert Mead is considered the father of "symbolic interactionism," following a series of lectures in social psychology he gave at the University of Chicago. Upon Mead's death in 1931, Herbert Blumer continued the lecture series and actually coined the phrase "symbolic interactionism." Nevertheless, the "term at least has the virtue of accurately reflecting the central significance of language in the social psychology of Mead" (Farr, 1996, p. 123).

For Mead, the communication act and symbolic exchange is the basic unit of human interaction and behavioral representation. Stryker (1997, p. 316) also summarizes the thinking of George Herbert Mead. Accordingly, Mead believed that individuals could try out and manipulate symbols internally in their minds, as well as alternative solutions to situations and problems in the mind in a day-dream sort of act. Then, they "could respond reflexively to themselves and treat themselves as objects (talk to themselves in another role like a customer) akin to other objects in the world (the self)." Mead argued that the source of the mind and self was an "ongoing social process in which persons required others in order to construct their solutions to problematic situations." Hence his well-known book *Mind, Self and Society* (Mead, 1934), or what we would like to narrow and redefine on a smaller scale in this work as mind, self, and the tourist customer.

The theoretical framework guiding this research effort is also built on the symbolic interaction theory of the Chicago School's Herbert Blumer, continuing Mead's qualitative tradition based on direct observation, where the individual is viewed as an actor, not a reactor. Such a model is not a stimulus-response theory explaining social interaction. Rather, individuals are symbol-using, symbol-creating, and symbol-designating creatures. This process, which follows an exchange in a relationship, is essentially conscious. "In its most basic form a social act involves a three-part relationship": a gesture or symbolic act initiated by an individual, perceived by another, and mutually responded to by both parties (Littlejohn, 1983, p. 47). Following in this tradition, we also apply an outgrowth of this theory. This emphasis is adopted from the Iowa School, centered on the work of Manford Kuhn, which includes the sub-area of role theory, in which individuals respond according to how their social titles define their social positions.

Both of these perspectives are integrated into our investigation of the service provider responding to the customer on the frontline.

However, neither emphasis curtailed the use of observational studies. "Many empirical studies in the symbolic interactionist tradition of social psychology at Chicago were participant observational studies," which appears to be the generic methodology for the study of social encounters (Farr, 1996, p. 28). Erving Goffman drew upon many of the unpublished dissertations after the Second World War to illustrate the "minutiae" and detail involved with encounters and social interaction. You are whom you associate with and what you do. In the end, the "theories of self-concept have emphasized that people's self-concepts are a product of their interactions and identification with other people" (Pelham and Hetts, 1999, p. 115). In fact, this influence created by other people is even more pronounced when a product or service is publicly consumed, as in the case of tourism activities (Amaldoss and Jain, 2008) – an interesting reflection of the theory makers themselves and the kind of eyes and ears harnessed to gather data on interacting beings.

There is a methodological difference in how those interactions are viewed, based on each school's perspective of self. According to Schubert and the interaction school, the social self is the creation of inter-subjective communication with the mind and the outside world. It is not a "solipsistic capacity", but an "inner experience" created in conjunction with the outside world" (Cooley, 1998, pp. 21, 23). In other words, "one's social identity develops itself through symbolically mediated interaction with one's surroundings." The mechanisms that mediate between the self and society are "communication, sympathetic introspection, and understanding" (Cooley, 1998, pp. 23, 161, 164). "The social self is simply any idea, or system of ideas, drawn from the communicative life that the mind cherishes as its own." "A self-idea of this sort seems to have three principal elements: the imagination of our appearance to the other person; the imagination of his judgment of that appearance; and some sort of self feeling such as pride or modification" transpiring between the persons. Adults "imagine the whole thing at once and their idea differs from that of a child chiefly in comparative richness and complexity of the elements that accompany and interpret the visible or audible sign" (Cooley, 1998, p. 173). Reflecting the insight of the early social interaction theorists at the turn and early part of the century, Troyer and Younts (1997, p. 720) point out that "social interaction is guided by our ability to read the interpretations others make of us and our actions (in or out of their presence) and adjust our behavior to correspond in a meaningful way to those expectations." They propose that both first-order expectations held by oneself, and second-order interactions held by others for oneself, guide social action. They conclude that the expectations of others matter most, but not under all conditions. Although their test results are not that inconclusive, the effects of a person's perceived social status did make a difference to how a person interpreted another's expectations.

Regarding those perceptions, symbolic functions can be subdivided, according to Dittmar (1996, pp. 157, 159), into "*categorical* symbols" expressing a person's social standings, wealth, status, and group memberships; and "*self-expressive* symbols" representing a person's unique qualities, including values, attitudes, and personal history. Consumer objects and travel are part of the way in which persons represent themselves to the world (Ahuvia, 2005), and travel consumption is intricately involved in our leisure activities, emotions, self-expression, and social relations (Plog, 2001). Influencing many of these consumer choices is our social economic status and also our values and attitudes about what how we view certain worldly activities and pleasures, such as certain kinds of tourist exchange.

As a follow-up to the earlier work of the theorists at the Chicago School, the new Iowa School of symbolic interaction took up the cause, using laboratory and innovative technology to analyze a social exchange between two or more individuals. The central emphasis is upon "how two people join their separate lines of behavior together to construct cooperative social interaction" (Hintz and Miller, 1995, pp. 355, 366). Such social acts are composed of three phases: opening, middle, and closing. The opening constitutes "the transitional phase between independent actions and interdependent interaction" (Hintz and Miller, 1995, pp. 357, 361, 262). Such action is not established until "each person acts in a way that does not challenge the other's definition of the relationship." Hence, this line of reasoning serves as a basis for beginning an exchange between travel customer and service provider. A certain taking for granted is assumed "in the context of some idea about how we fit together." As a service provider assisting a tourist, the assumed role is to help, assist, and care for the needs of the customer by communicating that the provider acknowledges that they are there to be at a customer's bidding. "Every time we fly somewhere, we deal with an airline or travel agency; very few of us fly in our own planes" (Gutek, 1995, p. 161). Airplanes are not just wings and engines, but are also pilots and passengers. Unlike animals, which respond directly, people respond to stimuli mediated by their symbolic world. What you see is not always what you think. Bower (1992, p. 203), in reviewing the work of some psychologists, suggests that "the desire to predict and control the world gets translated into inferences about the inner traits of others," often biasing impressions. Thus unrealistic expectations about human behavior, or even realistic expectations, are "often fostered by a lack of appreciation for the ways in which situations shape behavior further contribute to biased impressions." There is need to socially define or make sense out of our interactions and the situations when they occur.

"The stimuli impinging upon people are given meaning through cognitive processes and then responded to according to the attached meaning" (Albrecht *et al.*, 1987, p. 20). For example, Duck (1991, p. 42) reports on the classic late 1930s study that had male shills use their inter-subjective behavior to target ordinary females for attention as though they were highly attractive. The targeted women began to act, dress, and interact according to the definition coming from the men. This study helps show how perceptions of reality are often shaped through interpersonal transactions.

"Symbolic interaction is *inter*subjective to the core and envisions the development of language or ongoing symbolic interchange as fundamental to the human essence (and the human struggle for existence)" (Prus, 1996, p. 22). The study of interchanges between individuals also assumes and takes place within an organizational context, and some of the observations presented are confined to, or took place near, service front desks or in frontline situations. "Communication is the essence of relationships" and the medium of exchange. The process represents one individual to another and is "governed in part by interpersonal needs for inclusion, control, and affection. People define the situation they encounter, and adapt to those situations as defined" (Littlejohn, 1983, p. 191). In the end, the process seeks to know how the relationship affects your perceptions and needs.

In relationships, individuals monitor perceived costs and rewards. In a service situation, where dyadic relationships take place, interactive rewards and pleasure are very much the key social ingredient for maximizing customer satisfaction. It all begins with the "customers (who) 'see into' the organization through a unique window; the actions and words of frontline employees" (Bell and Zemke, 1992, p. 18). That is, "frontline employees are often the primary reflection of a firm's image" (Maxham and Netemeyer, 2003, p. 46). In an interactive exchange through dialogue, people communicate various forms of verbal behavior to express the social consequences of what they mean. Some are in the form of questioning and asking to have a need fulfilled; for example, "Where is the restroom?" or "Could I have a cool drink?" Others are in the form of a declarative report about your surroundings and the environment, as in "The weather is beautiful." Still others form communication links with the words and expressions that are said first by the speaker, who stimulates a repeated response in similar form in the listener. These expressions take the form of many ritualized greetings, such as "Good morning," and "Good morning to you," said in return; many of these expressions are polite exchanges in a fast-moving world of individuals and strangers interacting, and provide commonly accepted cultural exchanges. Finally, some verbal adjectives that modify a request such as "Could you do me a favor?" are then followed by your request. Such forms of expression make their way into our conventional daily communicating patterns and become part of our operating dialogue on "how we get by" and get along with others.

"You can never go wrong with face-to-face contact while there are other less direct methods of interacting; they will not be effective ... if you don't see your customers regularly" (Brown, 1999, p. 203). A social encounter begins when one person attends to another and ends when neither can attend to the other" (Hintz and Miller, 1995, p. 358). These social connections are the first step toward a relationship process with a company. In fact, in many cases, in the eye of the customer, the frontline employee "is" the service (Garrett, 2001). "If a customer interacts with a firm for the first time, then it is this initial encounter that determines whether a relationship is formed and continued" (Botschen, 2000, p. 280). There are four conditions listed by Botschen (2000, p. 281) that qualify: (1) you and another are behaving, (2) you are aware of the other's behavior, (3) the other is aware of your behavior, (4) as a result, you are both consciously aware of each other. The role performance structures a service encounter. "Each role that one plays is learned. One's confidence that one is doing the right thing leads to performance satisfaction.

"One's role specific self-concept is formed by reactions of others to the quality of one's role enactment" (Solomon *et al.*, 1985, pp. 102–4).

This process is called taking the role of another, in which the customer "anticipates the other's expected role behavior," allowing that customer to gauge their behavior to the service provider. In this context, satisfaction with a service encounter is seen as a function of the congruence between perceived behavior and the behavior expected by role players (Oliver and Burke, 1999; Sirgy and Su, 2000). In other words, customer satisfaction is an evaluative process (Mattila and Ro, 2008, p. 298), and therefore failure of the service interaction is failure of the customer and service provider in not understanding each other's actions and not playing their part in the service script. "Consumers can be thought of as possessing cognitive scripts for a wide variety of service encounters" (Solomon *et al.*, 1985, p. 106). That is, script theory contends that knowledge about familiar, frequent situations is stored in one's mind as a coherent description of events that are expected to occur (Bateson, 2002, p. 110).

The medium of exchange makes use of symbols that are both verbally spoken and nonverbal, including gestures and postures. Language embodies symbols that convey meaning (Brownell, 2000). "We plan, broker, initiate, guide, bully, love, terrorize, terminate, justify, or challenge through words. It is in words that we engage in social interaction and it is through a better *understanding of words and their use* that we begin to appreciate social behavior" (Semin, 1997, p. 294). It is through this medium that humans express themselves and their intention (Brownell, 2000). "Words and sentences do not express ideas or refer to things, but serve to get things done through people or have people refer to things" (Guerin, 1994, p. 143). Verbal behavior is just another kind of behavioral action that helps mankind function. The symbolic interaction model of George Herbert Mead, as singled out by Guerin (1994, pp. 144–46), sees language as having "no meaning residing in our words beyond their social consequences." Words also have no meaning without an active listener, who attends to the consequences of a message understood by all parties using commonly agreed upon symbols. And finally, verbal behavior is only generally reinforced, and not always taken as a direct command to act. Saying we should treat everyone in a certain manner has consequences when truly accompanied by other tangible actions. Nevertheless, "language and its strategic use is the paramount social reality within which all social psychology processing take place, are manifested and managed. It is the pursuit of the subtle but fascinating properties of this medium which brings us together, by which we cheat or influence each other, and by which we gossip or prejudge others, argue, help, or advise" (Semin, 1997, p. 302).

Social activity has given rise to "language acquisition and use ... at the core of human intersubjectivity. Only when people share sets of symbols are they able to communicate with one another and act in other ways that are mindful of the viewpoints of the other" (Prus, 1996, p. 11). In enabling the link between social behavior and interaction, Semin (1997, pp. 293, 297) refers to "symbolic communication" and the "language" forms seen as the "mediators not only of cognition and consciousness but of the self and social interaction." The messages coded and decoded through the use of language play a paramount role in the tourism sector (Dann, 1996). Levels of social classification are coded into the self and exchanges with others. Theories of the self contain both a more personal dimension, and also a more social group identification component, that Pelham and Hetts (1999, p. 116) see in explicitly how individuals consciously consider their role, and also implicitly how they associate nonconsciously in a group or social context. Both these dimensions of the self enter into the consequent influences that they have on a person's behavior. The authors focus their efforts on the implicit affects in three studies showing that "participants endorsed explicit self-conceptions consistent with their current cultural context, a finding suggesting culture's powerful influence on how people consciously think about themselves." Individuals' implicit self-concepts also influence their socialization, thus demonstrating the relative independence and persistence of implicit belief systems. Although culture may be a robust influence, individuals' earlier and other personal experiences also continue to influence perceptions of self. What kind of role they engage in will reflect those dimensions.

Social provider and customer

Our interest is rather narrow, and views the definition of a service provider's interaction with a customer as "face-to-face interactions between a buyer and seller in a service setting" (Solomon *et al.*, 1985, pp. 100–101). Service encounters are human interactions: "communication between a service provider and a customer is interactive; it is a reciprocal process rather than a linear one." "It is more accurate to think of the service provider as acting with the customer." And as a result, "the quality of the subjective product – the service experience – is the true outcome of a service interaction." The interaction conceptualization of meaning "is its stress on conscious interpretation," where the parties relating to each other compare, weigh, and evaluate their symbolic exchange. The interaction process results in "nearly all that a person is and does is formed in the process of interacting symbolically with others" (Littlejohn, 1983, pp. 50–51). This kind of approach to understanding what takes place in a social exchange is based on symbolic interaction premises that have come down to us via social psychology.

According to this perspective, which comprises the underlying model for the following chapters, role enactment(s) are comprised of the following characteristics, as spelled out by Zurcher (1983, pp. 13–14). They include a conscious and willful act. The interaction process taking place between individuals is not passive, since expectations are interpreted and modified for a particular setting or situation. The interaction is comprised of symbols creating communication using verbal language, gestures, expressions, and signs. Understanding emerges of our roles and self in the accumulation of interaction experiences through time in similar and different settings, or what we call situations.

Although roles often become institutionalized, individuals are still able to enact them by learning how to deal with expectations successfully through their exchanges with others in those situations. Such a reaching of understanding is based on the perceived negotiations between what we think is expected, and what others think is expected of us. In essence, the symbolic interaction viewpoint "assumes that roles emerge from, or are significantly shaped by, interactions in specific social settings" or situations. The medium carrying out these interactions is an individual or social self made-up of the "I" and "me" to use the terms of one of the founders of this approach, George Herbert Mead (1934). The "I" embodies our personal temperament, while the "me" entails our individual social self roles. Both components help to form who we are and how we act. For example, in an exchange, "The first couple of minutes of conversation is a point at which people attempt to get across to others the central features of their 'person', their essential 'me-ness' as they see it" (Duck, 1991, pp. 49–50). This is a way of quickly getting to know someone and what to expect from them in particular situations. The role of the service provider is just one of the many roles an individual may play that help to create who we think others see us as being. The service provider telling stories about playing other nonwork roles enhances bonding with the customer. These may be of a recreational nature in a tourist setting. In this way, "The self-definition and role performance of the service provider play a vital part in the service script, and that individual's appearance has the potential to affect his or her ability to successfully play the required role" (Solomon, 1998, p. 96). That is why "It is important to find out the current status of the customer contact personnel in terms of how they perceive themselves" (Jeschke et al., 2000, p. 209). This information can serve as a basis for improving the skills of the frontline and support staff. A checklist or even a questionnaire of who am I could be used to help the service provider. Allen et al. (1998, pp. 11, 19–20) define service focus "as an individual's beliefs about the value of direct customer contact for achieving desired performance outcomes in his or her own job." Those service providers believing in a customer focus use multiple social interactions to obtain insight about customers' needs, recognizing that there are multiple different types of customer, and that customer contact is shared responsibility in the organization, which is context-dependent (Gebhardt et al., 2006).

According to the tenants of mental accounting, the customer participating in an exchange weighs and judges the outcome of the interaction with the service provider (Prelec and Lowenstein, 1998). "It is impossible to conceive of an individual having meaningful perceptions or thoughts in the absence of sociality, or of social interaction and relationships existing without mental processing" (Smith and Mackie, 1997, pp. 308–9). Following in the symbolic interaction school, White and Schneider (1998, p. 4) also reference the early classic work of Thibaut and Kelly (1959) by pointing out that the social relationships discussed and analyzed by social psychologists provide a useful framework for understanding customer relationships in a service situation. The principle of maximizing gain and minimizing effort is one such norm that the customer uses in judging a service, or in other words, how they judge the value and cost of a service.

A recurring pattern in a social exchange on the way a service provider acts can be categorized as a rule approach. Role actions are "beliefs about what should be or should not be done to achieve an objective in a given situation" (Littlejohn, 1983, pp. 62–63). How one behaves, which will lead to positive reactions from a customer, is built on "appropriate behavior." Being careful to know and test what is acceptable in your particular customer situation is a must. "The greater the capacity for interaction, the more a person cannot help but to see his activities as interdependent with those of other people." (Lamb and Watson, 1979, pp. 168, 170). Three styles are identified as: (1) communicating by establishing reciprocal dialogue, imparting knowledge, sharing emotions, and investigating, (2) presenting by emphasizing, persuading, making positive demonstrations, influencing, and insisting–resisting, (3) operating by organizing people, spurring, delaying, controlling the actions of people, and also sharing one's own process of deciding and anticipating. These focus on the customer being "exposed to the physical, face-to-face contact with employees." While other channels of communication can facilitate a relationship, they are not as complex as direct interaction (Botschen, 2000, p. 281).

It was symbolic interaction theory that helped Botschen (2000, p. 279), along with more recent advances in interpersonal communication, to describe and refine encounters and relationships for a market situation. The theory, pioneered by the Chicago School of social psychology, is also being used by others in their approach to describing relationship marketing, if not directly, than certainly indirectly. This book relies heavily on this line of reasoning in describing and, more recently, explaining social interactions. "The literatures of psychology, social psychology, and communication theory have not infiltrated deeply into the marketing literature, although there is some evidence that they could contribute significantly to our understanding of RM (Relationship management)" (Buttle, 1996, p. 11). It is our belief that this is a largely untapped resource. When investigated, it appears that an "ideal method for analyzing the customer's and provider's respective roles is interaction analysis. Interaction analysis allows the researcher to determine the sequential probability of various behaviors occurring in response to other behaviors, such as the probability with which service provider smiles might follow customer smiles" (Ford, 1998, p. 38). Service providers exhibiting overt verbal communication cues and gestures pave the way. "Although symbols alone will not change a company's culture, they can reinforce shifts in organizational structure, operating policies, and performance measurement and reward systems, collectively signaling to employees that what is occurring is real" (Zeithaml *et al.*, 1990, p. 153). Lending support to this perspective,

Maxham and Netemeyer (2003, p. 46) state that "firms reap what they sow" in the sense that "employees' perceptions of shared values and organization justice can stimulate customer-directed extra-role behaviors."

The methods of detailing the interaction between a service provider and customer are unmediated. Many of the personal observations of interaction and exchange between the service provider and customer in this work are based on participant-observation. This "role allows the researcher to get infinitely closer to the lived experiences of the participants than does straight observation. Their experiences as participants may afford researchers with invaluable vantage points for appreciating certain aspects of particular life-worlds" (Prus, 1996, p. 19). Hintz and Miller (1995, p. 357) maintain that "observation of social encounters" is one essential tool for understanding the interaction process. Given this approach, symbolic interaction has been criticized for its view of social interaction as being unique and individualistic each and every time an exchange occurs. This conceptual belief, especially in defining a social situation, has been limited to the generalization of under-standing of the similarity of exchanges. However, as Gonos (1977) explains, modification to a rigid idea of newness and uniqueness has given way to a more empirical orientation that looks for the similar and common. He cites one of the more recent proponents, Erving Goffman, who finds that persons do not always create a new social situation, but adapt what is commonly accepted in the everyday norms and values of the community. To an extent, that is practical, but carried to an extreme it could be a frustrating practice because no-one could assume the verbatim actions of another. Every day, relearning to be a customer or to play the role of a service provider would be frustrating, given the different channels and manners of exchange that transpire. It is at this juncture that we see a weakness of the symbolic inter-action theory in its emphasis on rational thinking persons, and "neglects the contribution of emotions to behavior, particularly irrational behavior" (Albrecht *et al.*, 1987, p. 22).

Defining the social situation

The stage

Social situational definitions are comprised of at least four sets of factors to which the interactive participants attend when exchanging information (Sherif and Sherif, 1969, pp. 12, 124). First, they include the characteristics of the individual: sex, approximate age, social class, social status, relationships such as strangers or friends in a service context, etc. A second set includes the activities, problems, or tasks to be accomplished or resolved. A third pertains to the location, such as a recreational place in a tourist setting. And finally, the individual's relationship to the above three sets of factors and the role performance they are exhibiting – stressed, at ease, relaxed, involved, bored, etc. – that may characterize either the service provider or customer in that situation. As the factors in a social situation function *interdependently*, it follows that neglect of any one set will lead to conclusions that are in error or lack validity.

It becomes particularly crucial when we consider how we appraise other people, for other people are sized up in terms of how they are related to us. Many social relations and contacts shade our definitions of a human experience and how they handle the above variables. There is no leaving the social context or environment, whatever the predicament. "Socially constructed definitions of the self, the group, the situation, and the universe itself enter into our every thought, feeling, and action" (Smith and Mackie, 1997, p. 310). In attributing meaning to an interaction between persons, there are situational causes that "are things in the environment we believe account for a person's behavior and dispositional causes that are attributed to a person's personality, nature, or beliefs about the world" (Canary and Cody, 1994, pp. 157–58). The personal is what counts in service relationships that contain the human element, not the artificial impersonal.

When making comparisons between persons and systems, Connellan and Zemke (1993, pp. 30, 38), having examined both "thousands" of people and "hundreds" of systems, find "far more dumb systems than people." Companies far too often attempt through a systems approach to "sustain high quality service." In the 1998 American Customer Satisfaction Index (ACSI), developed at the University of Michigan, the hotel, airline, and restaurant industries are rated by the consumer in the lower third on customer satisfaction. Blackwell (1997, p. 80) claims that Americans are "living isolated, work-obsessed, technologically-centered lives" and that pets are filling in where human and social relationships endured. If this is so, then the tourist market needs to adjust to help accommodate those pets. At one of the largest US airports, both cars and pets are put up while the traveler enjoys their trip. "For the customer, the total time it takes to complete a transaction – including standing in line, waiting on the phone, or carrying out multiple encounters – is what matters" (Gutek, 1995, p. 153). Some of the worst offenders today are phone messages that branch through lists of options, or state that your call is important but that there is no one available in service who can take it at this time. Gutek (1995, p. 155) finds that in these service channels "completion time is poor, and process efficiency is abysmal." In a comparison study, the social situation or setting affected the way in which an individual sought to receive a self-enhancing message (Pelham and Hetts, 1999, p. 122). These researchers find that a personal response is more favored than a computer-generated response, indicating that there are limits to technology, especially in a service environment. In fact, many tourist services are only available locally in hotels. As a result, it is difficult to build relationships over long distances, so there are limitations to just how far companies can and may be willing to communicate and interact with a potential client.

At the nexus, "social interaction is seen by symbolic-interaction explanations as occurring within a common *definition of the situation*. The role taking occurs within the context of a social setting ('a basketball game') in the surrounding environment ('a gymnasium')" (Albrecht *et al.*, 1987, p. 21). Social interaction is influenced by the situational circumstances and the options customers may exercise as part of the interaction process. A good example is the airline passenger, as observed by Zurcher (1983, p. 229), who strives to be autonomous. "People attempt to negotiate their situation-specific identities, including the expression of feelings called for in the situation. They try to affect a compromise between how they want to present themselves and the presentation they perceive others to expect of them." The origin of this concept is credited to two social scientists, W. I. Thomas and F. Znaniecki (1918), both belonging to the University of Chicago School.

This change in explaining man's behavior began in the late 1920s and the 1930s, when the inner isolated self could no longer suffice as a scientific explanation. If people define a situation as real in their lives, it becomes real in its consequences for the way it eventually affects them and how they act. For Gonos (1977, p. 24), "The character of any situation is the result of the unique meeting of particular individuals, and their combined effects on one another." How simply that is structured, with one or a few individuals as well as departures and arrivals of new players in the interaction, determines its outcome. The key motives in the situation really hinge on the held beliefs, attitudes, and values that the individual customers are interjecting to define the situation for themselves (Vogel *et al.*, 2008). The service provider has to fit these different lines of demands together with the goals and objectives of the service organization to meet the needs of the client, to achieve a high level of satisfaction, and to exceed their expectation definitions of what will fulfill them (Oliver and Burke, 1999). "The world to which humans react and on which they act is a symbolized world, a world specified by meanings attached to the objects comprising it rather than that which may in some sense exist independent of its being symbolized ... The point of view of the participants in social interaction must enter decisively into satisfactory accounts or explanations of that interaction" (Stryker, 1997, p. 320–21). Again, the Chicago School's influence is felt in the definition of a social situation wherein the shared social meaning given to a social situation by those interacting in it includes the context and consequences.

The service provider is always concerned about the satisfactory or unsatisfactory consequences that may result for the customer in a service situation with face-to-face contact. "Consumers and employees expect certain behaviors from the service workers" (Tansik and Smith, 2000, p. 245). In many kinds of service situations, the service provider is expected to serve with friendliness, a somber demeanor, or even hostility, as in the case of a night-club bouncer. Feelings and emotions are involved unless the service provider is an academy award actor. Customers "prefer effortless" behavior (Grayson, 1998) that they define or perceive as emotionally involved (Tansik and Smith (2000, p. 245).

Situational identity action theory is premised on the social fact that expectations and normative behaviors are learned and demonstrated in any given social setting, which in turn defines the social meaning for customers and service providers alike. In other words, "situated identities are the attributions that are made about participants in a particular setting as a consequences of their actions" (Alexander and Lauderdale, 1977, p. 225–26). These actions are not pulled out of a magician's hat as a matter of chance. Public decorum and practices of interpersonal exchange mold the fabric of society, and the actions of the customers and service provider obviously define how they will be seen. Projecting and developing a favorable identity becomes a paramount consideration in interactive situations. A favorable image is fundamental, and the overwhelming majority of individuals realize through experience that a little sugar and sweetness goes a long way to help smooth out the bumps. Situated identity action theory is the updated version of the earlier symbolic interactionalists' reference to a definition of a situation. This theory hypothesizes that the social and physical context shapes how problems are conceptualized and solved, and how choices are formulated and decisions reached. It includes the physical context, the social, and the cultural as they are experienced by the customer. Such interaction involves recognition when customers interact with various facets of a situation. In the course of these interactions, a service-specific context experience is formed. Situated identity action theory basically "establishes practice or activity as the central theoretical concept ... that captures the interrelationship of context and cognition." As a result, this model "broadens the focus from individual activity to social activity, from static internal representations to collective processes, and from contextual mental computations to cognitive processing that is inseparable from the ongoing activities" (Gupta and Vajic, 2000, pp. 34–35, 40–41). In other words, "People are in social situations when they have established a mutual awareness that each is part of the other's conscious awareness" (Hintz and Miller, 1995, p. 356–58). Most greetings begin in pairs between a customer and service provider, but will expand when information is needed to clarify and articulate a need. In proceeding through an exchange, the service provider is often anticipating the need of the customer where a congruent social definition between the parties is established. This form of interrelatedness includes reciprocal attention, mutual responsiveness, and functioning congruent identities. And in most service situations, where cooperation is required, at least one common social objective needs to be established. Hintz and Miller (1995, pp. 356, 362) further state that "each of us organizes our activity in relation to the other in terms of a definition of our relationship and its meaning in this situation." This is recognized through repeated occurrences. Individuals often tend to take on compatible interpretations of situations and therefore act in concert. They apparently come to adopt a compatible "definition of the situation"; in symbolic interaction a definition occurs by having taken the role of the other or by adopting a group standpoint. In so doing, one learns what is expected of him; that is, he constructs his definition of the situation" (McHugh, 1968, p. 12). There are two para-meters to a definition of a situation according to McHugh (1968, p. 31): emergence, referring to definitions and "transformations" over time; and relativity, referring to definitions and "transformations" across space. In a small group study, emergence appeared in the majority of cases whose top reported attributes were a "theme" characterizing the situation, an "elaboration" of sequenced events, and "authorship" taking responsibility for an active role in the situation. Relativity was far less important in characterizing a situation where the top three characteristics included the "typicality" and "likelihood" inferring that behavior belongs to a certain category of people or the likelihood of that behavior occurring, and a "moral requiredness" characterizing the values held by a particular person's group orientation. These attributes are said to enter into how an individual deals with a social situation and the people that are participating within it. The characteristics defining a social situation all contain a social, conscious, emotional, and dynamic character.

Service situation

Those service providers in first contact with the customer are likely to set the tone for what follows (Netemeyer *et al.*, 2005). They are central to a service situation. These "frontline service employees are referred to as boundary spanners because they operate at the organizations boundary" (Zeithaml and Bitner, 2000, pp. 289–90). In defining a role "position" in such a manner, it becomes "a collectively recognized category of persons for whom the basis for such differentiation is their common attribute, their common behavior, or the common reactions of others toward them" (Biddle and Thomas, 1966, p. 29). We expect a frontline service provider in the tourist situation to be upbeat, happy, and positive, and also to be more than inclined to serve and give of their time. They are the medical healers of a time-worn, overworked society whose members are looking for a break – a vacation or holiday. It is not some trivial job that can be overlooked and ignored. These service providers, at each step in the tourist process, play a valuable role in healing the customers, at least for a brief respite. These roles are the necessary linkage with the internal operation of the organization. Such labor requires emotional com-mitment. Those attributes and expressions of "friendliness, courtesy, empathy, and responsiveness directed toward the customer all require huge amounts of emotional labor" (Zeithaml and Bitner, 2000, p. 290). Add to this customer assurance and trust, and the service provider needs to communicate reliably in order to build a solid reputation and image regarding what the customer can and should expect from their company (Kaydo, 2000). "Empowering, teach-ing, and supporting service personnel are particularly important in situations where there is little time to refer decisions to a higher authority, where direct supervision is difficult, and where the first-line service personnel are the company in the eyes of the customer" (Heskett *et al.*, 1990, p. 228).

Down that road to understanding and making a dialogue, frontline "encounters are situations which can be used both to send messages about a specific service or product and to receive and capture messages from customers (and other stakeholders), thereby creating a long-term purposeful dialogue" (Botschen, 2000, p. 282). For a better understanding, these "situations can be scaled in terms of impact, complexity, relevance, objectiveness, subjectiveness, and representativeness"; and be obtained empirically by having subjects keep logs on how individuals construe these daily life encounters (Endler, 1988, pp. 182–83). Knowing how customers in a tourist situation react and expect to be treated may change or reinforce practices a company expects of its service providers. "For both provider and consumer, the successful enactment of even the most basic service scenario involves the mastery of a wide range of behaviors" (Solomon *et al.*, 1985, pp. 102–3).

Many service encounters take place "in situations involving the execution of well-learned behaviors that possess a high degree of social consensus as to appropriate and expected actions" (ibid.). The authors used an example of a restaurant service exchange between a waiter and diner. The role exchange between the parties followed a set of exchanges and interplay that facilitated the serving of a meal. Successful businesses build a satisfied customer base on information and expected norms of their clients (Nininen *et al.*, 2007). In that respect, Manstead (1996, 1998), reviewing a previous body of empirical data, points out that social situations are powerful in influencing behavior. Both informational and normative situational influences are shown to alter behavior. Informational influence surfaces from the assumption that other people are often good sources of information about one's surrounding environment; if several individuals agree with each other, it is irrational to ignore such consensus. Normative influence stems from the perception that the opinions and actions of the majority in a social group constitute a group norm; by conforming to this norm, one circumvents rejection and/or increases acceptance. In the service situation of the "front desk," which may take many different physical shapes, the social interaction and expectation of being given direction, cared for, and treated courteously remain the same for the customer–tourist looking for verbal symbolic reinforcement, normatively providing service satisfaction, if not delight.

A crucial design aspect of a tourist situation might be to include an open setting that facilities self activity, and uses service providers as guides "to familiarize customers with rules and norms, encourage social interaction, and help customers to find their way in an environment" (Gupta and Vajic, 2000, p. 43). The social use of information and normative procedures is a complex social structure. To say that "we shop around and select those situations that are rewarding to us and attempt to avoid those that are painful," according to Endler (1988, pp. 181, 184), is a conceptualization; however, in Endler's evaluation that may be somewhat simplistic. Behavior is also "goal directed, we need to study persons' plans, and strategies and rules of behavior. We also need to study how people interpret situations, how they actively select situations, and how they react to situations imposed on them."

Service situations and how they are defined place norms upon the customer and the service provider in what is expected behavior (Vargo and Lusch, 2004). "Personalization of a service does not necessarily result in a more positive service experience" (Solomon *et al.*, 1985, p. 107) when the expected experience would be an advertised budget restaurant providing low customer care. This refinement would be seen as being deviant and unnecessary. Conforming to the role expectations of customers is rewarding. For example, "waitresses" not conforming to the type of restaurant situation received lower tips than those who played their expected role. In a high-service restaurant situation, personalization is a must, but that will not hold true for a hash-house diner, all-you-can-eat place.

Taking this organizational perspective on understanding the place of information and norms, Fritz (1999, p. 15) identifies three bureaucratic barriers that can derail customer service. These include the *"performers,"* who may be less than active in addressing the needs of the customer or find ways to make them more proactive and less reactive. *"Processes"* are another source where barriers emerge, so steps should be taken to deliver a service that is essential by removing unnecessary ones that may overly complicate how you deal with the customer. And finally, *"policies"* for guiding customer–provider interaction should be kept to a minimum so as not to bog down the service delivery process in cumbersome bureaucratic rules. These three Ps of the organizational situation, if not properly managed, can quickly turn a service delivery program in on itself. Functional autonomy is the ability of an organization to tolerate freedom within its ranks, and those organizations that demonstrate trust in their people to interpret a service situation can offer customized and the ostensible appearance of unique individualized service (Altinay *et al.*, 2008). For example, one well established hotel chain authorizes its frontline staff to solve problems, avoids steps in the check-in, check-out system, and makes every effort to keep policies in check by turning out satisfied customers and patrons.

Service acts are performed in complex bureaucratic organizations. Achieving situation goals is essential and is "critical to sustain superior service" (Connellan and Zemke, 1993, pp. 41, 43). Achieving those goals is reached by customers' experiences through their individual activities or process acts. In the end, both goals and processes are part of the customer satisfaction equation. Diller (2000, pp. 40–43) lists three sets of ambivalent goals and process situations that need consideration in the selection process. First, "opportunism" in price may be undermined or weakened by a need for "relief" for the customer. Strengthening the need for relief may be compensated by "guarantees of quality, creating personal relationships, club identities, and rewarding" the customer in ways that advance and enhance loyalty. A second situation involves "variety" and "continuity," where a need for "simulation" is counter-weighted by "the well known and familiar."

Continuity should be an option first exercised by a company that has market or global position, according to Diller. For resorts with this kind of exposure, these companies can create add-on selling links with the transportation and touring sectors, provided they can maintain agreed-upon interpersonal standards between the customer and service provider. Third, companies need to weigh just how much individual "autonomy" their customer needs, or how much "social integration" they seek through special offers treating customers as part of a group. These kinds of option are not appropriate for all service organizations, and each would have to test where the limits lie with their customer base. In this regard, "not everyone knows how to read the situation." Nevertheless, "most people would have little difficulty recognizing the fact that situations differ in their demands for sociable action. Some people, however, need ... intervention" from others. For example, relationships in a work environment are different from those in a leisure situation, "not because of what they are, but because of how they make people see one another" (Duck, 1991, pp. 35–37). Work can focus attention exclusively on getting tasks completed, but it may also increase emotional rewards by dealing with the process of interacting that achieves getting those tasks done "in a way that emphasizes the relationship between the participants rather than the tasks that they have to complete" (Duck, 1991, p. 39). In contrast, travel situations contain their own definitions of meaning, but they are not absolutely bounded. Kelly (1981, pp. 313, 314) finds "leisure situations are not without their own role expectations as well as incorporating those persistent role identities that each actor brings to the episode."

Negotiation and change are inherent in the interaction process. "In the immediate dialectic of the processual taking and developing of a characterization of a role, the reciprocal actions of others in the interaction provide feedback that not only continues the role-development, but yields satisfaction as the role-identity is established and verified." So it is not just the act of traveling, but also how the role emerges in the situation that brings satisfaction to the participant. This is especially true in leisure or recreational travel, where individuals are often seeking new experiences. In many situations, "one feature is that they have open-ended outcomes. In some, indeterminancy is a major feature of the activity," along with the temporary nature of the event. That is an appeal for engaging in such actions and situations, but is not without setbacks in working through the process as it unfolds without a set script. The process is ongoing as parties interact towards establishing an agreed-upon meaning or, as Kelly (1981, p. 316) says, "the meaning of the event is dialectical." It should be noted that "processual" and "indeterminancy" are correctly quoted. This emerging dialectic will grow.

Hanan and Karp (1989, pp. 166–67) predict and foresee "more leisure-time and discretionary options for its use through travel and entertainment." Travel and entertainment will increasingly become intertwined and interconnected. "Travel will become more convenient, affordable, and acceptable, and will undoubtedly rank high among beneficial forms of entertainment and education." Entertainment will become mobile and portable, complementing travel. The result will be "a market for benefit systems of infinite variety." At present, service situations may emphasize one kind of provider response more than any other for that particular setting. Bjarnadottir (1998) found that different service settings tended to emphasize one response trait over another disproportionately. For example, in healthcare, information and empathy are stressed; while in restaurants, redress and follow-through dominate the interaction. In a retail situation, customers place more weight on responsive behavior. When in the act of traveling, giving assurance and reliable assistance is a big part of a service provider's role. What this means is knowing the tastes and expectations of your customer. "Customer equity management demands an organizational structure built around the creation of, and capitalization on, customer affinity" (Blattberg *et al.*, 2001, p. 182). This means knowing the customer and what they value, but also how they should be treated in a positive manner. Such criteria are often overlooked. "If you have a detailed definition of what good service means – it is defined in the context of both the company and the customer" (Bell and Zemke. 1992, p. 66).

The individual customer's perception of quality, according to Edvardsson *et al.* (1994, pp. 32–34), depends on four service situation interactions. First, in the course of consuming the service, the customer interacts with different contact providers who influence how the customer defines the service quality. Second, the customer is affected by their interactions with other customers, which change the quality of intended service, such as boarding an aircraft or debarking to catch another flight. Third, interaction with the physical environment may be effectively designed, or not, thereby impeding the quality of a service outcome. Fourth, the service system put in place and implemented by service providers must be understood, attractive, and user-friendly for the tourist customer. Social support from service providers is a given in a service situation that is rendered by direct intervention by responding to the clear needs of the customer.

Social support also involves indirect support by being sensitive and listening, with positive feedback (de Ruyter and Wetzels, 2000). For example, Ford (1998, p. 49) reports on a study where bartenders report hearing personal problems from 16 percent of their customers on a standard shift of 100 customers. Their role also requires social support, engaging in humorous joking and light-hearted kidding. And finally, Ford (1998, p. 50) cites tangible aid by watching over a customer's "personal belongings, and providing cab fare or free meals." Such support in personalizing a service through a tourist network is the highest level of social support that can be achieved, provided the service has this operating network and normative connection throughout its staff. As indicated above, however, interpersonal interaction is of paramount importance in maintaining a personal caring service. A study undertaken by Tax *et al.* (1998) found that customers' perceptions of interactional justice have the strongest influence on consumers' overall satisfaction with a service provider. "Consistency is the key to delivering quality, ... on which a firm can rely" (Chakrapani, 1998, p. 41). Caring for a tourism customer and empathizing with them, communicating fairness and honesty in exchanges, and not diverting from a consistent pattern of exchange have been noted by other researchers as providing the measure of a reliable service outcome.

The customer holds sway over the outcome of a service act. "In its broadest sense, a customer is someone with whom we exchange value" (Timm, 1998, p. 3). That value occurs at many levels in a complex organization. Ashforth and Humphrey (1993) define the service context or situation as: (1) a customer service interface representing the frontline, (2) service transactions often being face-to-face, (3) dynamic uncertainty in the interaction between the parties, (4) relatively intangible because of the personal nature of that particular social interactional act. At best, a service organization can only crudely blueprint the kind of service situation that identifies them, given their structure.

Goodwin (1998, pp. 545–52) identifies four types of service experience often found in the tourist sector. These include, first, the Retreat, which offers "an escape, a separation from everyday 'mundane' role requirements." A service organization such as Club Med is an example where participants are screened to be included as a partner in the activities. Customers develop a sense of entitlement, a feeling that they are part-owner of the place, and often may want to see themselves as partial managers as well. Such an open environment is a managerial challenge. Second, the Dressing Room service creates physical but not informational privacy: where those using the service are free from observation and/or unwanted intrusion. Hotels and rental cars are examples where the customer can view the provider as a maid or valet, rather than a skilled professional. Customers enjoy the expected services when delivered properly, but uncertain outcomes can be upsetting. Providers can find themselves on the receiving end of a tongue lashing. Third, service can be viewed as a Depot, where informational privacy is maintained, but not physical privacy. Customers are "seen but nobody knows who they are" in real life. Customers being processed though an airport or train depot are examples. Service providers need to be trained to detect and resolve the demands of this situation, since customers pay for the right, and often demand more if the situation becomes too busy. The fourth and final situation is called the service Prison, where neither communication nor physical privacy is possible. An airplane is a good example, where the passenger is held in a fixed location with few options, and can be disturbed by their fellow passengers and crew members. In this situation, providers need to know that, if they act as guards, they may be dealing with prisoners in return. That is, customers will often consciously and subconsciously respond to the roles that they have been assigned in service environments.

In the service sector, there are situations in the hospitality area where the customer's role takes on aspects of the worker's role (Bendapudi and

Leone, 2003). These so-called partial employees are successfully socialized by the organization (Kelley *et al.*, 1990, pp. 318, 320–21). Examples include the restaurant buffet; conservation practices at some hotels where patrons monitor their own water consumption; and open seating on some airlines requiring the cooperation of the customer. The performance of these activities does not just happen spontaneously. They require management and organization in the way of "formal socialization programs, organizational literature, environmental cues, and reinforcement" of desired behavior. An outstanding example in the tourist and entertainment area is The Walt Disney Company's theme park management. "Prior to or upon arriving at Disney World tourists receive literature that influences their expectations for their encounter at the theme park." Some companies provide video disks outlining the activities, sites, and experiences that one can expect. In this way, customers who become successfully socialized have more valid and realistic expectations about a service (Burton, 2002).

Four criteria that aid in the socialization of customers include establishing a clear image in the customer's mind of an organizational climate for service. It is those service characteristics that distinguish the organization from others. By communicating the service actions beforehand through advertising, websites, and detailed literature, the customer receives a better idea of what to expect in the actual interaction process (Evans *et al.*, 2008). Certain steps will be taken and acted out for the customer. A second factor is the motivational effort and appropriateness put forth by the customer; research indicates that customers who are more motivated will contribute more to the technical and functional quality of a service. A third factor that contributes to greater service quality perceptions is generating commitment to the organization by turning ownership over to the customer by personalizing a service. By enlisting customers as so-called partial employees, where they become part of the service delivery process, the quality of the service tends to increase because the customer receives additional benefits, often resulting in lower prices, faster service, and greater convenience. The customer receives such additional rewards through their effort, which is rewarded by passing the savings in costs back to them. The system works in the hospitality area because it is self-reinforcing for the customer if the company recognizes and promotes its service as a partnership between itself and the customer (Dong *et al.*, 2008).

The symbolic interaction theory places the service provider and customer tourist in connection with one another for giving and receiving service. That frontline service often sets the general theme for a tourist experience, and the good or bad feelings the customer brings home. In today's largely impersonal world, going the extra distance as a service provider will bring greater satisfaction to the customer, and increased positive loyalty and recommendation.

2   Encountering interactive roles

Preview

This chapter begins to detail the roles played by the service provider and how that role is influenced by the social situation. Sometimes the service provider needs to play a passive role, while more active participation may be required in other situations. Despite the level of involvement, one goal always remains – to satisfy the customer or client. This chapter distinguishes the categorical differences between an interactive encounter and a relational service situation, and how these differences are played out, using examples from the tourist industry. The characteristics of the role players are defined and elaborated upon in order to put forth a plan for service providers and what is expected of them. The remaining part of the chapter deals with the bonding of the tourist customer service provider relationship through various emotions and motivations.

Role relations in service delivery

The relationship

What occurs in the face-to-face exchange between a service provider and customer forms the basis of a relationship. In a seminal article, Solomon *et al.* (1985) propose that the interpersonal interaction between a service provider and a customer is a critical driver of the customer's overall satisfaction with the firm. The service role is about people who are committed, turned on to people, and care about their needs. It is about people who take responsibility, know their business, are accountable, and are asked to improve the service each and every day (Peters, 1991, p. 4). No matter how modern service has become, "while instant execution companies eliminate touch from the process, they do not eliminate people; even in the digital age" (Yeh *et al.*, 2000, p. 177). These kinds of company deploy people more strategically to facilitate the needs and expectations of their clients.

The service provider not only remains the hands-on server but, in many cases, serves as the symbol of the company or spokesperson, publicist, and diplomat. "Service performers are a powerful medium for building brand meaning and equity. Their actions with customers transform brand vision to brand reality – for better or worse. Service providers make or break a brand, for the customers' actual experiences with the service always prevail in defining the brand for them" (Berry, 2000, p. 135). Thus service providers have the potential to enhance the competitiveness of the provider. That kind of interactive process between service provider and customer ultimately defines the meaning of the service for good or bad. The facilitator service provider such as Club Med is at one end of the spectrum, and is most active in interacting with the customer, while the caretaker provider (super-discount hotels) is at the other end, being very passive and uninvolved with the customer, and functioning to enable customers to learn by doing and to help them acquire the appropriate transaction-related procedures (Gupta and Vajic, 2000). In a category closer to the facilitator is the servant, who works for the tourist with kindness, grace, and manners to provide an experience of power and upper-class uniqueness to the personalized customer. In a very real sense, it is customers who define job descriptions of frontline staff. Frontline employees' actions are driven by what they need to do to say 'yes' to customers as encounters transpire (Drought and McLaughlin, 1995). That is a very difficult position to be in when weighing customers' demands, but forces the customer service representative to go the extra distance it may take to delight a customer. As noted by Gutek (1995), despite sometimes conflicting role demands, some providers are still eager to provide top-rate service and are willing to go the extra mile to satisfy their customers. This need remains an essential goal of service firms, to have frontline associates willing to take on extra-role activities to ensure customer satisfaction (Netemeyer *et al.*, 2005).

Barnes (1994) is convinced that the most important internal marketing effort in providing satisfactory service is the commitment to the best possible treatment of customers. And that internal marketing effort falls squarely on the shoulders and backs of the employees who have the central and pivotal role in the encounter process. Brown (1996), however, is also convinced that some companies rely on myth to explain improved customer satisfaction and success in their competitors. In those service companies, managers and employees alike mythically think that successful companies employ whiz-bang technology, that they are really just lucky, and that improving customer satisfaction has only limited impact on the performance of an organization. Such myths are convenient rationalizations for not developing a system of customer relationships or emphasizing customer contact.

Given the nuances of the role, frontline providers are facilitators of service offerings. The key differences between a provider in a relational rather than an encounter exchange are knowledge, and its delivery of benefits to the customer. In relationships, knowledge is entrenched in the individual provider, whereas in encounters it is embedded in organizational procedures and practices. More specifically, in relationships, the provider group often has control over the procedures utilized to enact the provider role; conversely, in encounters, the organization controls and defines the procedures in which the provider role is embedded (Gutek, 1999). A relational provider has more duties and is more flexible in delivering a service than an encounter provider, and develops a positive orientation to keep the customer satisfied because they know that they can be replaced. In an encounter situation, providers are judged on their delivery style against the criterion of whether they act as if they have a relationship with the customer. A number of role attributes are often associated with the encounter provider, among them appearance and attractiveness. Gutek (1995, pp. 113–31) finds that if this is true of a certain job, as in the case of flight attendants, then customers assume the job does not require skills or abilities. Encounter providers have little latitude over their work tasks and making decisions about the customer, other than what is scripted by the organization. Encounter providers are to be functionally equivalent with any other provider; the training is concrete and narrowed to just those service tasks for that position. Cross-training in duties is the exception. Moreover, as the quantity of expertise needed to perform a job declines, the focus on such personal attributes as physical attractiveness and the ability to interact with customers tends to rise to the surface (Gutek, 1995). Advancement is narrowed because jobs are defined by boundaries and, as a result, workers cannot demonstrate that they possess skills and talents worthy of advancement. The annual turnover or attrition rate can range any-where from 70 to 300 percent in the hospitality service sector. But, as expec-tations are so limited in defining these roles, and so little is invested in training, management can look to replacements if the local market has a sufficient surplus of labor. In Atlanta, Georgia, some years ago, when the labor market was tight, the Marriott Corporation began providing incentives such as on-site daycare and medical services to retain frontline providers.

In essence, an efficient frontline provider is an obedient worker who com-plies with rules and regulations, and delivers service with a smile. These, evi-dently, are not the key qualities required in professional, middle-management, or executive positions. In the encounter organization, the frontline associate is transacting in lower-level positions, with limited customer feedback, little variety, and little autonomy (Gutek, 1995). This results in customers receiving services from low-status workers. Gutek (1995) suggests that one antidote to this situation is to place "higher status" individuals in direct contact scenarios. In high-unemployment white-collar markets, such a practice may work while that trend exists, but may become unrealistic when markets are in demand.

We rely heavily on Gutek's (1995, 1999) works in this section because of the excellent distinctions that are made regarding encounter and relationship systems.

The encounter system consists of numerous roles: the providers, managers to supervise them, designers to configure and modify an encounter system to increase its efficiency, and personnel staff to recruit and train adequate staff (Gutek, 1995, p. 52–53). In most cases, an encounter provider situation con-tains a drastically weak link between provider and customer, and has heavily increased controls and limitations on the provider, in comparison with a professional service provider (Gutek, 1995, p. 165). The social interaction is not personal. The encounters are often anonymous. That is, the customers realize that no-one knows anything about them, and this is often comforting. The identity of the provider may also be hidden, provided (if at all) by just a first name (Gutek, 1995). Also, the themes of the encounters are mostly homogenous. In other words, all customers are treated in a uniform fashion. They are not differentiated on the basis of status, wealth, clothing, age, sex, or race (Gutek. 1995). Customers in encounter situations are essentially equivalent with regard to their function. They seek a similar service, and are therefore treated to a similar service outcome. Gutek (1995, pp. 33–34) likens encounters with a service provider to the clinical experience of encounter group therapy. A sense of safety and security for the customer is achieved through the probable chance of "never having to interact with the same people again" in that service situation in the future. In the same way, the bond between the service provider and customer is weak. Such encounters are generally brief, just direct meetings between two strangers, each playing a particular role. Since encounters are of short duration, nothing more develops. Also, encounters pose no requirement for a customer to return for another interaction (Gutek, 1995, pp. 41–42). At the center of the provider–customer interaction, "service encounters are where execution takes place. A set of service encounters usually creates and delivers a consumer or employee benefit that the internal or external customer uses, experiences, pays for or works for" (Collier, 1994, p. 279). In sum, an encounter entails the delivery of a standardized service process by functionally equivalent providers. On the other hand, a relationship is characterized by a history of shared interaction with the same provider over multiple service visits (Gutek, 1995).

Listing major disadvantages of encounter service, Gutek (1995) recognizes that the interaction between provider and customer may lead to negative consequences for both parties, because of the kind of exchange the service process relies upon to function in that role relationship. Specifically, a key shortcoming of an encounter strategy is that individual associates often have little motivation to deliver top-rate service because they do not anticipate future transactions with the same customer. Further, customers often have little desire to extend positive feedback to providers who deserve it, because they also do not anticipate future encounters with the same person. This is especially a problem in the tourism industry, where many resorts serve a guest for a single visit. The encounter interaction does not provide motivation for either the associate or the customer to be particularly personable. While encounter providers are, at least, slightly constrained by the organization's standards (and typically can be fired for being rude to a customer), customers have little incentive to be polite during the transaction. Thus both provider and customer are more prone to engage in stereotyping behavior, because neither possesses unique information about the other (Gutek, 1995).

A strong relationship is premised on an enduring number of exchanges over time that reveal the true public character and personality (Morgan and Hunt, 1994). Those personality and character aspects that both provider and customer wish to reveal within the context of their exchange take time to mature. Gutek (1995, p. 48) reports that waitpersons tend to be less open and more formal with persons who are different from them. The single exception is female servers, who male diners assumed would be more open and friendly than male servers. In two other reviewed studies, Gutek (1995, p. 50) finds that males are "generally served before female customers." The rationale given by servers is that "men need more help than women," "men are more serious buyers," and "women shop around more." Whether those assumptions are correct is open to speculation, but the fact remains that servers are acting on those beliefs; whereas in a relationship, associates possess the ability to deliver customized service (Gutek, 1995). Due to the valuable contribution of a customer to a business, or because of the specialized needs of the customer, service can deviate from the norm. In a good relationship, the participants are committed; they are willing to expend energy and resources to preserve the relationship. The customer may be willing to pay a premium to continue the relationship, and the provider may be willing to commit personal time to maintain it (Gutek, 1995, p. 17). The provider–customer relationship at first sight appears to be a very easy form of social interaction. "Relationships feel commonsensical and misleadingly appear to be natural and easy when they are going well. Relationships do not just happen; they have to be made-made to start, made to work, made to develop, kept in good working order and preserved from going sour" (Duck, 1991, p. 3). But they can be refined and developed like any other skill (Duck, 1991, p. 4). They are not immune from rational decision making and conscious manipulation in order to improve their effectiveness (Raimondo *et al.*, 2008). We do not find it a strange idea that professionals in the health-care industry and social services are taught to maintain a constructive bedside manner, and the same can be done in the hospitality professions. When one pays for a service, the expectation of benefit is real and not just left to chance. Therefore everyone in the company should accept relationship-fostering as an essential responsibility.

Customer satisfaction and continually improving the service is everyone's responsibility. Thus identifying all the points at which the organization has, or could have, contact with customers provides invaluable information upon which to base the design of service systems (Vavra, 1992). Small-group studies were employed in game situations to measure how players cooperate or diverge from each other. Gutek (1995, pp. 93–94) concludes that "a relationship breeds cooperation and mutual benefit when both provider and customer start out with good will, do not tolerate poor performance from the other, and quickly forgive the other's mistakes assuming he or she rectifies them immediately." The level of commitment and involvement is, of course, much greater in a relationship arrangement (Morgan and Hunt, 1994).

In essence, the continuum of commitment and involvement on the part of the service provider runs along the scale of encounters and relationship interactions that can be modified. That modification of a service interaction is based on the service being defined in a face-to-face interaction between a provider and customer in a service setting. The level of control or power on the part of the service provider is pivotal. "An obvious solution to power-lessness among providers is to make the delivery of goods and services more relationship-like" (Gutek, 1995, p. 174). This reciprocity of "you treat me with good will and I treat you the same" is not inherently part of the encounter process that is based on playing a single game. This will emerge as a relationship only after repeated playing with the same players. It is the prospect of future transactions that makes the qualitative distinction between a relationship and an encounter. Encounters, on the other hand, do not prompt cooperative behavior between customer and provider without systematic cooperative supervision. This dichotomy is not cast in concrete in real life, where management transforms the service encounter into a pseudo-relationship. Both are more like a continuum, with gray areas.

Service interactions are role performances (Collier, 1994, p. 35), where learned and consistent behavior is performed in order to accomplish a transaction. Whether trading for goods or services, these acts of barter, negotiation, and purchase are interdependent acts between individuals to satisfy their human needs, wants, and motivations. Such a viewpoint includes any "physical evidence" revealed in a social situation. Instrumental relation-ships are a big part of the service work role, in which interacting individuals are bent on dealing with the "ultimate function of the performance of a task." In order to realize the most successful outcomes, the service provider must enter a relationship with the customer, even though that relationship may be only minimally cooperative (Steele, 1979). Role expectations guide the ultimate outcome of the interaction, as in the case where the fulfillment of a customer's needs is an end in and of itself (Meuter et al., 2005). In the ideal case, we would project that a "friendly cooperative" process controls the parties' interactions among the service providers, and the same between the customer and the service providers. Deciphering service quality issues in face-to-face contexts is inherently complex. Both verbal and nonverbal behaviors (Sundaram and Webster, 2000) are critical drivers of quality, as are tangible cues such as employees' dress and other symbols of service (equipment, information brochures, physical setting) (Zeithaml and Bitner, 2000). The ability to interact is also superseded by the service role the provi-der occupies at that time, provided they remain true to form in the perfor-mance of their expected duties. The autonomy and anonymity of the customer is further enhanced because they perceive themselves as being among many who avail themselves of a standardized service. In the flow of the interaction, the service provider and customer are socialized to the same norms of social exchange to ease the transaction. Iacobucci (1998) also posits that the interpersonal facets of customer service cannot be overlooked because they are related to assessments of quality, satisfaction, and repurchase behavior leading to customer loyalty. Even when the customer has had multiple interactions with a firm, each individual encounter is important in creating a composite image of the firm (Boulding *et al.*, 1993).

Logic suggests that not all encounters are equally important in building relationships. The Marriott Corporation contends that the early transactions are pivotal (Zeithaml and Bitner, 2000) because, through time, customers accumulate positive experiences that can buffer a disappointing one (Hess *et al.*, 2003). Therefore, in the case of a new customer, the frontline is the first line of customer impression. A valued customer program includes as one of its key elements the interpersonal – the interactions the customer has with employees or, in some cases, with other customers (Grove and Fisk, 1997), as part of the total experience. This facet encompasses friendliness, courtesy, helpfulness, physical appearance, and apparent competence at performing particular responsibilities (Albrecht, 1992). Persons mentally explore possible outcomes of another's actions. Hence, through role taking (placing themselves in the other person's social position) and by assessing that person's role expectations they can react to achieve a desired end (Albrecht *et al.*, 1987). The expectations of a social role contain normative guidelines defining in our society what a service provider, for example, ought to or ought not to be doing in meeting those customers' expectations.

Zeithaml *et al.* (1990, p. 19) point out that there are four factors affecting a person's expectations. First, word-of-mouth communication is an extremely powerful force for influencing customers' expectations, when coming from friends, neighbors, relatives, or those who are respected in the community as opinion leaders and influential persons. The diffusion of innovations literature contains hundreds of cases of ex-customers telling others of their experience, good or bad. Communications also recognizes this channel of expression as being most powerful for persuading others, because it is thought to be genuine (Kaikati and Kaikati, 2004). Second, personal needs are controlling forces to the extent that a customer places limits on what they expect, or do not expect, largely in relation to how much they personally value a need. It is always a good idea to assess the extent to which a potential customer has a need, especially those who are very frequent travelers at one end of the spectrum, and the infrequent traveler at the other. Both will determine the effort required to satisfy their need. Third, past experience with the use of a service will also influence a customer's expectation level. Experienced travelers may be more understanding about some lapses in service, but very intolerant and very demanding about others, where they have an uncompromising standard. Thus the service provider should take the time to locate and identify those parts of the service experience that are most critical. Fourth, external communications from service providers are vital in shaping customers' expectation levels. Advertising is a must for critical examination, representing what the frontline providers are saying. The customer uses all of this input, both direct and indirect sources, to establish a level of expectation.

The old saying that "loose lips sink ships" was a reality in the Second World War; frontline servers and ads also can send the wrong message and sink a trip.

Part of this external input is price and cost, especially in the travel and tourism field, where decisions are often based on the amount of discretionary funds available to the traveler – but that is not where a social exchange stops. It is not enough to know what customers expect, it is also essential that service personnel know the motivational and psychographic considerations that drive their purchase behaviors (Blackwell, 1997). In that regard, Albrecht (1992, p. 197) recognizes William James, the psychologist, for pointing out that the "deepest need in every human being is the desire to be appreciated," and that includes not only customers, but also employees. Interpersonal acts of recognition or praise, compliments on good taste, and a positive, outgoing exchange lend support to this basic motivating need to be fulfilled. Since it is employees who have the most customer contact, they are largely responsible for driving customers' impressions. Personalized service delivered by a human is superior to any technology-based substitutes because zero-defect technology is not possible in service encounters due to the influences of numerous intervening variables (Tschohl and Franzmeier, 1991).

The service role is often placed in one of two categories. Specifically, managers will tend toward using a production-line approach or an empowerment approach to direct or drive transactions (Macdonald and Sirianni, 1996). It is prudent to note that overlaps occur depending on the nature of the service and customers' expectations. Nevertheless, in the production-line approach, skill levels are specialized and separated; in the empowerment approach, more flexible responses are needed to meet the demands of the situation. In our social service world, customers develop perspectives that entail individuals' definitions of rules, norms, dominant practices, lines of authority, consensual understandings, and other 'rules of thumb' that people develop to provide structure (Prus, 1996). These rules focus on the symbolic and verbal processes of how people communicate, link up, and deal with one another. Defining images of service providers, defining service situations, and resolving ambiguity with service are processes to which customers have been socialized within their cultural context, and of which they have certain expectations in advance. The process of exchange relies on norms of psychological reciprocity (McMullan and Gilmore, 2008). "If you don't show interest in your customers, they won't show interest in you. If you don't trust them, they won't trust you. And if you don't care passionately, sincerely, constantly about not just meeting but exceeding their needs, they won't see you as being any better or worse than any other organization they have done business with" (Bell and Zemke, 1992, p. 27). It is important to have employees caring about a company. Along these lines, when workers are guided by intrinsic facets of their roles, they are likely to exude extra effort when the organization needs it, whereas those motivated by rules and regulation have little impetus to engage in extra-role or boundary-spanning behaviors (Gutek, 1995). Again, it is the role of the service provider that remains dominant. The potential power frontline associates possess when it comes to customer retention cannot be overemphasized. For this reason, fostering a genuine customer-focus among all associates, which drives them to deliver consistent, reliable, responsive, and flexible service, is quintessential (Murphy, 1996).

Part of delivering that service is how close the service provider comes to fulfilling the exact needs and expectations of the customer. Ford (1998, pp. 41–43) helps to detail role interaction between the service provider and customer by recommending personalized service. High-end hotel chains such as Ritz-Carlton and Four Seasons lead the way in offering personalized service to their repeat customers (Court, 2005). The trend has begun to filter down to less expensive lodging. Increasingly, hotels and resort destinations provide the level of personal attention once afforded only by the rich and famous. Noe (1999, pp. 95–96) also contends that personalization is one of the key elements for enhancing service satisfaction. Ford (1998) begins by reviewing the interactive phases of the service provider: first, being attentive in their verbal and nonverbal body language; second, having the service provider actually perceive and interpret the intentions of the customer; and third, responding to the customer in a timely and appropriate manner. Ford (1998) concludes that, although personalized service may be the ideal form, few studies have examined it to date. Yet personalized providers attempt to fulfill each customer's unique needs, demonstrate active involvement in interactions with customers, share information, and show genuine emotions to communicate sensitivity to customers. American Express Travel Services is constructed around personalized service, and treats each individual customer and their special needs and problems with individual attention. They suggest that one of the most innovative forms of one-to-one customer service interaction is helping a traveler with a problem (Wiersema, 1996).

Problems happen and need solutions. That is the negative side of expectations, which Vandergriff (1999) describes as resulting in grief that is simply the distance between reality and expectation. And by the same token, if a person's actual experience of the service exceeds expectations, then excitement and elation are possible outcomes. This represents the expectancy disconfirmation paradigm in the services literature (Oliver and Burke, 1999). In understanding what customers expect, the provider must realize that when a customer's plane is late, s/he is annoyed, but when it causes a missed connection, they understandably feel victimized (Cannie, 1994). In that kind of situation, personalization and directly working with the customer can help ease the strain. On the positive side, steps can also be taken to help cement the customer contact. For example, sending a note simply thanking a guest for their stay goes a long way toward making them feel welcome now and in the future. Gilpin (1996, p. 151) cites this example from a colleague who wrote about a small hotel – but what if a large hotel could do something similar? The effect would reinforce what relationship marketing is built upon: "knowing the customer, listening to the customer, competing for the customer and finally thanking the customer." What a special way to make a connection with a customer, especially if the note is handwritten; or if an email address is known, the company could periodically keep the customer up to date if s/he so wishes. It takes that extra effort to raise the quality standard, and dealing with the customer directly is certainly one way to raise that standard.

A high service quality standard is a must in a service-oriented society where multiple companies are competing for the same customer. Chakrapani (1998, p. 225) cites quality experts from Deming to Crosby, who point out that the most effective way to improve customer satisfaction is to improve the processes through which services are delivered. Collier (1994, p. 7) also perceives the service quality challenge to be more complicated because service, information, entertainment, time, and people play greater roles, while the material, tangible product is only a single factor in the process. Human social interaction between the service provider and customer roles exist for the moment, and when organized, are broadly defined within the parameters of public norms: "In the final analysis, service is a relationship between employees and customers" (Bhote, 1996, p. 74). As a company, all resources should be geared toward making such a relationship work. It should be as legally binding as marriage, minus the divorce rate.

Customer confidence transpires as a result of the glitch-free interaction of people and systems; individuals interfacing with one another is what service is all about (Petite, 1989). SAS (Scandinavian Airlines), for example, contends that interactions with employees are often the true measure of the quality of service for the company. Customers seek information in "moments of truth," or interaction with a service provider to evaluate the nature of the service (Vavra, 1992, pp. 88–89). Armistead and Clark (1994, p. 90) designate service providers engaging in this function as "Boundary Spanners," linking the customer to the organization. The judgment of the customer regarding the value and quality of the service will be weighted largely on the basis of what happens during the interaction between the service provider and customer (Wang and Davis, 2008). Hensel (1990) truly recognizes the significance of effective service interaction. His attention is directed to service delivery scenarios in which human interfaces are critical to service delivery. In other words, interpersonal interactions are an important part of the service quality evaluation process. Interpersonal contact is essential to the quality of service; while automation has its role, it must take place where such tasks are more convenient for the customer than the company.

Evaluation of the service process should take place with the service employee. Service quality suffers when employees are haphazardly selected and poorly prepared to meet customer-defined service quality specifications. In service firms, quality is determined largely by the nature of the contacts between staff and customers. It takes both technical competence (skill and knowledge related to the specific service) and functional competence (skill in interpersonal relations) to deliver high-quality service. A successful strategy for developing competence mandates a description of the goal to be achieved by the company, as exemplified by SAS switching to a customer-oriented mission. In developing staff competence, it helps to recognize the capability of their staff. This natural ability can do as much to develop competence by delegating the right tasks and giving the right work opportunities as by training (Edvardsson *et al.*, 1994). It also takes the disposition of the employee and the service system. Service quality is created by the interaction of three distinct forces – the provider, the corporate processes, and customers. For example, a recent study conducted by Crotts *et al.* (2009), analyzing data drawn from four hotels, found that when staffing policies and systems are aligned with strategic goals (organizational alignment), employees are more highly committed and satisfied. Thus the existence of organizational alignment, in return, influences customer satisfaction through committed and satisfied frontline providers.

Many organizations make the mistake of emphasizing customer satisfaction to the exclusion of employee satisfaction when, in fact, the two are highly correlated (Goodman and Yanovsky, 1997). In that respect, customer satisfaction has to be balanced with employee satisfaction. Employees are internal customers; therefore employee satisfaction is critical to customer satisfaction (Chakrapani, 1998). To illustrate, Bitner and Hubbert (1994) operationalize the service encounter as the time in which the consumer and service interact. These researchers evaluated the responses of a sample of airline travelers' perceptions of encounter satisfaction, overall satisfaction, and service quality. They found that 95 percent of the respondents evaluated their satisfaction with the encounter, while almost 50 percent of those who rated their overall satisfaction also included the encounter, and 40 percent responding to the service quality also included reference to specific provider encounters. Although the three service interactions exhibited independence, this was particularly valid for overall service satisfaction and perceived quality, but not for a single service encounter. The significance of the person-to-person experience is certainly a determining, concrete event that structures a person's perception of a service satisfaction event, and even its overall impression and quality (Wieseke *et al.*, 2007).

"We must never forget that service businesses do not produce – they perform. They do not sell 'things'; they sell human performances" (Donnelly, 1992, p. 110). In the end, that is the bottom line and also the frontline of a service corporation. Where distinctions are made is when someone says how nice and friendly those resort, airline, restaurant, and hotel providers really are to us. It is a personal judgment because customers are receiving the output from these service providers, and the customer is the sole judge. Along these lines, Zeithaml and Bitner (2000) point out that because these services are intangible, customers are always searching for clues to the outcome they can expect from a service provider. Those clues come in large measure from the service people, along with the steps in the service process, and the physical attributes of the setting. Considering the big picture, people remain the ultimate service weapon. Since everything else can be copied and emulated, intangible attributes associated with frontline service staff are much more difficult for competitors to duplicate (Schaaf, 1995). Examples given are those of the Hyatt chain, which increased its staff considerably to be able to assign one person per major corporate client. Marriott, as well, assigns a person to a corporation to work on site to deal with their client's travel needs. More and more, such partnering practices are becoming quite common, giving pleasure travelers the advantage of being offered bonuses or reduced prices to pick up excess capacity. This may lower profit margins, but still leads to a profit in the end.

There is a growing segment of wealthy people in the USA who have little time for leisure or tourism. They get their pleasure or indulgence by flying business or first class. Thus they are being served by the middle class who, according to Reich (1998), are receiving less personal attention. Since their jobs have changed, service employees are measured by catering to the professional class and the quality of their attentiveness to people who are wealthier than themselves and their peers. That is a price for a service economy that managers must be aware of in dealing with their employees' loss of status and income. Their employees are not like servants from the other end of town, as in the Gilded Age, but a novel type of social divide seems to be forming, just the same, between the classes. Such a divide can threaten the division of labor. Carr (1990) uses an example of a 200-bed hotel with an occupancy rate of 85 percent, providing a full range of services. A rough estimate is that those guests will have 20 points of service contact each night, making approximately 4000 to 5000 chances of potential service failure. Zeithaml *et al.* (1990) indicate that a large number of frontline employees, as well as many others, are named as to blame for America's service malaise, but they categorically and flatly disagree with that conclusion. When service roles are not given proper attention by upper management, and placated by middle management, who is to blame? If frontline employees are provided little sense of how their roles fit into the big picture, of what their customers expect, or why their work is important, whose fault is it?

It is a major mistake to forget that today's highly educated workforce presents a mismatch with the prevailing encounter system. "Skilled workers who would be very effective in relationship interactions are bored and frustrated by the lack of feedback, challenge, variety, and autonomy in encounter-style provider jobs" (Gutek, 1995, p. 174). Schaaf (1995, p. 68) asks the basic question – how do we get ahead on the corporate ladder? And rhetorically, he answers that question by stating: "We get the hell out of customer service positions just as fast as we can, don't we? Nothing good happens 'down there.' The pay, the perks, the power, the prestige, the celebrity of a career accrue to us as we work our way farther and farther away from the customer … We say we want to help the customer, but we reward people for something else, the power lines are in all the wrong places." The organization has some design deficiencies. Tschohl and Franzmeier (1991) note that, in our society, service jobs are often not perceived as worthwhile avenues to pursue.

Consequently, when the worker accepts this view, the attitude is transmitted in their lack of performance. The former highly respected Ritz-Carlton chief Horst Schilze would never accept this premise, and the service standards set by Ritz employees make them outstanding winners of the United States' highest customer service award. "Service workers performing 'Everyman's or Everywoman's' skills are vulnerable to the embarrassment of everyday failures, but have few opportunities to display skill of a higher order, even if they often use such skills to accomplish their tasks. Thus, their daily work experience is often one of a series of minor complaints assuming major proportions for the customer, or empty 'thank yous'" (Macdonald and Sirianni, 1996, p. 17). The relationship between the service provider and customer in the travel sector is an intangible bond that can be brief, such as in an encounter, or more enduring, as in the relationship. However, the nature of this relationship, if positive and enduring, becomes an intangible asset in the long run (Roberts, 2001), enabling the provider to compete better and more effectively in the marketplace.

Social behaviors behind positive service acts

Motivations

In addition to how persons define a situation, meaning is also moderated by motivational and psychographic variables, by past experiences, and by the objective facets of the situation (Endler, 1988). Motivations in a socially interactive world are multi-dimensional. "Three basic motivational principles include the desire for mastery (understanding the universe to obtain rewards), the desire for connectedness to other people and groups, and the desire to maintain and enhance a positive view of the socially extended self (the individual self as well as other persons or groups connected to the self)" (Smith and Mackie, 1997, p. 310). The many potential influences of feelings from both the customer's and the employee's perspective must be considered in service delivery (Liljander, 2000). Anger, frustration, fear, etc. ... as with social bonds, commitment, trust, and satisfaction foster rapport-building (Liljander, 2000). These are factors affecting customers' relationships with a company. The essence of a customer service job involves feelings, and having felt things about the customer. It is not emotionally neutral. While it may not be a love–hate relationship, some of the emotions that can be involved are not weak. In their effects upon us, customer contact jobs in particular involve a high degree of emotional labor (Furnham, 2002). In fact, as noted by Donnelly (1992), they are often the bricks and mortar of the job itself.

At its core, Bennis (1979) asserts that the expression of interpersonal feelings is basic to the existence of the relationships among individuals. Such characteristics as self-esteem and level of aspiration often have a heavy influence on a frontline provider's style (Duck, 1991). The kinds of comparison for derived benefit in a relationship need to meet or exceed the expectations of the individual for them to achieve a satisfaction level in an exchange. Self-esteem and aspirations for achievement, too, can affect a relationship, especially if a person is down on him/herself or holds out little prospect for the future. This is not a good situation upon which to build a relationship or encounter. In a relational contact, emotions and control play a larger role. In general, providers are expected to mask robust feelings about customers and minimize the manifestations of their own feelings, whether those feelings are positive or negative. For them, emotional labor entails setting aside actual feelings and displaying others. Such displays of emotion in encounters, however, are "not considered a skill," and typically providers are "not monetarily compensated for it" (Gutek, 1995, p. 81). Skill in masking these stronger feelings is not readily open to examination, despite the interaction. There are emblematic expressions of emotions such as anger, happiness, and others, but these have rarely been examined in empirical research, probably because they are not easily elicited in laboratory conditions (Feyereisen and de Lannoy, 1991). An important reason why on-site observations of the customer and service provider are conducted is to get a feel for the real-life interplay. Harris (1991) finds that passion, enthusiasm, or zeal is a necessary ingredient for customer rapport-building. While it cannot be directly taught, emotional expression is contagious, and can be transmitted within a group of service providers who provide an uplifting experience to the customer. This is especially important for providers in the tourism industry, where customers expect to be made happy and satisfied when taking a break from their daily lives. Transactional standards are about the human-to-human dimensions of customer contact and, unfortunately, are not easily expressed in tangible and measurable ways (Anderson, 1999).

Such standards are difficult to craft and design, as well as to form and communicate. These kinds of transactional facets are vital in garnering exceptional customer ratings. Nevertheless, this is a variable standard or norm, largely built on previous past experience (Hess et al., 2003). For the most part, "the spirit of service lives in almost all human beings to some extent, but it is a highly variable level of energy ... Some people can easily find the kind, generous, caring part of themselves all or most of the time. Others may be less self-loving and self-caring" (Albrecht, 1992, p. 89). To teaze this out of the social self, Southwest Airlines encourages its service providers to be themselves. For example, Southwest Airlines takes the position that an active sense of humor helps alleviate frontline stress and bolster both employee and customer satisfaction (Wiersema, 1996).

Trust is another important emotional interactive bond between customer and service provider that characterizes the sustained success of service firms (Berry, 1999). Competence is critical to developing customers' trust in a service company. It is a very big challenge to maintain consistency of service, since labor-intensive services are more vulnerable to failure (Fisk et al., 1993). It is not like a product consumed outside the factory. The service product is consumed within the service factory and in real time, with no chance of replay (Michel, 2001). Cultivating trust relationships is important because there will be times when failure happens. Given a high-trust customer relationship, such an unfortunate happenstance will be more than likely viewed as an aberration. Trust increases the tolerance of mishap that occurs in all service endeavors at some time – even the most competent. Trust is also part of the interaction between employee and company. Berry (1999) likens high-trust organizations to healthy extended families in the kind of caring, compassionate, carefree behavior that is often necessary. We, as humans, are ever rewarded by the special good words and deeds of others, which help sustain our psychological spirit, not just our physical needs. Families have friends who are also sustained in trusting interactions. "Relationship companies look for ways to please their customers, to do something extra or special for them, just as friends would do for one another. As in friendships, relationship companies do not take advantage of customers. They respect, honor and trust them" (Fournier *et al.*, 1998). If a company achieves such a level of mutual interaction, customers are likely to feel an emotional attachment and take emotional ownership, where they act as voluntary advocates and defenders of the service. Trust is the cement that acts as a bond between customer, company, and service provider, who look after and are concerned about each other's interests.

Successful companies encourage and anticipate superior achievement from their employees. For illustration, Berry (1999) describes Cora, a waitress in a café in Appleton, Wisconsin. She developed her rules for success, such as treating customers like family, by being cheerful, smiling, chatting, and including everyone in the conversation. She also developed her listening skills to the point where personalized, customized service is provided, given the customer's time frame. If they have the time, she will chat; if not, she will have them on their way quickly. Hochschild (1983) observes that service employees are expected to display emotions in the course of interacting with the customer. Such emotional labor for the flight attendant is the accommodating cheerful, friendly, outgoing, bubbly disposition that is put on display. At Delta Air Lines, a flight attendant notes that they are trained to treat passengers as if they are guests in their own home. The fact remains that behaviors are human activities that can be seen, measured, or described. The precision of terms describing behaviors such as being "customer-friendly," "neat," or "cheerful" may be too general. More specific actions may need to be detailed in a customer service situation, such as connecting behavior to customers' requirements (Connellan and Zemke, 1993). Behavioral possibilities, such as greeting customers within 30 seconds to make them feel comfortable, or linking actions to the specific role identity, such as middle-aged or teenager, are added examples that can take on emotional consequences.

The emotional performances of the service provider fall within the context of the social role that typically refers to the behavior expected of individuals who occupy certain social categories. Roles are behavioral expectations for what a person should do. Understanding what should be done is part of a person's social self, including recognizing expectations for a role in a situation, along with exhibiting their own temperament and personality dispositions. The enactment of a role is part of the process of interaction taking place between a service provider (airline steward) and customer. During such an exchange, "needs and motives are encoded in the transaction-related vocabularies that define the roles (Zurcher, 1983). In today's world, roles are not as clearly defined as in the past. Modern societies are typically not as coherent as those in the past. First, "they are congeries of organized role relationships ... some overlapping, some conflicting, and some isolated and some not." Service roles, especially, are not clearly defined position descriptions, save for the paper they are written on. They are often unable to be dealt with in a uniform manner each and every time since service situations change, just as the customers move through them, sometimes quickly and sometimes slowly. Second, "the forms and contents of social life are social constructions, the products of collective activities of persons as they together develop solutions to problems in their daily lives," and they are not fixed in cultural concrete. Third, "the human being is an actor, an active agent who acts on and alters the (social and non-social) environment that impinges on her or him, who initiates transactions with that environment and responds selectively to it" (Stryker, 1997, pp. 317–19).

In a service situation, social interaction exchanges either benefit or detract from the customers' satisfaction or happiness each and every time they occur (Boulding *et al.*, 1993). Involved in these daily exchanges are motives that are basic to an understanding of the emergence of the self. Included is the need for positive regard and coherence (Pelham and Hetts, 1999). Positive regard is seen as including the approval of others and gaining the esteem of others, while the need for coherence endorses the notion that individuals desire to reside in environments that are coherent, predictable, and controllable. Seeking these social endorsements and social situations molds the self into an interactive person who functions as a self-identity with others. Given the global world of tourism today, service providers need be careful about the recognized social status or esteem enhancement of their programs and how they make different cultures feel at home. Playing the role of the tourist maximizes understanding of those programs.

For the most part, the customer self maintains a somewhat reserved emotional role. Barnes (2000) reports that qualitative data indicate that customers do not typically employ the term "relationships" to describe the interactions they have with the service provider. That kind of social definition seems to be reserved for more personal levels of mutual interaction. Barnes's summary from the research literature includes mutual trust, commitment, communication, empathy, self-disclosure, emotional openness, shared values, cooperation, caring, affection, and sincerity, which are part of social process between the service provider and customer. Achieving this level of involvement in many mass-market transactions seems very unlikely, unless the service provider is willing to personalize what they can offer to the customer. For some customers, privacy and being left alone, without being fussed over, is what they most desire. The most public kinds of interaction are conducted in the open market by the customer, who is a stranger, and who expresses his or her needs and expectations through appearance, verbal communication, and body language. The frontline service provider has to be alert to the messages being sent by the customer, be they happy or disappointed. To assume that something is part of human interaction does not mean that in fact it is truly a part of the exchange process. Altruism or empathy may be part of the basic interactive process. An article by Batson (1995, pp. 333–82) addresses this question. The studies reviewed showed that they did not promote an empathetic relationship. Batson (1995, p. 365) concludes by quoting Adam Smith: "How selfish so ever man be supposed, there are evidently some principles in his nature, which interest him in the fortune of others, and render their happiness necessary to him, though he derives nothing from it except the pleasure of seeing it." Therefore probably a central and most significant motive in generating human contract is altruism. Seelig and Rosof (2001, pp. 934, 956) refer to five different types of altruism, one of which we find most important for our purposes – what they call "generative altruism." This refers to "nonconflictural pleasure in fostering the success and/or welfare of another." Altruism of this kind is helped by forming a connection with the development of empathy in the individual, which is an outgrowth of interpersonal interaction. The mother–infant relationship is used as a primary example where pleasure is sought and given to satisfy. The authors, however, contend that although "empathy is necessary for the genuine altruism, it is not sufficient. The ability to assess the needs of another and to determine if and when to fulfill those needs is also a component of mature altruism." Someone having achieved normal altruism through socialization and interaction, who values this self-definition, will "recognize and respect" the "autonomous wishes and pleasure or success" of another. They are able to assess the other's needs, and empathic motivation reinforces that analytic interpersonal skill. Regarding our memberships and associations in society, "a close relationship can make us respond to other people's needs as our own, producing cooperative and altruistic or even self-sacrificial helping" (Smith and Mackie, 1997, p. 311). A condition may arise in interpersonal relationships where a lack of consensual exchange is a source of anxiety because valid communication does not take place between individuals. As Bennis (1979, p. 116) states, "the presence of anxiety indicates the lack of 'empathy.'" The key connector for altruism is empathy that is grounded on meaningful communication leading to social dialogue.

The emotional disposition of empathy acts as a magnet for generating power for a social relationship, as is the case between a service provider and customer. Ciaramicoli and Ketcham (2000, p. 25) quote the psychologist William Ickes as defining empathic inference as everyday mind-reading. And "without empathy we would not be able to connect to each other in any meaningful way." In the service situation, the essence of empathy is communicating through personalized service recognizing that customers are special and unique (Zeithaml and Bitner, 2000). The provider's actions, interactions, and exchanges represent the customers' self-perceived value. Lowenstein (1997, pp. 198–99) lists a number of functions that frontline staff need to carry out with the customer. Among those listed, other researchers cite the following: do the frontline staff listen, empathize, treat customers as individuals, solve problems for the customer, ask the customer if they are satisfied, serve them positively so they will want to return, and function as part of a service team to address a customer's needs? A most important part of empathic listening is to allow others a chance to explain themselves and to communicate their thoughts and feelings fully (Ciaramicoli and Ketcham, 2000). Such a practice is an art that can be continually improved upon. Focusing not only with the ears, but with the eyes and body, is also part of the process that leads to meaningful exchanges (Sundaram and Webster, 2000). Giving the other person a chance to respond by asking indirect or open-ended questions also demonstrates empathy because it communicates respect for the person's derived reactions and responses. Moreover, when the frontline provider asks an open-ended question, it communicates the message that s/he desired to learn from the other person, and that the provider is genuinely interested (Ciaramicoli and Ketcham, 2000).

Communicating is balanced by the ability to listen. Canary and Cody (1994) maintain that listening increases the probability of achieving transaction-related goals by increasing understanding of the other individual's needs and wants, by gleaning new insights into problems and solutions, and by garnering feedback regarding behaviors. A valuable form of listening is empathetic listening, in which the speaker's words and gestures are understood as if they were your own. Empathetic listening fosters maximum comprehension of communication from the speaker's perspective and is essential to communication effectiveness. Effective communication requires perceptive communicators who are cognizant of how others perceive their actions, and how they should decode others' actions (Bell, 1987). This act is facilitated by responsiveness. A responsive person possesses the ability to generate appropriate script to extend another's comments, and has awareness of his or her role in an interaction. Bell (1987) further reports that responsiveness is negatively correlated with neuroticism, social anxiety, and communication apprehension in groups, but is positively related to sociability. Communicatively, the empathic individual signals understanding and concern through verbal and nonverbal cues. Overall, responsiveness is often positively correlated with various relationship-oriented dimensions of person perception (Wheeless and Lashbrook, 1987). This primary research effort on empathy suggests that empathic responding is signaled by numerous behaviors, most of which are considered cues of involvement. These include facial grimaces of distress or anxiety, body gestures, smiles, laughter, leaning forward, eye contact, vocal intonation and quality, facial expressiveness, open arm and leg positioning, nonverbal mirror imaging, head nods, closed body orientation, and appropriate touch (Pease and Pease, 2004). Moreover, empathetic responding also encompasses references to the here and now, topic centrality, and vivid/ metaphorical language. These research findings indicate that nonverbal behaviors account for twice as much variance in perceived empathy than verbal behaviors, despite verbal communication being a unique human facility and expression.

Box 2.1 Considering culture: eye contact and head nodding

The use and interpretation of various body language cues varies cross-culturally. Eye contact, for instance, is generally construed in a positive fashion in North America as a signal of honesty, openness, and integrity. On the other hand, it is often viewed in the Japanese culture in a negative fashion, due to perceptions of intimidation sometimes associated with its practice. Similarly, head nodding serves as a further example of a cross-national body-language difference. While in North America head nodding is interpreted as "I agree," in Japan it typically means "I am listening," and in parts of the Middle East the downward motion communicates "I agree" and the upward movement signals "I disagree."

When the social theme of empathy is examined, Gergen (1994) finds that expressions of happiness are the most common reaction by far (70 percent) to perceptions of empathetic listening. Empathy takes many turns, and for a service process, it begins right at the very start. The social process begins at the beginning, and "you must start at the very first contact point, which is probably an advertisement, and ask yourself if that is pulling in the same direction as the rest of your efforts. You must then, putting yourself in the customer's shoes, arrive at your premises and view them from the outside" (Brown, 1989, p. 51). Remember that when the customers arrive, they will be assessing, perceiving, weighing, and evaluating every step of the frontline staff and operation. Through that process of "customer-orientating, a business means wearing customer spectacles and seeing with the customer's eyes. It is a matter of listening actively both to what the customer says and to what he or she does not say" (Edvardsson *et al.*, 1994, p. 119). In evaluating the level of commitment toward an organization, it simply means moving through various stages from customer, client, support, to advocate at the top. Not only are advocates repeat users like the supporter, but they openly engage in word-of-mouth advertising for the organization. Advocates of the organization are those who actively extol the virtues of the firm to others. What affects them most in achieving this level of commitment is empathy. The establishment of customer empathy as a company value is necessary when competing in a global marketplace for customer support. To understand what it takes to acquire customer support and response, managers must refine their empathic response by: (1) studying their market on a periodic basis, (2) interacting with their customers themselves to obtain first-hand insight, and (3) tapping the frontline's experience with the customer to help model more empathic customer relations (Locander, 1989).

For individuals and service providers alike, attitude plays a key role in shaping human cognition and behavior. It affects how they selectively perceive, interpret, remember, and guide behavior (Manstead (1996, 1998). If service providers are empathetically disposed and outgoing, with positive attitudes to all members of the human race, they are more than likely to be outstanding contacts with the public and team players. Attitudes and expectations often play a large part in how the customer defines the provider's actions. Many service situations, especially those termed pure services, are marked by a large degree of human contact (Solomon *et al.*, 1985). A big potential influence on customer satisfaction is the kind of expectations customers have toward the employee who will be serving them (Gremler *et al.*, 2001). The interactions between employee and customer often psychologically become the service itself in the customer's mind. Such an impression can have a large impact on the perceived quality of service and satisfaction experienced (Mohr and Henson, 1996).

The responsiveness of the employee in performing the service was the focal point of the customer's concern and target of evaluation. How they performed in providing a service task was really the focal point of consideration. A study conducted within the restaurant industry (Andaleeb and Conway, 2006) also found employee responsiveness to be the leading determinant of customers' evaluation sentiment. Along these lines, "part of the positive interaction strategy British Airways has developed includes increasing contact between passengers and the in-flight crew, and otherwise creating a feeling that each passenger's individual needs are being proactively addressed" (Lowenstein, 1997, p. 57). The long-term value of the company is largely determined by the value of the company's customer relationships, which Rust *et al.* (2000, pp. 4, 33, 55) call the firm's "customer equity." Measuring the impact of a customer on a company's continuing relationship with him/her is determined in part by the nuances of the transactions. It is therefore important to recognize that the customer begins to form a relationship with the firm itself, whether through formal relationship/retention-type programs sponsored by the firm, or through relationships with individuals with whom the customer has had interactions. These relationships form the basis for retention equity. Hennig-Thurau *et al.* (2000) also report the results of findings based on a study of perceived customer benefits and motivational responses to becoming or remaining involved in a customer relationship. This specific empirical study corresponds to the earlier work of Gwinner *et al.* (1998). The authors find that essentially three types of benefits or motivational responses emerge in the relationship process. These are "confidence benefits," where the customer trusts the firm in keeping its word and promises. In evaluating the merits of these types of customer benefit, the results show that confidence benefits are indispensable for most service and become an important part of the customer relationship agreement. "Special treatment benefits" include reward programs, clubs, and recognition programs. And finally there are also "social benefits," which take a more personalized interest in the customer as a friend. They bring a need to provide, within limits, "emotional support, privacy, and tolerance for other friendships" (Hennig-Thurau *et al.* (2000, p. 387). The offer of social benefits is not without caveats. They may imply counterproductive side-effects that could endanger the development of true relationships and should be carefully evaluated, but the authors conclude by stating that companies should evaluate the possibilities that fit their individual "business context" (Hennig-Thurau *et al.*, 2000, p. 388). Perhaps the benefit that counts most is that which produces the most reliable outcome.

There are limits to customer adventures. Gutek (1995) reports that a body of research indicates that customers are also more highly satisfied when they experience minimal uncertainty in an interaction. Cohen (1972, pp. 167–72) also linked the familiar with the novel at either end of the tourist market for motivating travelers wherein "the security of old habits is combined with the excitement of change." The answer seems to be: "give it to them straight," no unpleasant surprises and "give it to them often" (Broydrick, 1994, p. 9). The travel tourist experience has the potential to be too uncertain. So it is wise that the service provider details the limits of the situation. The above studies suggest that moderation is the applied norm.

Part of the tourist situation is molded in a service relationship in the concept of a marketplace (Czepiel, 1990). Images of teeming, noisy places for dealing in goods and services are wonderful situations that bring out the joy in people. Today's community is a dot.com world, where there is a real problem of retreating into a shell and not risking our human side. In a symbolic world, we learn to define emotional experiences by "learning cultural recipes for defining situations in emotional terms" (Prus, 1996, p. 177). We take on emotional identities in "recreational involvement(s)" when traveling and touring, and even assume "styles of expressing particular emotional themes" (Prus, 1996, pp. 182, 184). Emotional interaction is created by defining the "immediate situation" and dealing more with the agents of interaction, namely the service provider and the customer. In a satisfaction analysis of Bodrum, a Turkish resort area, the investigators included for evaluation not only the site situation, but also the supporting contexts that were necessary to support the tourist activity. They found that the tourists were more highly satisfied with the resort area than the town. The factors receiving the highest ratings related to their interpersonal contacts, such as the friendliness of the town, the knowledge/experience of the resort staff, and the resort's hospitality. By the same token, one of the least appealing factors included the airport checkout, again highlighting the importance of the human element in the service situation (Pinar and Rogers, 2000). Achieving satisfaction in this wider context includes not just the immediate service situation, but identifying those factors in the tourists' expectations of wellbeing. Most resorts can hope to control the more tangible demands of the tourist by defining the limits of their tourist situation.

The human element cannot easily be ignored, discounted, or taken for granted. The first line service role represents a major part of a corporate investment in the travel hospitality industry. Social interactions are not so simplistic, but are rather complex between parties. Neither the provider, customer, or management can control the inclusiveness of emotions and motives – the dispositional elements of human behavior.

The travel tourist experience opens up choices to a customer with a range of expectations not common in daily life. Fulfilling these customer goals in a tangible way rests with the frontline to a large extent. From the customer's initial decision-making process to the curb and beyond, the service provider's presence and performance remains essential. Achieving customer satisfaction in this situation presents a real challenge.

3 Knowing the travel customer's role

Preview

This chapter raises the necessity of understanding market segmentation and how it relates in a service-provider tourist–customer exchange. The chapter stresses that tourists come with different credentials, levels of experience, and resources, crossing all levels of the socioeconomic spectrum. Depending on the targeted market, it becomes essential to know what kinds of leisure expectations are required of that particular market segment. The relationships between quality standards and customer expectations are discussed and examined. These include varied kinds of practice that service providers have available to them to ensure they will stay ahead of their targeted customer. The activity profile of the traveler and other marketing data information is presented as an important tactical tool. Although this section of the chapter is not very extensive, it identifies the most important sociological group profiles for serving specific tourist customers and their primary and secondary roles. These social affiliations define general dispositions that are a reflection of a party in that role – seniors, singles, families with children, and certain cultural groups. Knowing the identity of the customer at the most basic level helps to reduce uncertainty and the risk of missing the most obvious requirements due to lifestyle.

Recognizing the travelers' importance

The market base

It is not enough to organize a service company that deals with travel and tourism by merely identifying market segments. In addition, it takes understanding of how the structure of the organization fits the needs of the customer. "Reorganizing the company around the customer has therefore become compulsory from a competitive viewpoint – it is a must, not an option" (Ahlert, 2000, p. 263). For example, Edvardsson *et al.* (1994, pp. 127–28) believe that the customer should be the centre of the business, which means that "rather than 'top-down' or 'bottom-up' perspectives, we propose … an 'in-out' or co-service process perspective. This involves defining activities externally – for the customer and other interested parties/actors in the market – and focusing on the service process in relationship with the customer." To help get a handle on sorting out differences in customers, a few basic steps are necessary to run a more effective marketing plan. Company service personnel must recognize that "all customers are not equally valuable," and a "customer pyramid" approach is helpful in identifying the various levels (Venkatesan and Kumar, 2004). Customers in different tiers have different characteristics, and segmentation analysis assists in profiling the customer. And finally, customers in different tiers view quality differently, so firms must focus on what drives quality in a tier, and develop strategies to meet that need, but focusing most heavily on the upper tiers (Rust *et al.*, 2000, p. 202).

Because individualized service is cost-prohibitive in a mass society, segmentation makes it possible to design a service system for those customers who have similar needs and familiarities. Very simply, market segmentation can be described as "the process of dividing a market into groups of similar consumers and selecting the most appropriate group(s) for the firm to serve" (Peter and Olson, 2002, p. 552). "More recently segmentation is on the basis of lifestyle," where each segment is somewhat customized to the particular social class or status level. By appealing to a large market segment, services can be adapted and refined to meet the needs just of that segment (Edvardsson *et al.*, 1994). This is not a random act by a travel service that appeals to all segments. Some are fortunate to include overlapping levels, such as Disney, or are more focused and particular, such as the gambling industry. The strategy is clear in that "leaders have discovered the secret to accelerating and sustaining growth: Pick the right customers" (Reichheld, 2001, p. 85). By being particular about who you are serving, many service costs can be focused and even reduced by appealing to a single lifestyle rather than multiple interests.

Blumberg (1991) indicates that there are four steps in developing a successful strategy based on market segmentation. The first step is to identify and define the user group(s) to be served. The second step requires determination of the requirements and needs of that sector. The third step establishes a service policy that meets these requirements and needs; while the fourth step specifies the manner in which the policy affects the customer. These four initiatives are focused through the eyes of the travel customer, but that is only half of the customer marketing strategy. The other part of shaping a customer base includes identifying what type of customer you, as a company, want to serve. Carr (1990) suggests that firms ask themselves six questions when considering which customer segment(s) are most suitable for frontline interactions. How sophisticated a customer do we want? How wide a variety of customer do we want? How much do we need to depend on repeat customers and word-of-month advertising? How much do we want to depend on the honesty and integrity of our customers? Do we want customers who like a friendly, personalized atmosphere or those who prefer a formal, business-like one? Do we want customers who work closely with us to improve and develop service attributes, or are they simply customers? Essentially, the first four steps are what Vavra (1992) describes as aftermarketing, a procedure that identifies the customer base and comprehends their needs and expectations. The service providers form a relationship that recognizes individuals, shows appreciation for their patronage, quantifies customer satisfaction, and provides channels of communication to help achieve and maintain a market following. A good example is the Fairfield Inn subdivision of the Marriott Corporation, which targets the "road warrior." They appeal to customers on a limited auto touring budget, or businessmen seeking consistent quality and economy for their corporate dollar. Marriot determined that those guests desire hospitable treatment and clean rooms at a reasonable price. Management evaluates their service on the hospitality of check-in and check-out, cleanliness of guestrooms, and overall value of the customer's experience (Heskett *et al.*, 1990). The responses are also incorporated into the employee's quarterly performance evaluation process, with implications for the annual award of bonuses.

Customers occupy a special category. "Customers come first; everything else ... comes later" (Carr, 1990, p. 193). Rosenberger (2000, p. 358) makes a simple, but yet a most profound, point by stating that "in any test on customer orientation, the role of the market partner is defined as buyer, customer, client, or user, but never as a 'human being.'" This is a point well taken: for customers do not leave their feelings, fears, joys, and stresses behind. No tourist is seeking a disappointing experience, so the service provider is dealing with heightened expectations and increased sensitivity to pleasant encounters. Kelley *et al.* (1990) reaffirm that the customer has a set of normative expectations surrounding the service transaction for what the frontline associate should do (employee technical quality), and how the service employee should behave (employee functional quality). In other words, according to script theory, information about the service process is held in the memory of a consumer as a sequence of actions that transpire in a particular order, and this knowledge is called a script (Bateson, 2002). The customer then develops perceptions of the actual behavior of the employee and compares these with the normative expectations, to determine a quality of service including what they contributed to the service act and how they contributed that through their interaction. The tourist's positive expectations and emotions are the guiding light.

The Walt Disney Company refers to its customers as "guests," while SAS (Scandinavian Airlines) serves "travelers." "If people were known as customers, Disney management feels they would be viewed as part of a faceless crowd ... " (Liswood, 1990, p. 29). Their corporate names are positive and illuminate their primary role function as perceived by the service provider. Given what is transpiring between the roles, the tourist customers are recipients of goods or services. And ideally, "a good customer in an encounter is one who takes the least amount of time, has all the pertinent information available, and provides that information without question, enabling the provider to complete the transaction and get on to the next one" (Gutek, 1995, p. 98). Tourist customers decide when to avail themselves of the services offered, and are prepared to do some work themselves – complete forms, provide credit card information, and check travel schedules, to name a few. Gutek (1995) reports that Americans spend about four hours of research for every 100 dollars spent, or about 9 percent of their nonworking, nonsleeping time, doing personal research before purchasing a future service or good. Given customers' lack of time, and business factors encroaching on Americans' non-working lives, it is important to expedite tourists' potential decision-making processes.

Box 3.1 Considering culture: perceptions of time

Some cultures are more time-bound than others. That is, in mono-chronic-time countries, such as Germany or Switzerland, time is divided into small increments and high levels of attention are given to the passage of time. Hence promptness is a priority and public clocks are relatively easy to locate. Conversely, in polychronic-time countries, such as Brazil and India, there is a loose notion of being on time or late, and wide latitude is afforded to the starting and ending times of business and social gatherings.

The first major customer objective begins with the identification of your core market segment, with whom you must achieve total customer satisfaction (TCS). TCS will help you hold onto your privileged status, and it will help you expand and extend your privilege (Hanan and Karp, 1989, p. 3). Achieving this status level is the only alternative for a successful tourist provider; the repeat process is rather uncomplicated. Customers enter the core customer stage after they begin a regular repeat-purchase cycle. The firm's product or service meets their required specifications and value. Unless a major problem arises with the purchasing process, these customers rarely ever re-evaluate their choice. "Core customers – the firm's most highly valued customers – are critical to overall profitability" (Blattberg et al., 2001, pp. 16, 153).

In a relatively free enterprise system, profit ensures support for the business. Rust et al. (2000) remind us that the premier customers need be served above all, as they represent the most profit, and work is constantly needed to strengthen their relationships with the company. Staying with this core segment and emphasizing what the company does best is an essential element. Every manager's standards of performance should require the total customer satisfaction of core customers. This will be the wellspring for up to 80 percent of profits. That is, the 80–20 rule of marketing states that 80 percent of a firm's sales are often generated by 20 percent of its customers (Hallberg, 1995). This standard is so imperative that it cannot be violated or ignored (Hanan and Karp, 1989, p. 5). But it does not mean that once the core market segment has been identified and customer expectations known, all is categorically set. According to Collier (1994, p. 203), service monitoring means being open to change and evaluating the effectiveness of the client–customer encounter relationship on a continual basis. In comparing the budget of a super-budget hotel with that of a luxury hotel, Collier (1994, pp. 264–66) demonstrates that different skill sets are needed for the two contrasting enterprises. "For luxury hotels, the consumer benefit package and associated service encounters are customized and personalized to the individual, involving appearance, manners and effective communication skills." For super-budget hotels, the average hotel guest is identified with the market segment, and the skills of the employee are directed more toward those operational skills necessary for the physical operation of the facility – maintenance, cleaning, etc. But customers also have corresponding roles to play in these service situations. "Customers need be educated or in essence 'socialized' so they can perform this minimal role effectively. Subtle ways can be found in a tourist situation such as signage, information brochures, personal information from the frontline employee, and web sites without detracting from the customers experience. The role of a customer may also be seen as a 'productive resource,' 'a contributor to quality and satisfaction,' or as 'competitors'" (Zeithaml and Bitner, 2000, pp. 333, 322). However, those roles requiring more active customer participation may have little potential in tourist situations, where many are looking for leisure and relaxation, except maybe the more active outdoor sports and wilderness-park experiences.

Answering the question: What comes first in the service system? "The customer comes first! What does the customer want? Find the answer and then produce and deliver in a fashion that will create a lasting bond" (Griffin, 1994, p. 153). One must realize that this not a hit-or-miss process. Rather, sustaining high-quality service is not simply doing well whatever it is you do; instead, it is comprehending what drives value for the customer and doing those things well (Connellan and Zemke, 1993). An additional requirement for delivering high-quality service is the development of performance standards mirroring management's perceptions of customers' expectations. However, executives commonly report that they had a problem trying to translate customer expectations into quality standards (Zeithaml *et al.*, 1990). That condition may be more a result of a lack of sincere commitment to service quality on management's part, or a lack of specific customer input that clearly identifies quality attributes. Data and quality information are a necessity for quality implementation. In obtaining information on service systems, customer service expectations should be measured along with the relative importance of service quality attributes (Berry, 1995). Both these measures, when combined, are the heart and soul of customer feedback, because the expectations of the customer are comparison standards for judging the effectiveness of the real service attributes (Oliver and Burke, 1999). Customers' expectations are not readily known by the firm, but consumer research dedicated to understanding the customer, rather than being operations- or systems-driven, should aid in alleviating unnecessary stumbling blocks in customer relations (Gilpin, 1996).

Much of what is not done in the hospitality field is because of poor use of routine data-gathering techniques, thinking guest cards are valid and reliable channels of information, and under-utilization of computer technology that, as well as tracking a hotel guest's purchases, could also note their requests for service (Piccoli, 2008). Guests need to know that such information will be held in the highest confidence, even as in a doctor–patient relationship: that it will simply be used to improve future service, and personalize future stays, and above all will not be sold in secondary markets. These assurances are necessary to motivate guests to participate in such a program because consumers are becoming increasingly concerned with their privacy, and are therefore becoming more protective of their personal transactional data (Knutson, 2001; Fisk *et al.*, 2004). The collected databases could also have two levels – a basic one, used to help refine general segment market tastes; and another at a more private level, when granted by the guest, especially if certain dietary needs or other health considerations are essential for an enjoyable and satisfactory stay (Magnini *et al.*, 2003). Learning specific details about customers and their needs and wishes allows the service provider to customize the service and more accurately adapt the service to the situation (Berry, 1983). Data gathering with the traveling public as part of the up-front decision process "puts customers on your team" (Furlong, 1993, pp. 170–73). Companies need to contact their customers directly about the goals of their marketing research efforts, and identify specifically those details the customers are interested in. Firms are advised to involve customers as part of a "work" team, seek their "appraisal" of what is being delivered, and reward their efforts. Evidently, the end goal is discovering what affects customer satisfaction, and avoiding what produces dissatisfaction.

When attributes measured pertain to customer satisfaction in areas in which the firm excels, these data provide valuable information (Chakrapani, 1998). It is the roadmap on which to build. Emphasis remains on the customer. Hanan and Karp (1989, p. 19) point out three requirements that every manager must do in assessing their customer's needs. "1) Know the customer's checklist of what is important; 2) know the meaning of each category of satisfaction as the customer defines it; and 3) know the customer's assessment of each of his suppliers in each category on the checklist." The customer perceives and interprets the quality of a service. Customers' expectations are what motivates an active interaction with service representatives. Expectations derive primarily from customers' needs and wants, but are also influenced by the company's image or reputation in the market, the customer's prior experiences, and the firm's current marketing efforts (Edvardsson *et al.*, 1994). Consequently, to deliver top notch service, a business and each manager in it have to define who their customers are, and understand their consumption-related psychology. Bell and Zemke (1992) posit that, when delivering exceptional service, firms need to fulfill the customer's wants and expectations, be flexible with the service, treat the customer as a partner not as an adversary, and make it easy for them to do business with you. They also go on to stress the importance of identifying customer values, setting standards, and monitoring results. For example, timeliness, accuracy, and responsiveness were identified as the most important service values to a surveyed group of bank customers (Liswood, 1990). For hotel guests, however, clean, quiet, comfortable, and reasonably priced set the tourist standard. In a nutshell, firms must align their values with those of their target customer segments.

Zero-time companies that can respond instantly to the requests of their customers know "what drives ... them." It is their customers' "needs, values," and attitudes that drive the service process (Yeh *et al.*, 2000, pp. 52, 255). In their process, the customer is the decision maker who has multiple travel choices. "What the business thinks it produces is not of first importance – especially not to the future of the business and to its success. What the customers think they are buying, and what they consider value, is decisive – it determines what a business is, what it produces, and whether it will prosper" (Drucker, 1977, p. 90). Keeping those customers committed to reconfirming their decision on your patronage is paramount for success. "The first job of a loyalty-based effort is to enable the firm to find and keep the right customers. The right customers are those to whom the best value can be delivered by the firm over a sustained period of time" (Reichheld, 1994, p. 239). Marriott Courtyard employees know that their hotel was designed based on cutting-edge research exploring what their target market segments desire in a travel-related hotel (Collier, 1994). Given that perspective, it makes the interactive process between the customer and frontline provider more relaxed, as the values and standards are established in advance.

Involving the customer opens up previously unknown areas of interest, attributes, and quality considerations of the travel customer: "When you involve your customer in the development of your strategies, you reap an additional benefit: the ability to focus more clearly on meeting their needs" (Brown, 1999, p. 31). In that way, collaboration with customers will produce services that fulfill their needs (Yeh *et al.*, 2000). In obtaining feedback from customers on service, the Marriott Corporation now uses a comprehensive approach, which involves randomly selecting and sampling recent guests. The firm adopted this approach because it determined that scattershot distribution was not yielding an accurate measure of customer sentiment. In other words, the firm came to realize that those most likely to complete response cards were either the very satisfied or the very dissatisfied (Broydrick, 1994). Marriott Corporation uses extensive marketing research that has resulted in the development of numerous lodging brands, such as Spring Hill Suites. Reliable and accurate data used to unravel the needs of the market segment will be significant in achieving customer satisfaction (Anderson and Fornell, 2000).

Brown (1989) emphasizes that open channels of communication are essential to monitoring the satisfaction process, but are also important for picking up on emerging problems, and anticipating changes by discovering customer–service interactions that deviate from the script and truly improve the existing service process. Evaluating customers as recipients of goods and services does not mean that they are passive in the service process. The customer can offer immense insight into poorly designed organizational service processes. Lengnick-Hall (1996) argues for a customer orientation that empowers a more involved customer, thereby leading to a more binding and satisfying relationship. The process is not a one-way dimension, but a give-and-take, so that innovative ideas can be introduced and old service processes refined.

Besides visually inspecting what a customer likes and enjoys, "A more powerful way of assessing the client's requirements is through conversation." "Effective client communication starts with the realization that communication is not a separate activity from rendering a service; communication is a *component* of how you render service" (Bly, 1993, pp. 47, 105). In essence, it is what firms say and do that counts. But the service process of communication is not a tangible, material object. Therefore individuals often perceive greater risks when buying services than when buying products (Heskett *et al.*, 1990). Social interactive activities, as in restaurants or vacation locales, for the most part are in the middle range of difficulty for customer evaluation. Information-based pseudo-relationships can be developed, however, through a customer-contact or preference-tracking database (Thelen *et al.*, 2004). For example, some interactive inputs may occur between frequent flyers and airline clerks. Nevertheless, by assessing records showing a customer's personal preferences for food and seating, the reservation clerk achieves a degree of instant intimacy that would normally result from a history of shared, person-to-person interaction. The customer, however, may be less inclined to have an unknown reservation clerk know their "political, religious, ideology," and other attitudes about life (Gutek, 1995, pp. 201–3). Such more intimate facets of a person's personal life often are major lifestyle predictors in determining a customer's action. "Interacting and relating are almost synonymous" and communications are "based on descriptive information *about* the customer" (Day, 1999, p. 159). Clues to the customer's expectations are essential to defining the particular market segment to which a service company in the travel and tourist field needs to respond, so that their message and what they have to offer is being heard by the proper market segment.

Crane (1991) describes an evaluation survey that assesses various phases of customer service from the service provider's perspective. The information obtained from the survey is used to improve phases of poor performance and help change and modify the service process where it is needed. The various departments responsible for the service are shown where they are strong and weak in the service process. As a result, they can take corrective measures that have been found, on average, to be both efficient and cost effective. The CEO of SAS (Scandinavian Airlines) tells Heskett *et al.* (1990) about one of their partner airlines that was developing a resort for senior citizens. While they asked their target clientele what they wanted, they didn't accurately listen and digest the information, and in the end they were left waiting for customers. Berry (1995) reports that, even in companies that conduct sound service research on the customer, an information dissemination system is necessary, especially for decision makers. Unfortunately, corporate research findings often do not reach the frontline service provider who is most often responsible for implementation. Mostly they reach down only to middle-level management, if that. Information and data on the market segment does no-one any good if it is not being used to direct decision making. Berry (1995) finds that service leaders listen to the sounds of the business. Not only do they listen, but they share that information with the service providers who can make difference, and also receive input from them, to ultimately improve the quality of the travel service.

Social and service quality correlates of the traveler

The travelers' activity profile

In a generic definition of the tourist, Cohen (1974, p. 533) defines their role as "a voluntary, temporary traveler, traveling in the expectation of pleasure from the novelty and change experienced on a relatively long and non-recurrent or rarely undertaken round trip." These dimensions of the tourist role are certainly real and must be factored into the role expectations a tourist possesses. Nowhere, however, is there even a hint that a traveler is a customer, which opens up questions about how to deal with the traveler role and yet fulfill their expectations in service situations. That can easily be ignored when the role of a traveler is confined to general, universal considerations, but not when dealing with the customer role in a service situation that requires dealing with expectations. These are necessary in order to understand how travel providers must organize themselves to meet travelers' needs. Adding to this, Cohen (1972, pp. 167–72) describes the tourist with paradoxical role expectations – they want excitement but also seek the familiar. "The experience of tourism combines, then, a degree of novelty with degree of familiarity, the security of old habits with the excitement of change." In appealing to the tourist, "made necessary by the difficulties of managing and satisfying large numbers of tourists, the attributes of a destination tend to be simplified … ." Such a practice reduces the level of expectations and fear of unnecessarily shocking the customer where they have no social anchors to hold onto. Pleasant surprises do boost customer satisfaction and add novelty to the situation, but care has to be taken in their presentation.

Symbols become important in defining parameters for a service situation. Since specialized population segments have real growth potential, many companies are hiring upper-level employees who are highly visible members of that specific group (Blackwell, 1997), or they are supporting ethnic cultural events, festivals, and recreational–sporting events. Tourist destinations have long since promoted their cultural diversity, food, and entertainment options as a way of attracting vacationers.

The 69 million Americans over the age of 50 today are joined every eight seconds by another boomer. This cohort of age 50-plus represents only 26 percent of the US population, but their economic impact is far greater (Alea and Chekouras, 1999). They collectively own 55 percent of all golf shoes, 51 percent of all recreational vehicles, and 47 percent of all cameras that relate directly to travel tourism activities. And they are the fastest-growing segment of the tourist marketplace. Baby boomers are a dominant population group and will dominate the minds of marketers well into the first few decades of the twenty-first century. According to the U.S. Travel Association, baby boomers generate the most travel in the USA, recording over 268.9 million trips, more than any other age group. The empty-nesters whose children have grown and moved frequently indulge in travel, restaurants, and related cultural events (Blackwell, 1997). In that regard, Brock (2002) points out that the 50-plus market is the fastest-growing segment of the US population, controlling 48 percent of discretionary spending. They "come close to having it made" and are referred to as the "young again" market, averaging higher per capita after-tax income and greater levels of net worth than younger customers (Blackwell, 1997, p. 92–94). While the above trends are correct, today's current market makes those observations and data all relevant.

The young-again segment places increased focus on experiences such as travel, activities and staying in touch with others. The segment is also benefiting from advances in healthcare. This market is especially interested in comfort, security, and convenience, partially accounting for the growth in vacation time-share options, cruise-line vacations and holidays, and senior days at certain resorts. They perceive assurance to be a paramount service quality value, and are particularly emphatic about the relative importance of reliability (Crompton and MacKay, 1988, pp. 371–74). Service companies must constantly monitor demographic and service quality changes to gauge the potential size and value preferences of their role market. Knowing the future size of a population, their socio-economic characteristics, and social attributes such as age, sex, household make-up, and ethnic ratios, is just sound general market analysis (Lin, 2002). Blackwell (1997) predicts that fertility rates will remain low in the USA, but sees upward trends in domestic ethnic markets such as the Latino, Asian, and African-American sectors, while the Caucasian population is expected to contribute little to growth after 2030. The travel industry is experiencing a growth in the 50-plus market that is a result of the shift in the US demographic base from a younger to a more middle-aged and older market. As a result, there is a shift in lifestyle that Clark (1989) believes will need to be taken into review when dealing with them as a customer. These include a greater balance in work and leisure, a convergence of men's and women's roles, a greater need for security, increased convenience of customer service, and an increased interest in healthy living. But age and ethnic affiliation may not be the only factors that will influence the travel market.

In many cases, however, lifestyle characteristics actually trump age and ethnic group characteristics, making our understanding of customer expectations more precise (Blackwell, 1997). Simply put, lifestyle information allows firms to narrow general market segments, such as baby boomers, into more specialized niches based on psychographic variables. By closely monitoring how consumer activities, interests, and opinions are changing, firms possess the ability to tweak the demand chain to better meet the needs of their desired consumers. The values and beliefs of the customer shape lifestyle characteristics (Dolnicar and Leisch, 2003). The life-stage or age cohort also shapes these values (Du and Kamakura, 2006). In conducting lifestyle assessments, firms should center efforts upon changes that could have a direct impact on future business. Pertinent variables may include time clients spend at work and on work-related problems, types of hobbies and how they spend their free time, and what types of social gathering they attend. Such quantitative data on customers has the potential to elicit concrete insights into current and future trends in the marketplace.

Blackwell (1997, p. 100) believes that there are a number of questions worth reviewing that are crucial to understanding the kinds of activity a lifestyle may include.

Box 3.2 Lifestyle questions

- How and why has an activity increased or decreased in popularity?
- If a new activity is dominating the time of tourist customers, what activity/ies are receiving less time?
- How much time, money, and interest is a tourist customer spending on an activity, and will it increase or decrease?
- Are there needs or problems created by an activity?
- Does a lifestyle trend account for sales in an activity?
- What types of new service could spur increased interest in an activity?

Such questions cannot be overlooked in trying to understand the expectations and needs of a lifestyle customer segment. In a survey of leisure preferences based on gender, Gruber (1980) found that some activities tended to be more male- or female-dominated. Although that is the case for some sports and hobbies, it is certainly not the case for many leisure activities that are associated with travel and tourism. Of the leisure activities examined, both snow- and water-skiing are enjoyed by both genders, reinforcing the services of many resorts that also include such favored unisex activities as golf, horse-back-riding and board games. Although gender differences endure in some leisure activities, those associated with travel and tourism are neutral in that regard, and lifestyle considerations are probably more persuasive. These situations are usually service-intensive because most of these activities are commercially underwritten so that competition for customers can be keen.

The tourist experience is not merely for fun, pleasure, and recreation, but the role of the traveler can also be affected by the social interactions experienced – lifestyle and the social segment of a role is not just a static part of a social dimension. Neumann (1992) goes so far as to argue that the self can be influenced and changed. A tourist experience confronts the self with new situations that, more often than not, differ from everyday life. Indeed, part of the promise of travel is self-discovery. It is as if the individual leaves behind the daily routine of the old self built on multiple roles, and dares to experience a new, transcendental self. The activities of "driving (sightseeing), hiking, climbing, and contemplation have the potential for transcending the conditions that hold a stable self in check and for providing conditions where another dimension of self emerges" (Neumann, 1992, p. 189). Tourists describe themselves as being pleasantly lost in the flow of new physical and mental activity, with accompanying social interactions with others that may be very different from those in their everyday job, family, and community. That is another dimension of tourism – the experience of new people and situations, offering a refreshingly new, though brief, image of self.

Many of these tourists attempt to disassociate themselves from the camera-toting, tour guide-led travelers. They actually see themselves as crossing the trails of other people; "see themselves as self-sufficient explorers in serious pursuit of adventures, freedom and meaningful experiences." In the end, "travel brings people into a world of unpredictable possibilities that can reveal new ways of knowing the self" (Neumann, 1992, pp. 194, 200). In some cases, tourists discover something new about themselves that they take back to their daily lives in small measure by reliving those tourist experiences in their daydreams, thoughts, and interactions with others. In illustrating a role enactment or performance, Zurcher (1983) discusses how a commercial airline passenger acts or may act within the limits of their role expectations and performance. The behavioral expectations associated with the passenger role are extensive and restrictive. The process of arriving at the airport, checking in, boarding, taking off, flying, landing, deplaning, and leaving the airport are all highly structured for the safety of the passenger, to meet time schedules, and to deal with large numbers of people and luggage. Customer satisfaction is achieved by converting this conformity to expectations to a functional autonomy wherein the passenger takes advantage of the process. They learn shortcuts: they know the most reliable way to the terminal; know where infrequently used check-in points may be located, know which flight gate check-ins to use, and are aware of other efficient ways to avoid the big lines and crowds. Zurcher (1983, p. 98) notes, however, that the novice passenger can be "numbed into passivity. Passengers simply flow with the lines and the moving crowds. Their luggage is separated from them. They absorb the boarding time and gate number, and are verified with a boarding pass. They accept seat assignment without expressed preference ... They take their seats placidly in the waiting room, and remain there until instructed to board the plane, even if the room is jammed and uncomfortable or the plane is delayed."

Unfortunately, the service provider often also remains inert in this process, and offers no satisfactory alternative for this passenger segment. The employees often act as robots programmed with a limited set of rules, exerting them as power symbols over the heads of the passengers without any regard for the real situation. Employees abusing their position to play power games may often leave the customer looking for another airline. For the most part, however, the lead role remains with the flight attendants who structure the in-flight activity. Yet passengers are still in control to some extent in rejecting expectations by doing flight routines in advance, being nonchalant, and refusing meals when offered. The passenger knows where gaps in the service exist, and orders special diet meals in advance, has flight crews check on connecting flights, and knows how to work the crew in the galley; some even take a negative approach by complaining out loud. All these interactions serve to let the crew know what passengers expect and what they think they are due.

Enacting the passenger role takes several steps in the flying routine. Experienced passengers may opt for autonomy with regard to their choices or activities that enhance privacy, personal space, comfort, convenience, and prestige (Zurcher, 1983). They attempt to maximize their personal satisfaction and use their knowledge of expectations to benefit themselves. In achieving that goal, "the airline passengers studiously avoided involving much of themselves in the passenger role" (Zurcher, 1983, p. 231). Expectations of the service situation are determined to some extent, for some passengers, by better tracking of taste. Levels of expected service could be exceeded in the airline industry by keeping computer track of frequent flyers. By monitoring the customer's previous interactions, Gilbert (1996) states that personnel armed with this information can anticipate future actions. For the infrequent traveler, whose general social segment, lifestyle and demographics, or what personal interaction the customer may be seeking emotionally, may be unknown, the service provider should be actively considerate and sensitive to signals of discontent, and should make it easy for the customer to complain. It might sound obvious, but customer care of the traveler is basic and essential to the goodwill sown by a service team. Despite what may be written and said, the customer is a human being.

4 Managing the travel situation

Preview

This chapter explores the service manager's role in the service system from a social interaction perspective. Each section in this chapter lays out specific management techniques for use with the service provider. It discusses and enumerates the many and varied kinds of interactive role a manager must try to master, and how their ranking in the service organization affects their function within the exchange process. The second feature of the chapter explores a managerial program vision for a travel service company. How a vision is defined for internal and public consumption brings order to a social situation. Its design and development are investigated and laid out for the service provider, and help to define how to cope with and solve problems. For management service vision to be successful, it must embody positive management applications, which are described in detail. Part three of the chapter recognizes the importance of the frontline employee in maintaining customer satisfaction and the ultimate success of the management plan. This part warns of fostering role ambiguity, overlooking the lack of proper skills, and the loss of autonomy, which reduce the service provider's effectiveness.

The service manager role

The role

A true customer service administrator is not a general in an army. "Service leaders are not bosses; service leaders are coaches." The best service leaders love the business that they emotionally lead and are enthusiastic about "creating something special" (Berry, 1995, p. 12). Such personal commitment places a premium on integrity. In fulfilling that commitment, management must function to provide the tools and means for providing customer service. Timm's (1998, pp. 123–28) plan focuses on building the service system around central structural policies and processes. (1) The organization has to own a theme that presents and represents the type of service offered. The theme should be in key words that lay out a goal and objective that both the internal (service provider) and external customer can identify with and embrace as guaranteeing their satisfaction. (2) A service strategy needs to be developed which focuses direction. The organization should begin by laying out a service sequence and experimenting with different customer interactions to produce the best results for the customer. (3) The firm should also give service personnel an organizational model that identifies their role and gives them the authority to meet the customer's expectations. Ritz-Carlton employees, for example, are encouraged to take ownership of a service interaction – to do what it takes to satisfy the customer. (4) It is also imperative that firms attract the best people for the frontline, and then develop their knowledge, behavioral skills, and service ability. (5) Finally, mangers need to control the direction a service company takes by adopting tried-and-tested policies that produce loyal customers. In doing so, they must prevent the daily problems that are part of running an organization, including absenteeism, internal disputes, and other in-house problems, from disrupting the quality and value of the service.

In essence, managers play four roles in the service system. First, they design the service system; second, they implement delivery in the service system; third, they enforce or control the delivery system; and, finally they may alter the delivery system to increase its efficiency (Gutek, 1995). Managers establish the mind-set and style for a company. "If style is best described as the living culture of a company, then it is often fashioned from the mindset and actions of owners, founders, and senior executives. Thus, the leader sustains style and is the change agent. In succeeding with a style of standards, values, and principles that are held out to the public, the superior leader will be proactive with their employees, customers, and they will listen to frontline staff" (Lowenstein, 1997, pp. 121–25).

The role of a manager is not just that of a passive participant. Armistead and Clark (1994, pp. 107–9) define that role as including four active functions: first, the manager needs to be a systems architect, with frontline and back stage support staff linked in concert with the customer. Second, the manager needs to be a role model – research has shown that service providers are strongly influenced by the observed behavior of their leaders. Third, the manager must act as a psychologist, and recognize and identify the needs of the customer and service provider. Fourth, but not least, the manger is the team builder, who is called upon to coach through being innovative and supportive, limiting employee burnout, and sharing customer problems. The necessity for an active role is further reinforced in the article by Panter and Martin (1991), in which roles for management and middle-management levels are specified for the most part in order to indicate the kind of technical support needed at the frontline. The organization begins with The "Director," who coordinates the middle-management and frontline roles. As such, customer-contact employees, and the roles they perform, are held in such high regard among astute directors that they can be conceptualized as an additional market segment. In an analogous manner, these employees are "valued as customers" and their roles are "prized as products."

Research indicates that tourism and hospitality managers who are committed to service quality and demonstrate an empowering leadership style foster a transformational environment that communicates their commitment to quality to their frontline providers (Clark *et al.*, 2009). Such a style yields employees who are more prone to share organizational values, who understand their organization, who perform at higher levels, and who are more satisfied (Clark *et al.*, 2009). Panter and Martin (1991, pp. 52–53) propose that the first middle-management role is that of a "Rifleman" – the marketer who targets the sought-after primary customer segment. In preparation for the customer's arrival, the next key player is the "Environmental Engineer," dealing with those tangibles that affect customer satisfaction – the physical layout, props, and scenery. Then there is the "Legislator," who sets the guidelines or norms of acceptable behavior for customer interaction. Such norms may address "inappropriate dress," "behavior threatening health and safety," or behavior that infringes upon the "rights of others." These three behind-the-scenes roles provide necessary support to the frontline employee.

Being managerially involved also conveys a persuasive message to the customer (Harris, 1991). A more difficult responsibility may be in training the service provider in developing interpersonal skills, and how a service provider takes into consideration the customer's feelings, values, and needs. Teaching basic listening skills to the service provider is necessary to reduce the likelihood of misunderstandings spawned by communication difficulties (Armistead and Clark, 1994). For example, teaching the service provider to rephrase the message and asking for more details both signal perceptive listening (Ramsey and Sohi, 1997). Probably the most obvious way to ensure managers play a proper role in customer service includes writing those functions into their position description. Cant (1992) thinks that a clear statement detailing the role functions a manager should play in customer service relations is an essential link, as it relates to their particular situation in the service chain. Recognizing that they are but one link, their role actions need be geared to the specific element of service they provide. "Service leaders do the right thing – even when inconvenient or expensive. They place a premium on being fair, consistent, and truthful with customers, employees, suppliers, and other stakeholders, thereby earning the opportunity to lead" (Berry, 1995, p. 15). Management's role in service can be heightened by conscious involvement and participation, sending the message that customer service satisfaction, customer loyalty, and service quality are every employee's responsibility.

In summary, management's responsibility is to audit all service policies and program execution to determine if they measure up to the company's expectations (Roscitt, 1990). Evidently, the service providers must be included in the organizational plan. Most service jobs are high in discretionary effort content, meaning that it is up to the individual employee how much effort to invest. Role conflict and ambiguity can substantially zap or neutralize this energy (Nygaard and Dahlstrom, 2002). If not supported by management, service providers can lose the energy to serve. In time, their motivation can be deflated, and all is lost (Zeithaml *et al.*, 1990).

Service role processes

Managers seeking to harness human potential must not have an oversimplified, mechanistic view of the workplace, but rather should be skilled in managing the human side of the organization (Heil *et al.*, 1997). As noted, the service professional manager sets the tone for the organization, respecting and valuing their people, learning what the service does, offering training opportunities, and demonstrating that they also value and respect their customers (Petite, 1989). Conrad (2001) makes it clear that the successful organization must manage for the customer and deal with the good employee. Opening customer listening posts and educating the customer on the services offered, while also involving the frontline employee, will likely mean repeat business and future goodwill toward the company. Throughout this process, firms should integrate customer satisfaction and preference data into management decisions and daily operations (Vavra, 1992). Naumann (1995, p. 213) suggests that hoarding customer service information does not enable service workers to benefit from those sources to make better, empowered decisions. Managers need to be at the forefront of such efforts. "Flexibility, creativity, and good interpersonal and communication skills will continue to become more important. Managers will need to walk their talk." Such a role process will encourage employees to do the same, with the goal of improving customer service.

> ### Box 4.1 Considering culture: comfort with psychological empowerment
>
> In collective societies, such as China, where individuals are socialized in childhood with proverbs such as "the lead bird gets shot," or "the tall grass gets crushed by the wind," it can be comparatively difficult to teach frontline service providers to feel comfortable with decision-making authority. In such collective societies, service providers often desire to ascertain "the mass view" before making decisions. Conversely, in individualistic nations, such as the USA, frontline service providers often embrace decision-making authority and use empowerment as a source of work-related motivation.

Customer care is not a one-time effort for a company. There is more to what the smiles and pleasantness truly symbolize and represent in the experience of the customer. Clutterbuck (1989) finds that it has been suggested that

85 percent of quality problems are caused by managers who do not develop quantifiable standards or spend too little time on customer care. This lack of input is recognized within the service sectors of the company and is seen in the lack of customer response, and ultimate loss. Service leaders need to assist frontline employees who depend on the services that they receive from employees in other departments. Therefore relationship marketing should not be limited to frontline employees, but should be extended to all personnel (Liljander, 2000). Teamwork and management direction should definitely be a functional ingredient of any customer-oriented service program.

Over and over, we keep getting the message that management must be involved in customer service. Macaulay and Cook (1993) propose that this managerial involvement must be evident in service training initiatives. They find that training of frontline staff is most effective when management also participates and, as a result of that training, demonstrates changes in service policies and/or employee relations. To realize those pay-offs, Harris (1991, pp. 8–9) identifies a number of interactive processes that manager and employee should pursue to ensure customer satisfaction:

Box 4.2 Management/employee service initiatives

- Top management support of customer service.
- Constant determination of the customer's thoughts.
- Listening to what the customer is saying.
- Looking for ways to reward the customer.
- Incorporating customer attitudes into new service ideas.
- Centerpiecing customer service at every meeting.
- Viewing all corporate decisions as customer impacts.
- Resolving customer complaints to affect future customer decisions.
- Hiring customer-oriented employees.
- Treating customer service as your most important asset.
- Implementing purposeful customer-related actions on a daily basis.

Being flexible in exchanges is important – very easy to say, but difficult to accomplish. "Policy manuals often don't take into consideration legitimate, non-routine requests, and/or unique customer requirements. For example, no matter how committed a hotel clerk is to meeting an important guest's request for a one hour extension on late checkout, service quality may be jeopardized because approval is needed from a manager who cannot be reached for the next three hours" (Hensel, 1990, p. 51). There is a good deal of friction in the service contact relationship, and manager expectations and customer demands can be real sources of stress. Service managers, as a result, might consider dedicating attention to inherent customer-contact stress factors (such as incompatible requests), and communicating the extent to which employees can be empowered in those situations (Babin and Boles, 1998).

In terms of role definition, managers should be obsessed with customer service and see themselves as a company model; frontline sales and service providers should view themselves as company owners upon whom everything depends (Levinson, 1988). If that is the case, then the organization should assist and support the service provider, since any number of problems and mishaps may occur (Magnini *et al.*, 2007).

Channels of communication need to be open constantly, not only to the service provider, but also to the customer. Direct phone lines to the desk in hotel corridors may circumvent many minor inconveniences, while other channels may be explored prior to, during, and after a customer visit. Middle managers are close to problems and are key players in their resolution. They are "in the center of everything and can either run out of fuel or send in the gas tank." That is precisely why promoting the right kind of people to these positions is a major responsibility of top management (Zeithaml *et al.*, 1990, p. 140). Instead of a top-down management system, Blanchard (1989) suggests flipping the management pyramid on its top, so that the energy and orientation of management is directed toward the customer. In this kind of management system, the clear purpose of the manager's role is to support the service providers on the frontline by ensuring they have all the necessary resources for doing the job. When the frontline staff recognize that management is pushing for them to win with the customer, they will stretch and push themselves to get the service job done (Maxham and Netemeyer, 2003).

Service leaders trust in the fundamental capability of individuals to achieve and conceptualize their own role as setting a standard of excellence, providing the tools needed for success, and encouraging leadership behavior throughout the organization. Since service leaders have faith in the people who work with them, they place communication with them in high regard (Berry, 1995). In order to foster such an environment, however, managers must lead by example (Brown, 1989). If the goal is for associates to be polite and cheery, then the manager must be the model of politeness and cheerfulness. "Probably the best way for managers to express firm commitment to customers for keeps is to get off mahogany row and talk to the people on the frontline." In other words, they must get off their "duffs" (Furlong, 1993, pp. 183, 185). Talking to customers face-to-face enables management to personalize, identify problems, and specify customer needs. According to SAS airline officials, the role of middle management revolves around "translating the overall strategies into practical guidelines that the frontline can follow and then mobilize the necessary resources for the frontline to achieve its objectives" (Carr, 1990, p. 90). In the simplest terms, they need to foster an environment in which honest errors are viewed as learning opportunities, and in which employees are empowered to use their native intelligence when transacting with customers (Carr, 1990).

"Vision is the destination" and organizational procedures are the strategy. For example, British Airways instituted five organizational practices: first, understanding customers' wants and needs: second, focusing the workforce's training on serving the customer: third, creating a friendly customer process that can be delivered globally; fourth, building an infrastructure to deliver superior service, and fifth, presenting an advertising campaign to promote this customer service image. This Putting People First program set the tone for the airline. The CEO also set a personal example by attending corporate seminars to convey this perspective and the importance of what they hoped they could do for the customer (Weinzimer, 1998, p. 36). To this day, British Airways enjoys consistently high levels of customer satisfaction.

Managers ensure the values that an organization communicates are consistent with the views of the employee. If a caring, friendly, and helpful environment is projected through management marketing, but employees have regard only for speed and efficiency, these inconsistencies will eventually deteriorate customers' service quality perceptions (Kelley *et al.*, 1990). Management commitment to quality service reinforces support for encouraging innovativeness among employees in the performance of their service roles (Hartline and Ferrell, 1996). "In considering any question (as a manager), you should ask how does this help us add value for our customers" (Woods, 1999, p. 9). In all the companies investigated by Berry (1999, pp. 23–38) there is a set or soul of core values that places a company and its employees apart. These values include excellence, innovation, joy, respect, teamwork, integrity, and social profit or helping the less fortunate. In this context, true commitment cannot exist without trust. It is worth mentioning again that frontline providers have to believe in the integrity of their managers (Liljander, 2000). Essential to a strong employee affiliation with a company and employee commitment is a perception and proof of a company's good and honest intentions and business practices.

This same kind of customer treatment should be reflected in the treatment employees receive from their managers (Bell and Zemke, 1992). In other words, "firms reap what they sow" in the sense that "employees' perceptions of shared values and organizational justice can stimulate customer-directed extra-role behaviors" (Maxham and Netemeyer, 2003, p. 46). Cannie and Caplin (1991, pp. 148, 151) cite a tenet followed by Marriott and other outstanding customer service organizations: "Customer relations mirror employee relations. The way you treat your employees is the way they will treat your customers." Essentially, that means the manager showing respect and providing positive rewards or reinforcement has an impact on customer satisfaction. Likewise, calling employees by a name they prefer, reprimanding only in private, providing clean facilities, saying please and thank you, listening to, and trying to understand, employees' opinions, providing the staffing, resources, and knowledge they need to do their job effectively, giving fair pay increases, accepting responsibility for mistakes, defending subordinates in front of others, and focusing on correcting problems, are all reflected in consumer sentiment ratings.

Taking an additional step, managers must also derive ways to increase employee self-efficacy and job satisfaction, because those perceptions affect the interface between the service provider and customer (Goodman and Yanovsky, 1997). Managers convey the service task goals, provide training to associates to achieve those goals, and monitor providers' performance. They also change production standards and how many associates will be needed to provide the service; in addition, they monitor customers' reactions to their service system in post-transaction surveys. Finally, they may need to specify the job tasks better, by breaking them into finer, more easily delivered service elements, making the tasks more specialized and easily performed by the provider (Gutek, 1995, p. 171). Given the close correlation between satisfied employees and customers, Armistead and Clark (1994, p. 104) contend that a manager can give positive input by talking to employees about their work situation. They need to relay what the company is trying to achieve, encourage cooperative work efforts among employees, and give feedback on what customers are saying about the service offered. This dialogue is essential for teamwork.

When celebrating success, it is the role of the manager to lead rather than delegate. Service providers recognize their own organizational importance when "the chief is out there patting them on the back" (Bell and Zemke, 1992, p. 186). "Managers should do their best to keep employees in good moods and to make sure that they enjoy their work" because this "motivates" employees to interact positively with the customer (Tschohl and Franzmeier, 1991, p. 192). Heskett *et al.* (1997, p. 222) observe that companies are increasingly becoming aware of the fact that it is essential to "keep the best talent near the customer," and are broadening fulfillment opportunities and promotion recognition on the frontline.

While most managers would say that they embrace the more humanistic aspects of Drucker's writings, lip-service is rife. "America's CEOs would not be smacking their workers with one hand, while awarding themselves huge pay raises with the other, if they understood Drucker's social concept of business" (Lewin and Regine, 2000, p. 50). Stated differently, it is not uncommon for those working in the service sector to fall into that category characterized by claiming high levels of support for service quality, but doing little to implement the necessary operational tasks (Peccei and Rosenthal, 2000). That is especially true when it comes to recognizing the potential impact of the service provider's role.

Managing data usage

Fitzgibbon (1988) recognizes that, while many managers and administrators are removed from direct contact with customers, their actions or inactions can seriously affect the level of service quality and satisfaction felt by the customers. They can contribute to service understanding by institutionalizing feedback communication from the customer through surveys, documented personal exchanges, and systematic interviews. In getting a better handle on understanding customer service needs, "good research is the key to good customer service." Nevertheless, "marketing research is only an input to management decision-making, not a substitute for it. Tourism managers who understand this point will better meet their customers' demands for goods and services and simultaneously use fewer resources to provide those goods and services" (Baker *et al.*, 1994, p. 4). Management involvement is needed to complete the assessment process. Managers must use reliable information-gathering tools to determine what their particular customer service needs are, for this is a central function in a market-oriented firm (Kirca *et al.*, 2005).

Understanding customer profiles is also a part of management's role (Sharma and Lambert, 1990). The customer role could be assessed by applying an approach used by Callero (1992), in which judgment on a semantic differential scale of countervailing adjectives is used to describe a customer profile. A modification of this technique uses a series of relevant action items, such as active/passive, associated with how customers see themselves and how they perceive the service provider. The advantage of such an approach is that the actions are less ambiguous and more intuitive. To be sure, this method stresses interpersonal relations. Any action item could follow a semantic format on a questionnaire or interview schedule. The customer can indicate their preference toward either end, or remain neutral. This approach is useful in testing an interpersonal interaction defining a customer provider role that influences a customer's level of satisfaction.

They must also ascertain what service elements are being used, and to what extent. Further, they must also acquire data that define the dimensions of the service program, and finally obtain information that evaluates the services and links all of the above to customer profiles, to understand better the type of customer being served. In a simple world, a company would hope to attract one particular market segment. Unfortunately, the world is more complex, and many companies in the travel and tourism market also serve secondary and even tertiary clients with ever so slightly different needs. Sharma and Lambert's (1990) approach and research also provide a practical example of how to conduct segmentation analysis within the reach of management implementation. Although this study was conducted in a high-tech, product-dominated market, the emphasis on customer preferences and measuring customer service attributes that are specific to this business sets a good example for all service providers. Research must be detailed to fit a specific service situation. Zeithaml *et al.* (1993) posit that levels of personal expectation are related to the levels of desired service the customers seek. They use the example of a customer with high social needs, hoping that a hotel will have live music and dancing. Another customer may have more personal needs, hoping for merely a clean, quiet, comfortable room. Service providers and mangers need to have strategies in place to care for both customers at once. Care must always be taken, for managers are often ignorant of customer expectations because of a "lack of marketing research orientation," where information and data never get to the top or middle levels of an organization, or are not gathered; "inadequate upward communication" from the frontline provider to middle management; or "too many levels of management separating those on the frontline who may know what the customer wants and needs." Zeithaml *et al.* (1990, pp. 52, 59) illustrate the need for customer data by calling attention to a successful executive who spends up to 80 percent of his time attempting to understand the needs of his customers.

Role ambiguity transpires when employees do not possess the information or training necessary to perform their jobs adequately (Zeithaml *et al.*, 1990). Managers need to clarify roles by providing accurate communication about what is expected, feedback to reinforce what is being done correctly and correct what needs to be changed, and finally training to improve competence. It is especially important to note that, in many companies, managers possess more accurate information about what customers want and expect than frontline staff. Zeithaml *et al.* (1990) speculate that often managers are, in fact, not communicating and sharing this information with their staff. Evidently, the potential for top-rate service increases with customer knowledge gathering, interpretation and dissemination. It can be speculated that because knowledge is power, managers mistakenly believe that in order to maintain their status, they need to hold on to all their customer information. Such inaction not only hurts the customer and frontline staff, but adds nothing to the performance rating of the upper-level management. Managers, especially middle-level, must be encouraged to share marketing and customer survey data with staff both above and below. "Getting close to customers entails listening to what they have to say, and listening to what employees are saying about what customers expect" (Horovitz and Panak, 1994, p. 29).

Another twist in the misdirection of communication is that managers do not always agree with customers on the particular importance of a service element. A study by Marr (1994) shows that there is no unanimity between managers and customers about the elements of service in a product-oriented market. We do not know whether this would be the same for those just providing a service. But what the two roles did agree upon was the central importance of service. Part of the problem is that the particular management role held by an individual "shades" the way they see the customer. Clear communication and cooperation between management roles would surely spawn an enhanced understanding of customer service needs and the resulting costs of providing these needs. Service programs sometimes miss the target customer, or do not appeal to them, despite what the hands-on service provider is doing. Chakrapani (1998, pp. 172–73) lists five service gaps that service management providers must be attuned to in communicating with their contact providers on customer feedback: (1) a *service quality gap* exists when customers perceive that they are receiving less than they expected to get in return; (2) an *understanding gap* confuses when service encounters are poorly defined and executed; (3) a *design gap* hinders progress when the steps in a service process are not presented to the customer effectively from beginning to end; (4) a *delivery gap* undermines the interaction in which the service providers miss the mark in treating the customer; and finally (5) a *communication gap* misdirects meaning in what is actually being transmitted to the customer from what should be transmitted, so that the intended message of management is being incorrectly received. Often, even the best plans of management break down at the point of service contact, exposing such gaps. Therefore steps need be taken to have frontline staff involved in carrying out the grand design of the marketing program. This requires human interaction and feedback by concerned service providers who are treated as an important asset in the management process.

Designing the service setting

The program vision

Harris (1991, p. 1), describes customer service as an attitude that begins at the top, where the president (CEO) must get actively involved. "One of the most important tasks of leadership is to articulate a vision that can be understood by every employee and transformed by them into specific actions" (Weinzimer, 1998, p. 23). It is profitable to create a vision statement. Companies with a clear vision, which employees feel part of, generally outperform companies without a vision. The vision must be an image that employees and customers can "visualize," providing a sense of "purpose," that offers an expectation(s) of "success" (Weinzimer, 1998, p. 24). "A vision is a vivid picture of an ambitious, desirable future state that is connected to the customer and better in some important way than the current state" (Smith, 1999, p. 61). A vision functions to provide a unified purpose and guide decision making toward a customer service goal (Baker and Sinkula, 1999).

A number of important questions to ask of any service organization seeking to achieve top quality service (TQS) need be addressed by customers, managers and service providers alike. Customers are mentioned first in achieving TQS because they are the key part of the organizational service situation. Questions should emphasize the importance of customer expectations (Timm, 1998, pp. 142–44). (1) *What do customers want?* The answer to this question lies in data gathered by highly reliable and valid methods and techniques. There is no substitute for strong, scientific customer data. (2) *How do we best provide for the customer?* This entails exceeding customer expectations and perceptions of value by testing newer and refining older business practices. (3) *How do we get all organizational members involved to focus on the service system?* This essentially involves making everyone in the organization responsible for the customer by sensitizing, educating, and training all employers to think how their behavior affects the customer. (4) *How can we improve and adjust service?* Keep the quality mantra before the employee at all times through newsletters and weekly (but brief) cheer-leading sessions, and by recognizing and rewarding innovative service ideas and practices. (5) *How do we know if our service programs are improving?* It is not enough to undergo routine cost audits, it is also necessary to conduct behavioral audits to measure customers' responses to service providers and the service situation.

No service provider is perfect, nor is any service organization totally without errors (Magnini *et al.*, 2007). The challenge remains to reduce the chances of making mistakes. Active customer care involves knowing those common practices identified by Edvardsson *et al.* (1994, pp. 131–32) in their study of approximately 100 successful customer care companies: (1) company service providers listen to customers and seek to comply with their requests; (2) the companies possess a vision of (specialized) customer care; (3) the companies monitor the frontline in specific detail on how they are delivering a service; (4) the companies employ service-minded individuals who are trained and skilled in using their knowledge, and are given the authority to do so; (5) the companies reward their employees for providing customer service and care. In building a strong customer relations program, Perris and Scott (1991) also outline necessary steps toward achieving service success: (1) clearly define customer goals; (2) spell out the functions of customer service employees; (3) train employees in the procedures of effective service; (4) maintain the vital links of communication between the customer and service teams; (5) resolve complaints quickly and effectively; (6) institutionalize customer opinion polls; (7) reward loyal employees and customers. The ability to modify and redefine customer service roles requires data and information in order to be successful.

The outstanding service companies that Berry (1999, pp. 65–67) investigated, besides sharing a core set of values, were focused primarily on the customer. They emphasize "serving a specific market need rather than ... marketing a specific product for that need." Without exception, they "serve underserved market needs." They "serve their chosen markets in a superior manner." And finally, they "focus on the core strategy." They do not try to be all things to all customers, and their employees know and understand what they are about because their strategy is so clearly expressed. This, however, does not mean they are locked into the past; they are also relentless innovators in future development. The Marriott Corporation is such a company, well-known for its strategy-implementing prowess. From detailed kitchen recipes to the 66 steps required to clean a room in a half-hour, Marriott continually sets high standards for service by knowing its customers.

Customer care programs should include predictability/consistency, reliability, fairness, continuity, and stability for the customer (Petite, 1989), the fundamental bases of the RATER system. The RATER system is a defined social situation, specifying the (R) reliability of the promised service; (A) assurance of employees providing trust; (T) tangibles or physical appearance of the people, facilities, and material; (E) empathy provided by employees in attending to customers personally; and (R) responsiveness to the needs of the customer – being there for them. In the companies that Zeithaml *et al.* (1990, p. 66) reviewed, they found that frontline people are more accurate in predicting those tangibles that satisfy the customer, while managers are better predictors of customer reliability, responsiveness, and assurance. Interestingly, however, both frontline staff and managers perform the same in the area of empathy. Today's customers put a high premium on reliability, assurance, responsiveness, friendliness, clear communication, and security in their service transactions (Liswood, 1990). Add to that the essence of empathy conveyed through personalized service, and the notion that "customers are special and unique" (Zeithaml and Bitner, 2000, p. 85).

Implementing the above tasks is not an easy accomplishment, and often faces many impediments. That is, let-downs can occur with any and all service experiences. It is not unusual for gaps to exist in the perceived closeness customers experience with a company. Barnes (2000, p. 101) suggests "two-way communication, trust empathy, mutuality of goals" to intensify that contact. Peters (1991) also concurs with the observation by many in the service sector that customer perception, listening to the customer, and being empathic to the needs of the customer are all the intangible realities of customer service.

In addressing the participatory role of a customer in the delivery of service, Kelley *et al.* (1990, pp. 315, 320) refer to "organizational socialization" as a customer playing the role of a partial employee. The literature containing maps and signs that Disney World sends to a customer helps them navigate through their facilities. These informational techniques facilitate the service encounter and enhance tourists' perceptions of the quality of service they receive at the theme park. Another socialization practice is a published customer bill of rights. It tells internal customers (employees) what is expected of them; it also is a statement to customers telling them how they will be treated (Brown, 1995, p. 75); and finally, it is a basic statement of expectations concerning the services to be delivered. For a hotel chain, clean, quiet, comfortable, convenient, fairly priced, and receiving cheerful efficient, hassle-free care and compassion during a stay might be the basis for a consumer bill of rights (Brown, 1995).

Establishing and communicating "service standards are essentially the rules a firm writes for getting the work done. They are tools for designing and delivering a service experience that's what the customer wants, even when – perhaps especially when – what the customer wants is different from what the service provider's personal preference might be" (Anderson, 1999, p. 89). The dramaturgical symbolic interaction model provides Deighton (1994, pp. 124–25) with an approach to theoretically describe distinct role performances. The first is the contextual performance that is done to fulfill an obligation in which the service provider holds themselves to a standard. The Sir Francis Drake Hotel in San Francisco, for example, "launders all its coins each night so that the hotel can give its guests clean money" the following day. The second, a staged performance, is put on to impress the consumer. A thrill performance, as cited by Deighton (1994, p. 127), fits into the travel and tourism mode, for example, white-water rafting expeditions and safaris. Another type is a festive performance, with deliberate staging and costuming, such as cruise vacations and Mardi Gras. These social situations provide the social, cultural, and physical environment for such acts to occur with staged realism within the normative boundaries of "good taste" and perceived consumer satisfaction.

"Viewing services as staged performances is not metaphorical" (Deighton, 1994, p. 137). It is of the essence of service management that the customer and all the actors who are involved in delivering the service share and sustain a single conceptualization of the situation in light of numerous potential disruptions. An experienced tourist customer service provider does not design a universal outcome, but rather designs enough flexibility in the situation "so that customers who have different knowledge structures and preferences can create their own unique use environment during interaction and, therefore, their own unique experiences" (Gupta and Vajic, 2000, p. 38). A personal limo driver working for the Ritz-Carlton exemplifies the personalization of service. He is available not only for sightseeing, but also for specialized day trips – antiquing, art galleries, or historical architecture. He can expedite check-ins, city travel, and reservation availability. Loyal customers refer to him as the "go-to guy." Love of the job, a genuine delight with people, and a personal clientele represents the best in frontline service. Through situational design features, limitations and constraints are placed on customers to interact within set design parameters, such as passengers flying in an airplane or diners seated in a restaurant. Yet excellent, experience-minded companies such as Disney, Club Med, and Starbucks allow each customer to feel they can create their own use environment, within limits, to suit themselves.

Another factor is the level and intensity of interaction with the tourist service provider who makes the customer feel like a member of the crew or family; in other words, the customer can serve as a value co-creator (Claycomb *et al.*, 2001). Such service strategies bolster the sense of belonging and help to foster a sense of being a group member, which in turn generates memorable service interactions (Gupta and Vajic, 2000). "By no stretch of the imagination is the customer always right: instead, an essential task of everyone from design and marketing, to the frontline, to upper management is to teach the customer how to be right – and simultaneously create financially viable environments in which the customer's odds of being right are as high as possible" (Schaaf, 1995, pp. 23–24). If customers are truly treated as being co-members of the team, then the interaction takes on a new level of meaning. This new dialogue mirrors the reality that customers expect not only to be treated as a tourist, but also to be respected for their self-perceived expectations of care and service. As an extreme case, there are some medical services available in London that combine meeting medical needs that require hospitalization with upscale dining and accommodation commensurate with the tourist industry. This unique service is a variation of the spa and health resort theme, but is certainly mainstream in competing for customers; the core instrumental service of doctoring couples with the secondary service of dining.

The same is true for Southwest Airlines, which manages expectations effectively and provides service consistent with these expectations – low fares, no meals, superior on-time record, no seat assignments, and efficient baggage handling (Blattberg *et al.*, 2001, pp. 110, 157). Southwest also brings fun to the workplace, where service providers are able to act out joyful routines for the customer that provide "cheap and fun" no-frills entertainment, such as peanut bag-tossing in mock competition (Ivins, 1999). On the interpersonal side, this brings a sense of humor and light-hearted merriment to a flying experience that can otherwise be tedious and boring.

We have used the distinction between the instrumental (primary attributes) in comparison with the expressive (secondary) attributes of a service. SAS (Scandinavian Airlines) is an example of a company in the primary business of flying customers between destinations, while the instrumental activities of ticketing, providing ground transportation, and access to telecommunication systems are secondary and activities that support their goal. SAS is now one of the outstanding customer-oriented airlines in Europe, but that was not always the case. The tide shifted in a favorable direction when its CEO decided to turn an $8 million loss into a $71 million profit by simply making "sure you are selling what the customer wants to buy" (Brown, 1989, p. 34). Managing expectations at its hotels in the USA, the Marriott Corporation has made its core services and perks consistent within each individual division. American Airlines has made it a practice to standardize unit services in order to provide a baseline consistency, making it easier for the customer to relate to and make known their needs. Creating a similar service delivery system across all locations, regardless of where they are, eases interpretation for the customer. In this way, encounter-based organizations create a loyal following by delivering standardized and consistent service (Gutek, 1995).

Customer reward programs are another potential way of increasing customer support, such as frequent flyer programs or hotels that provide bonus points. But some of these programs have excessive limitations (Heney, 2008). If the reward restrictions are viewed as too onerous, such programs can backfire and become disincentives. However, true discounts and special offers, if legitimate, will tend to increase customer support. It is even better to know a customer's taste preferences in advance, and then reward them in the hotel with a light-filled, open, nonsmoking room, or one that accommodates smoking, or to provide that complimentary glass of their favorite beverage. Such infrequent and intermittent practices are pleasant and thoughtful surprises.

The frontline service provider also needs to be aware of disruptive customer behavior that negatively affects other guests (Tax *et al.*, 2006). Zeithaml and Bitner (2000) report that, in a study of critical service encounters occurring in tourist attractions across central Florida, researchers found that customers have a negative impact on each other when they neglect either explicit or implicit rules of conduct. Customers reported such negative behaviors as pushing, shoving, smoking, drinking alcohol, being verbally abusive, or cutting in line – impersonal, rude, unfriendly, or even spiteful. But an important up-front way to help mitigate this undesirable behavior is to communicate behavioral norms clearly in advertising, personal selling, and other company messages.

The instrumental–expressive distinction defines two attributes for judging the effectiveness of service. The advantages of approaching satisfaction from the perspective of instrumental and expressive attributes is that the information that could be obtained from such an approach to service satisfaction can allow service provider to not tolerate the poor performance of instrumental factors (Uysal, 2006). Because of the tangible nature of instrumental factors, service providers and managers can develop appropriate service amenities and features and maintain them at the performance level that will be expected. The degree to which service providers control the nature of the interaction between instrumental performance and the psychological meaning and interpretation of such performance eventually influences customer satisfaction and the corresponding development of successful amenities and features, and monitoring and mechanisms (Uysal and Noe, 2002).

The setting in which the interaction takes place between the service provider and customer has the potential to play a role in enhancing or reducing the level of satisfaction that customers experience in their consumption of tourism goods and services. The setting in tourism and hospitality encompasses a combination of physical, social, and technological elements. Because of the simultaneous production and consumption of most services in tourism and hospitality, service providers should pay careful attention to the physical and aesthetic features of the setting. Customers' reactions and their perceptions of the existing features of the setting would definitely help the frontline employee to function properly and take pride in what is being offered in the setting. The presence of any instrumental factors, such as availability of enough parking spaces, clean bathroom, or access to the internet may not add much to satisfaction, but their absence will certainly detract from satisfaction. Both the instrumental and expressive factors of the setting collectively or independently contribute to overall satisfaction (Uysal and Noe, 2002). This point becomes even more relevant in hedonic (pleasurable) consumption of services such as dining, sightseeing, attending a festival, or taking a trip to Yosemite National Park (Bonn *et al.*, 2007; Joseph-Mathews and Bonn 2009).

Blueprinting is another model for judging service satisfaction. "A service blueprint is a visual definition of a service process" or a kind of social system model. It "displays each sub-process (or step) in the service system, linking the various steps in the sequence in which they appear. A service blueprint is essentially a detailed map or flowchart of the service process (Zeithaml *et al.*, 1990, p. 158). Customer service interaction blueprinting focuses on the process of delivering a service by segmenting it along a time continuum. The blueprint contains a time sequence of social interactions with service providers, and an invisible part that identifies those engaged in service activities behind the scenes that support the on-stage performance. On both aspects of the blueprint, "fail-points" (Vavra, 1992, pp. 94–101) are indicated where service may break down, since they pinpoint emotional and qualitative judgments about the value of the customer's perception of the service received.

As Liswood (1990) notes, firms should make it easy for customers to do business with them. Moreover, a firm should never inconvenience a customer for the sake of the organization or an employee (Donnelly, 1992). Blueprinting can serve as a useful process for addressing these issues. Houston *et al.* (1998, p. 748) point out that "a single positive experience cannot overcome regular poor-quality service. The failure to find a relationship between the quality of the service encounter and evaluation of overall service quality follows this interpretation." A consistent blueprint pattern of the frontline provider's interactions is responsible for either a positive or negative judgment of a tourist service.

Service precaution

Many companies are simply content to play the numbers game by counting how many customers are served, trip tickets written, etc., and ignore key job performance variables that influence service quality perceptions (Hensel, 1990). It is just so easy for a company to slip into counting heads, rather than focusing on the more important factors that affect service. Behavioral measures can help direct employees' actions toward meeting customers' expectations because variables such as courtesy and professionalism often drive employees' loyalty. Nevertheless, employee selection typically affords insufficient attention to such interpersonal skills. On the contrary, selecting "the right person for the right job" is perhaps the most controllable factor in ensuring quality service encounters (Lee-Ross, 2001, p. 90). "Competence" in employee skills is one way to ensure effective customer service, including the knowledge and experience required of that service provider to meet the objectives of delivering top-rate service (Healy, 1996). "Prolonged contact with customers can lead to deterioration in service performance or *burnout*." Team coordinated efforts, adequate training and backup support, plus respite helps control the negative consequences of customer service burnout. There are also other factors that affect burnout in our economic systems. In a comparison of leisure time use by Americans and Europeans, US workers led the list of time spent at work in figures gathered by the Economic Policy Institute taken from mid- to late-1990s data. Stress and burnout are being reported more frequently in the literature as a worker problem (Bakker *et al.*, 2003). Respecting and investing in employees can help safeguard against these burnout issues, but unfortunately, often that is not done.

Wharton (1996) defines emotional labor as requiring workers to display what they may not necessarily feel privately, which is often felt to be damaging to the worker's performance. The findings of his study, including recreational and food counter roles, show that service workers "are no more likely than other workers to suffer from emotional exhaustion … On average, workers with low job autonomy, those who work more hours per week, and those who have spent fewer years in their jobs report more emotional exhaustion than other workers" (Wharton, 1996, pp. 91, 101, 106). The type of labor is not inherently responsible for poor performance. It is more likely that service roles are considered to be of low status.

Customer service jobs for the frontline are situated at the bottom levels of company organization charts. Not enough time is spent hiring and training people at this level. As a result, they may lack the necessary skills to serve customers properly. Many service firms experience high turnover among contact employees and therefore sometimes fill openings quickly, even if they must hire persons with background or skill deficiencies (Zeithaml *et al.*, 1990). Managing this situation is difficult because there is no long-term incentive for the younger, part-time employee. "Because service providing employees are relatively young, single, and more often part-time than employees in other workplaces, managers might not recognize potentially deleterious effects of work/non-work conflict. Common restaurant, hotel, and retail services, which include irregular schedules, limited weekend time off, and alternating schedules with little or no notice, affect the work/non-work interface" (Rowley and Purcell, 2001). To the extent that these situations can be minimized, the payoff is decreased turnover (Babin and Boles, 1998).

Role conflict and role ambiguity are also conditions affecting the performance of frontline personal in service situations. "A striking result" in the companies studied by Zeithaml *et al.* (1990, p. 112) is the universal presence of role conflict. Employees feel that expectations of them are inconsistent or too demanding. Role conflict often results when the expectations of the company and the customer do not coincide. Employees feel they are asked by management to "push services" on customers, which detracts from their ability to serve the customer in the time allotted to them. Managers can also create role conflict situations when too much paperwork is demanded from frontline staff when they are trying to serve customers. Role conflict and ambiguity cause stress in a service worker that can affect job performance, job satisfaction, and quitting intent (Chebat and Kollias, 2000). Role conflict results in competing demands being made on the individual; role ambiguity is characterized by uncertainty about the expected behavior in a situation. Babin and Boles (1998, pp. 87–88) examine the difference between male and female adjustments to role ambiguity and conflict. They find that female service providers' performance is affected more negatively by increased role conflict or role ambiguity. Further findings also suggest that "job satisfaction affects quitting intent differently among female and male service providers … The path estimates suggest a stronger relationship for men than for women" and "contrary to traditional role expectations, men did not exhibit stronger job satisfaction. In contrast, a slightly more positive and significant relationship was observed among female service providers." And finally, "the results indicate that women are affected more severely by increased stress."

Ambiguity in the performance of a service role, and perceived role conflict between the key frontline provider and supervisor and customer, should be minimized because of the serious negative effects they can have on service quality. The negative effects of role conflict and ambiguity are "so profound, reducing them may be half the battle in delivering high-quality services" (Hartline and Ferrell, 1993, p. 40). Reducing these negative effects can be accomplished, in part, by management having a demonstrated "commitment to quality." Employee training also significantly reduces role conflict and ambiguity (Saks *et al.*, 2007). On-the-job training opens up possibilities for role conflict because of conflicting information coming from management and experienced employees. More formal training outside the work situation, and self reinforcement of the new employee's efforts to please, positively stimulates greater role assurance. Cohen (1984, pp. 379–82) contends that the tourist situation is transitory, with local hosts catering to the hospitality needs of a transitory visitor who can be taken advantage of through dishonest practices. To ensure an unblemished reputation, a professionalization of the tourist industry is suggested, which guarantees to "surmount the potential conflict between the economic and the social components of the service role." Standards of conduct, normative practices, and personal practices that are reinforced by the local situation can hope to ensure a more stable role relationship between tourist and service provider. Internships and training help support this goal. "Service processes must be rigid yet flexible, efficient yet effective, serious business yet fun, controlled yet free, stable yet changeable, objective yet sensitive, and standardized yet customized" (Collier, 1994, p. 114). Finding the correct balance is the real management challenge.

There are lines of visibility that the customer experiences, and then there are behind-the-scenes lines of support. Coordination of these efforts is essential to service effectiveness, and also to avoid "fail points" in the service diagram. Management oversight must pay particular attention to the role service providers, as they largely influence customer satisfaction or dissatisfaction.

5   Positioning the travel provider

Preview

This chapter addresses how to go about properly positioning the travel provider in the mind of the consumer. The strong linkage between customer and employee satisfaction is used as to anchor this discussion. The quintessentially vital roles of employee empowerment and managing accurate and useful customer information are also explained. In terms of theory, this chapter explicates how justice perceptions, particularly the interactional justice dimension, drive customer sentiment toward a service provider. That is, interactional justice entails perceptions of interpersonal sensitivity and being treated with dignity and respect. The chapter concludes by offering ten recommended actions for service providers that can predictably lead to specific customer reactions. These action-to-reaction causal paths are laden with managerial implications for firms seeking to excel in the area of customer service.

Perception of the service role

The linkage

A major focus in any hospitality and tourism service model should be the personal linkage between the service provider and customer. For the most part, however, employees in direct contact with the customer, the service providers on the frontline, have received far too little attention. Liljander (2000, pp. 162, 171) echoes this sentiment in stating "one marketing relationship which has a direct affect on customers, and which has received too little attention, is the one involving the company's personnel." In essence, we wholeheartedly concur with this observation and judgment that, in any service industry, the service role is basic and essential to performance. The organizations supporting tourist service include transportation systems, hotels, resorts, restaurants, shopping establishments, historical and natural parks, and entertainment in the arts such as music and the theater. The systems and human infrastructure supporting them are even more specific, including all manner of artisans, social events, and physical places, including beaches, wilderness areas, theme parks, resorts, festivals, fairs, and seasonal recreation and sporting venues, as prescribed in various cultures throughout the world.

The social processes bonding these social systems together are the service providers. The frontline service role is very demanding and is often found to be more stress-filled than many nonservice professions (Furnham, 2002). To use an old adage, it may not be rocket science, but in many ways, it's like riding a rocket every day, and employees as well as managers should be conscious of the demands. "Serving customers directly can be demanding, stressful work. The service provider is 'onstage,' performing in view of customers expecting them to know the answers to a thousand different questions and managers expecting them to give respectful and professional service even when their customers are disagreeable or rude" (Berry, 1999, p. 87). Initial front-desk contact personnel set the standard in the service industry. These people often set the tone for a customers' ensuing perceptions of satisfaction. The customer service representative carries the responsibility of providing the service level in a face-to-face situation that the customer unequivocally expects. Brantley (1988) sees them as the embodiment of the organization. Because of that role, they are very influential in affixing a company's customer service image; and because they are on the spot, in real time, they have to deliver the goods demanded given the immediacy of the situation. There are also behind-the-scenes personnel whose contributions are significant, but they are not necessarily recognized by the customer as an essential part of the service team. They encompass the desk clerks, waiters, door and bell staff, maids, stewards, and repairmen.

Organizations requiring enduring periods of emotional labor on the front-line must recognize that service employees need to step "out of character" to relax and regain composure, away from the front stage of customer interaction (Ashforth and Humphrey, 1993, p. 105). The behind-the-scenes areas often function as oases to which to retreat for needed rest, recovery, and consultation during a work shift. However, these same organizations need to go a step further by offering a balance of work with free time and a life away from the job, as work–family conflict is a leading cause of job stress among frontline hospitality workers (Karatepe and Sokmen, 2006). Burnout is cited as a negative factor affecting service performers through emotional exhaustion, a depersonalized self-image of being talked down to by customers, and feelings of lack of work accomplishment. Such negative feelings stem from an overload of interpersonal contacts and lengthy work schedules without adequate support or relief (Ford, 1998). Withdrawal from the situation and perceptions of self-conflict may also be a result of stressful work interaction situations with too few providers and resources to meet customers' expectations. In addition, emotional exhaustion can also reduce recovery performance (Karatepe *et al.*, 2009). Controlling the above negative impacts on service workers makes their work–life balance more managable.

No customer expects to be dissatisfied or disappointed by the service they receive. We expect satisfaction at least, and delight at best. In our large, impersonal, urban world, where a sense of community is missing, the individual may disappear into loneliness and become nothing more than a credit card number. All service organizations must recognize that the individuals they deal with have feelings and make judgments. The service personnel representing that organization have the responsibility of recognizing their customers as responsible human beings. Liljander (2000) cites studies showing that all frontline workers influence customer satisfaction, and that being in tune with customers' needs and wants gives those employees a sense of accomplishment and satisfaction. This interactive work process is itself a rewarding experience, as should be the more tangible benefits. Employee happiness, economic benefits, family care, and job security serve to maintain and promote employee loyalty and a spirit of wellbeing (Liljander, 2000, pp. 176–80). Unhappy employees compromise the service act by taking their frustration out on the customer. In the end, all parties lose, and satisfaction's alter ego, dissatisfaction or noncommittal neutrality, reigns.

Dealing with the employee as the internal customer is the first step in the service process. Successful management and employee relations live by "the golden rule of service: do unto your internal customers as you would have them do unto your external customers" (Brown, 1995, p. 11). "Tell the truth" means telling the employees the whole truth and not withholding information to pump up one's status (Blanchard and Bowles, 1998, pp. 51, 160). In their reported case study, a company was saved from foreclosure because telling the truth led to trust, which built self-esteem among employees. This may sound like a simple recipe for success, but people are more than willing to move forward when they are given a meaningful role in the company's success. In another example, the founder of a hospitality company including 300 restaurants and nearly 40 hotels says the following about his employees and motivation: "Our employees are people, and people have moods and feelings which they cannot simply divest in the cloakroom when they arrive in the morning to start work ... If employees are to perform well, they must have the feeling that they are acknowledged and accepted as people. They must feel they are accomplishing something and that their achievement is being recognized" (Horovitz and Panak, 1994, p. 34). Such respect is necessary for everyone, from the frontline to the top line of the organization. The motto of "ladies and gentlemen serving ladies and gentlemen" was developed by the Ritz-Carlton Corporation in an effort to disseminate this essential respect throughout the layers of the organization (Michelli, 2008).

Service providers hold the success or failure of a company in their hands. It is they who are the difference, and they should be recognized as such by managers and co-workers. "Treating people at all levels with dignity and as human beings who can make a contribution releases ... and reinforces their inner motivation." Even the most self-motivated frontline providers need to be regularly shown appreciation (Geddes, 1993). It is all too easy to ignore that frontline employee. Broydrick (1994, p. 113) reports on a Lou Harris poll taken among employed adults, asking what they thought led to employee satisfaction. They ranked the following as contributing to a satisfying job: (1) good salary, (2) job security, and (3) appreciation for a job well done. Petite (1989, p. 65) found service roles at multiple organizational levels that were valued and respected. The valued employee than was able to understand their role better, learn new service skills, and make customers feel valued and respected. This kind of performance loop breeds employee satisfaction.

A hotel survey by Hartline and Ferrell (1993), which included managers, employees, and customers associated with three mid- to high-price hospitality services, found that employee job satisfaction is the key determinant of customers' service quality and value perceptions. These results also produced other beneficial effects, such as being positively related to hotel occupancy rates, that in turn affect a hotel's return on assets. Employee self-efficacy was also measured and found to be related to customer satisfaction, while employee innovativeness revealed a positive effect only on service value. In another later empirical study by Hartline and Ferrell (1996, pp. 61–62) on hotel employees, managers, and customers, some of the critical factors affecting the employee–customer interface were examined. Self-efficiency, job satisfaction, and adaptability were hypothesized as positive factors affecting the service interaction, while role ambiguity and conflict are thought to be negative effects. The study reports that "employee self-efficacy and job satisfaction increase customers' perceived service quality." Since the service is consumed on the premises, confident and satisfied employees are likely to perform better in the hotel than those who are dissatisfied and incompetent. Second, "there was "no evidence of a relationship between employee adaptability and customers' perceived service quality." Third, "role ambiguity appears to have the most prominent effect within the employee-role interface, because of a negative relationship with employees' self efficacy, and job satisfaction." Fourth, and unexpected, was the positive relationship between role conflict and self-efficacy that may be based upon an employee's self perceptions of coping with divergent and even contradictory demands. Fifth, the negative relationship found between self-efficacy and job satisfaction may be part of "the nature of the customer-contact position, in which employees are typically underpaid, under-trained, overworked, and highly stressed." The employees in this study are typical of retail service workers in that they are "young, well-educated, and likely to be holding the job while attending school." The employees' part-time position and higher-level aspirations may be part of the cause of this negative relationship. "Because employees can control their behaviors more easily than work-related outcomes, behavior based evaluations gives employees more control over their evaluations." These types of script can be easily changed on the basis of staff profiles and actions. The major observation of this study remains that "attitudinal and behavioral responses of customer contact employees are the primary determinants of customers' perceptions of service quality."

Management needs to recognize that they cannot always offer superior service, but they can be very selective about who they place on their service teams. For example, Southwest Airlines utilizes highly refined character and personality screening mechanisms, and hires only about 4 percent of applicants (Reichheld, 2001). Senior executives and even CEOs also spend as much time as possible in recruiting top-notch employees since they know the firm's outcomes depend upon them. Loyal employers reap benefits from their workers, who end up being more customer-oriented and essentially demonstrate more respect for their customers. Southwest Airlines has never had a layoff and has lower turnover rates of workers than the rest of the industry. Meyers (2001, pp. 1, 4) reports other companies with similar employee programs that have an impact on the customer interface.

Loyal employees also promote a more accommodating service situation. "Although there may be a stronger relationship between customer and employee loyalty in professional services, and in services involving frequent personal interaction, having loyal employees should be important to all firms" (Liljander, 2000, p. 172). Management and the worker philosophy of a company that involves its service providers at all levels will breed loyalty. "People who are truly in control work for organizations that value them as persons. Their thoughts, feelings, needs, and dreams are respected, listened to, and acted upon" (Blanchard and Bowles, 1998, p. 85). That kind of interaction translates over to the customer, who is similarly enjoined, so a better, more affable service situation is likely to take place (Maxham and Netemeyer, 2003). The service role is about maintaining self-esteem for the lowest in the chain of command and the least in the company. Enhancing the self-value and worth of the frontline employee is critical to corporate success (Peters, 1991, p. 4). Babin *et al.* (2000) also find that a work climate perceived as being trustful and accountable by the employee is also one that is less stressful and yields more committed workers. As a result, both role conflict and ambiguity are less prevalent, ultimately enhancing the productivity of the employee. When you treat an employee with respect and dignity, especially in a service situation where interpersonal contact takes place, the employee in turn passes that aura on to the customer (Maxham and Netemeyer, 2003). "In sum, a satisfied workforce will generate a satisfied customer-base, and a satisfied customer-base will buy more and help the company grow" (Macaleer, 1995, p. 29). "People who feel they are doing a good job, providing a service that is considered valuable by the customer, tend to enjoy what they are doing. They are more productive, stay with the organization longer, have lower rates of absenteeism, and have higher satisfaction with themselves, their colleagues, and employer" (Connellan and Zemke, 1993, p. 5). Satisfaction links both service provider and customer in a mutually beneficial relationship.

The service act in a tourist situation has to be built on a solid formulation, since the service situation is not always acted out between familiar participants.

As a start in managing this process, Day (1999, p. 62) indicates that the Marriott Hotel corporation has a "fanatical eye for detail." "This begins with the hiring process that systematically recruits, screens, and selects from as many as 40 applicants for each position ... ." Matching the correct employee with the customer is a first step in the satisfaction process. An enduring, mutually reinforcing relationship between a satisfied employee and customer produces what Heskett *et al.* (1997) call the "satisfaction mirror." The result produces employees who become more satisfied by dealing with satisfied customers, and customers in turn become more satisfied by dealing with satisfied employees. This reinforcing social effect was found in each of the service organizations for which data were available. Building that cycle of capability for the satisfaction mirror, two companies in the travel sector each oriented their hiring practices primarily for attitude and secondly for skills. Rosenbluth International and Southwest Airlines hire "nice people with good attitudes," who enjoy serving people.

But the goal of achieving satisfaction does not stop with hiring. It continues with monitoring: keeping the customer–employee interaction connected requires constant listening to their changing needs. Heskett *et al.* (1997) cite Disney, Club Med, American Express, Southwest Airlines, British Airways, Fairfield Inns, and Ritz-Carlton Hotels as having direct interests in the tourist marketplace. There are ways in which these companies engage in various customer information and data-gathering efforts that determine how well or poorly they are doing in fulfilling customer expectations. Ritz-Carlton, for instance, requires that each property conducts at least 33 telephone interviews with customers per month (Michelli, 2008). They monitor employees' attitudes, personality dispositions, and skills as a part of controlling the service act – it is understood that what is being acted out on the service stage has a direct impact on satisfaction.

Role exchange and interaction process

Acting

Service should be an integral component of everyone's job description, not just the responsibility of the guest services department (Tschohl and Franzmeier, 1991). If there is any all-inclusive role that is an absolute requirement of the service provider, it is simply that they must truly possess a deep love and concern for the customer (Hallett, 1990). The strength of that relationship will be most important as time constraints continue to put pressure on families' and individuals' use of time for travel, relaxation, and pleasure. So everyone, not just the doorman or desk clerk, but even the CEO who walks through one of their corporate social situations, has to be conscious that they are on a service stage. In an excellent summary of Erving Goffman's work relating to interactive expression, Morisaki and Gudykunst (1994, pp. 52, 59) agree that communicating expressions is not intrinsically lodged in the face or body, but rather in the interaction and encounter taking place in an exchange. Goffman sees humans as playing theatrical roles, as if they are on a stage, the ultimate social analogy. Moreover, the drama is played out in real-life experiences. The social interaction of the players actually plays a major role in generating meaning. It is not just a static view of the face that communicates. Most western researchers interpret the face as an "independent construal of the self." This is defined as the individual being a unique and independent entity. It's how you use it in the exchange process that takes on meaning. It is the looks, smiles, nods, and shifts in the head that project what we are trying to convey (Pease and Pease, 2004). Humans ultimately use verbal communication, in which messages are conveyed through language. These verbal and nonverbal media transmit the intended message. It is through *interacting* that narrative skills are developed and refined. For example, "a stability narrative" may be part of a person suggesting honesty or a "progressive narrative" suggesting success. The important point here is that these implications are realized in action and they become subject to social appraisal. "Others may find the actions and outcomes implied by these narratives (according to current conventions) coherent with or contradictory to the telling(s)" (Gergen, 1994, pp. 188, 207).

This interactive process is judgmental, and service providers are very much being judged by their performances. First, the words and stories being told in the interaction process are the realities that the service provider and customer wish to convey to each other. When information is transmitted in a social context, its interpretation is influenced by the recipients' perceptions of why the information is being transmitted, as well as its literal meaning. As a result, recipients attempt actively to interpret messages in a way that makes them informative. The motivation and meaning in a communication act are reinforced by a second and third process in an interactive exchange constituting "accuracy" in a conveyed message, and also "politeness" stating that communications should not offend the listener (Wyer *et al.*, 1995, pp. 16–18). In transmitting messages in these social contexts or situations, Wyer *et al.* (1995, p. 25) refer to the research of others who see that stories are a fundamental way of individuals identifying with one another in a social situation. "We typically respond to descriptions of another's personal experience by recounting an experience of our own that has similar features, and use this story to understand the experiences the other has had" at that time. Such stories are often used to bridge the gap between the service provider and customer to ease an initial, uneasy stranger exchange. Together the gestures, looks, posture, and words lead to an end result. The communication media through which the service provider works attempt to meet or exceed the customer's expectations.

Communication is influenced by context or social situation. Contexts vary not only in the type of service offered and the physical surroundings, but in the characteristics of the actors in the exchange. Variables such as the gender, age, appearance, mood, education, occupation, personality, and racial or ethnic background of customers and service providers may significantly influence the service approach (Ford, 1998). For example, research indicates that in service encounters, females typically place greater emphasis on inter-actional justice, which encompasses interpersonal sensitivity, than do males (McColl-Kennedy *et al.*, 2003). These social identities frequently lead to biases based on titles, ethnic heritage, race, or religion, (which) invariably cause confusion and hostility, which spawn challenge in the exchange (Ciaramicoli and Ketcham, 2000). Thus keeping age groups moderately separated in leisure situations is a "no brainer." Family units are also part of the boundary maintenance experience, whether for dining, play, rest or relaxation activities. Firms should be considerate of young or older families, those with children or none, and those in between – communication source categories that are looking for messages to fit their lifestyle. In one study, a clerk's behavior was observed at check-out counters to determine if racial identity had anything to do with the selection of a clerk by a customer. The results McCormick and Kinloch (1986, pp. 552) indicate that the type of racial situation, rather than the clerk's race, defined the nature of the interactions. "The results indicated that both white and black clerks were more friendly (pleasant, cheerful, and smiled) in mono-racial settings and more perfunctory (reticent, acted bored, avoided eye contact) in interracial interaction." Interestingly, the "behavior in interracial interaction was remarkably similar for clerks of either race."

The Walt Disney Company contrives situations with different quests (customers) in its training situations. In mastering the act of communication, Disney finds that no role is really too small or menial. "All employees are taught to be enthusiastic members of the cast" (Liswood, 1990, p. 52). According to Solomon (1989), training at Disney does not stop after the cast members learn their role's orientation. The message is stressed that the customer is a guest who must be happy, and that providing a safe, courteous, efficient, showy experience is the continued role of each cast member. For example, projective techniques are used to sharpen employee/cast member skills. In one case, an image of elderly guests with a small child with tears in his eyes, standing in the rain at Disney World, is shown for reactions. Cast members are then given an opportunity to suggest what might be done to improve the situation (Heskett *et al.*, 1990, p. 217). The situation places a service act in a different social context, where steps are suggested by the service provider that should lead to smiles. The service provider must always be sensitive, alert, and open to the customer. Tourist plays are not random acts between players. Indicators exist for the service provider in dealing with a social situation even though the social backgrounds of the actors change.

Research indicates that emotional responses to the physical environment can be transferred to people and/or objects within that space (Turley and Milliman, 2000). Timm (1998, pp. 104–11) cites seven check-points when dealing with the organization's stage for customer performances. (1) Make sure service providers are groomed and appropriately dressed to represent the kinds of tasks they will be willing to perform. (2) Make sure the appearance of the service area is clean, bright, and airy, that it smells nice and is tastefully decorated, and that it provides comfort stations such as restrooms and places to sit or to get a drink of water. (3) Correspond and communicate with the customer on a regular basis to let them know you have their interests at heart. Provide 1-800 numbers and online notification, notifying customers of upcoming sales and bargains. This is especially important for off-season use of facilities, which might appeal to an older or younger, more cost-conscious tourist. (4) Get the customer involved by handing them an information package about the services you offer, physically orienting them to their surroundings, and showing them how things work, especially technological gadgets that may be new and intimidating. (5) Make the social situation fun for the customer and have the employee feel that they are at play. Southwest Airline personnel have been known to dress up in costume for holidays, or to provide little treats or rewards to make the experience more memorable and pleasant. (6) Reward your frontline providers with real value for handling customer transactions that meet and exceed customer expectations. Recognition of their good work with service awards or employee-of-the-month photo displays for the customer to see instills confidence and esteem. Being considerate of employees' material needs also encourages employee *esprit de corps* to deliver quality service. (7) Stay close to the customer after the initial sale. Invite their input on how you could have made their service experience better through focus groups or interview questionnaires. And definitely report back on any changes that were implemented because of their input. Such actions demonstrate that the customer is indeed a "real" part of the service process. A social situation helps define the service play and stage that the service provider and tourist customer use to formulate a meaningful act.

The interactive process is at its most fundamental between a single service provider and a customer. "When two actors have reciprocally acknowledged each other's attention, any action taken by either actor can be seen by the other as being related to one's activity." "This is why the first action that occurs in the context of RAA (Reciprocally Acknowledged Attention) must offer some explanation for the actor's allocation of attention and some indication of the actor's availability for continuing interaction" (Hintz and Miller, 1995, pp. 360–65). The authors note that social encounters are hierarchical, beginning with the simple and advancing to the complex. A hierarchical building process exists in which social accomplishments are contingent on the successful construction and maintenance of the more basic levels of meaning. Also, part of the interactive process involves mutual responsiveness that is interrelated with attending to another person's actions. It is not possible for an individual to respond to another's behavior without first attending to it. In fact, attending and responding are simultaneous in most situations, except when one of the actors deliberately ignores the other, perhaps serving to offend. Smith (1999, pp. 62–64) outlines a series of steps for the service provider in conducting an interaction exchange with the customer by first, greeting the client, putting them at ease, and setting a favorable tone. Second, the process with the service provider showing how much they "value" the customer by recognizing them as the single most important part of the organization. Third, asking how they may be of help and assistance to that customer by taking note of their personal and individual needs. Fourth, listening to the customer – this means interpreting not only the verbal message, but also the tone of voice and the body language. Fifth, helping the customer by targeting the services they request, and pointing out how they satisfy and benefit them. Sixth, inviting the customer back to use the services offered, and always thanking them for their patronage.

Box 5.1 Considering culture: volume of speech

The degree to which individuals adjust the volume of their speech in given settings is known to vary between cultures. Americans, for example, have a large degree of fluctuation in their volume depending on the physical surroundings. For instance, they typically significantly reduce the volume of their conversation in populated areas, such as classrooms or service environments. Chinese, on the other hand, often do not noticably reduce the loudness of their voice in such areas. Armed with this knowledge, service providers are less likely to interpret loud verbal exchanges as anger.

It is important to note that the service interaction process does not just happen. Service can be offensive when a hierarchical management style puts frontline employees at the lower end of the corporate ladder and then ignores them. An organization style ensuring positive contacts with the customer is premised and based upon employee and management mutual interpersonal respect. In communicating with customers, Desatnick (1987, pp. 20–26) sets out five steps in which lack of respect for service employees is demonstrated by thoughtless supervisors and managers. Very simply, employee respect leads to customer respect in reverse order. (1) When "there is an acute awareness that if management solves employee problems, employees solve customers' problems. It is as simple as that." Employees ask how they may be of assistance. (2) Management needs to spell out service guidelines for employees. "All the things employees want and need to know are ensuring ... that their customers ... will get the proper service." Employees can then demonstrate that they know what kind of service is offered, and are not left guessing. (3) Management "rewards customer-related actions beyond the call of duty and publicly praises those who set examples of personal accountability." Employees who exercise personal responsibility and are empowered to do so are recognized for their positive contributions for the benefit of the customers. (4) "Companies develop profound problems in employee morale through the overt lack of respect for individual employees demonstrated by the thoughtless supervisors and managers." Such thoughtlessness destroys the spirit of service for others. (5) "All of us can think of times in our careers when we have had a non-supportive boss, someone who inevitably passed the buck on to us for whatever went wrong, and worse still, took personal credit for our contributions." Employees who can count on management not to pass the buck, and to reward them, will have customers looking to them with the same kind of acceptance.

Though there is a socially interactive set of communicative actions to achieve the needs of customers following on a hierarchical process, it is built on a supportive organizational context between service employee and management, mutually respecting and reinforcing each other. Service is part of everyone's explicit or implicit performance descriptive in order to keep the tourist customer in focus as being the paramount goal to satisfy.

Getting the service role right

Performances

Gitomer (2000) suggests that customer service begins with employee satisfaction. This may sound very obvious, but it is often overlooked for time and cost reasons. To reiterate, a company building a service-minded organization must (1) select the right service providers, (2) train providers to deliver service quality, (3) structure the support systems needed, and (4) retain the best providers (Zeithaml and Bitner, 2000). Certainly, outgoing and caring people come to light in a service situation, and the research shows that those individuals who are helpful, thoughtful, sociable, and also socially adjusted, likable, have social skills, and are willing to follow guidelines make good service employees. As already indicated, Southwest Airlines, a leader in customer service, "looks for people who are compassionate and who have common sense, a sense of humor, a 'can do' attitude, and an egalitarian sense of themselves (they think in terms of 'we' rather than 'me')" (Zeithaml and Bitner, 2000, pp. 293, 297). In selecting customer-contact employees, Liswood (1990) contends that sound decision-making ability under stress, a desire to be liked, a problem-solving mindset, and an optimistic mindset are desirable traits in frontline providers.

How do these specific traits translate into specific social interaction exchanges? In providing one answer, Armistead and Clark (1994, pp. 84–85) strongly assert that the following points "should" be considered in face-to-face contact personnel. First, "People who regularly deal with customers should be recruited for their interpersonal skills," those who exhibit a personal disposition to ensure the customer's expectations will be guaranteed and exceeded. Second, "Some basic customer awareness training will be worthwhile, particularly if this includes some controlled exposure to real customers." For example, shadowing more experienced workers is a useful training tactic in the hospitality industry (Magnini and Ford, 2004). Such training should be given not only to new hires who have frontline responsibility, but also to those employees who have intermittent contact and interaction. Third, "Positive service attitudes are more likely to be produced by positive motivation and management example than by sets of commands."

Finally, personnel recruitment has become more intricate, with the use of testing, extensive interviews, and on-site trial periods. Personality testing has become more commonplace in the workplace at all levels. "In addition to determining whether applicants have particular technical skills, employees also are asking whether the applicant has the 'right' personality to motivate and develop teamwork among employees from the bottom to the top of the corporate hierarchy" (Mook, 1996, pp. 65, 72). Tests such as the Minnesota Multiphasic Personality Inventory (MMPI) provide an overall profile of the test-taker. The burden is on the employer to show that the tests used are relevant to the job position and consistent with the business's mission, and that the test is reliable and valid. For example, (Mook, 1996) reports that psychological testing has shown value in evaluating applicants for airline flight crew positions.

Communication apprehension, believed to be most likely a learned phenomenon, is another factor that should be considered in the employee selection process, because it renders open and effective communication impossible. "People develop expectations with regard to other people and with regard to situations. Expectations are also developed concerning the probable outcome of engaging in specific behaviors (such as talking). To the extent that such expectations are found to be accurate, the individual develops confidence" (McCroskey and Richmond, 1987, pp. 145, 148). If the individual is not able to manage this situation, and fails because expectations are inaccurate or they cannot develop new alternatives, their anxiety and fear are reinforced. The only universal effect that has been discovered is a feeling of discomfort. As a result, a willingness to communicate is predicted to decline. As always, some situations may be more of a problem while others contribute less. The Personal Report of Communication scales, such as the PRCA-24 (B), are also recommended by McCroskey and Richmond (1987, p. 151), and appear to be more valid and flexible in application to many service situations where communications is key to customer service. In addition, subjecting job applicants to behavioral interviews during the selection process (in which they are asked to respond to situational and/or past behavior questions) seems to aid in filling frontline positions with capable individuals (Andrews, 2008).

In their study employing various qualitative techniques, Panter and Martin (1991) identified six frontline employee roles for managing customer behavior. The "Matchmaker," has the function of grouping different and incompatible income, sex, or age/generation groups to avoid self-encroachment. There is the "Teacher," who is used to socializing individuals to the location of functional areas and the norms of appropriate behavior. The "Santa Claus" role rewards the customer for cooperating with the organization through their congenial behavior. The "Police Officer" enforces the rules that will not disrupt the service process. The "Cheerleader" acts as a host or hostess by bringing people together. And finally, the "Detective" investigates what satisfies and what is dissatisfying to customers on a routine basis to keep the organization on guard for needed change. These roles are held in such high regard that the recruitment process is on the same level of importance as targeting the customer segment. Others, too, have suggested the requirement for fitting organizational roles contains a similar continuity in function. In that respect, Baldasare and Mittal (1997) identify four service roles that need serious thought when implementing a service process. The first is that of the "Coach," who essentially teaches or guides the user into the service provided. Second is the "Facilitator," who informs the customer about how the company conducts itself, its general culture, *modus operandi*, and general philosophy. Third, the "Integrator" teaches the customer about the services offered and what departments to tap into to obtain a particular service. And finally, there is the "Student" role, where the associate is put at the disposal of the customer to learn where the weaknesses and strengths are within the service process, to create improvements.

Very particular role functions that specialize in the scope of employee limits should not transcend those more encompassing requirements. Once a service interaction has commenced, the service provider may utilize strategies for directing the flow of conversation during the interaction. One is a "script," like a theatrical schema, that directs the flow of interaction between service provider and customer. It directs the behavior and interactions in a given scenario (Ford, 1998). Such actions and behaviors mold into patterned role behavior for the service provider. Some researchers are beginning to evaluate different service role performances in a particular situation. Three service scripts were considered by Hall (1993, pp. 457, 461–62) for restaurants, with the service provider being friendly, deferential, and flirtatious with the customer, along with providing the basic service of waiting in a timely and efficient manner. Both male and female servers in each of the service situations reported that the service providers perceived women customers as being more difficult to service and also as being more unfriendly than men. In each restaurant, female service providers were seen as being more friendly, and saw themselves as personally being more friendly by smiling, looking happy, and enjoying themselves, but the type of restaurant setting also determined what constituted "friendly." Hennig-Thurau *et al.* (2006) indicate that not all smiles are equal: the kinds of smiling, for example, at an upscale café and a coffee shop are worlds apart. Despite "the type of restaurant, servers framed the problem of customers who abuse their power as being treated like a servant." Customers treat "waitresses like servants" "because customers don't take waitresses as seriously" (Hall, 1993, pp. 462–63). In the trendy restaurant, usually "a look, a glance, the tone of voice, I'll be right with you" and providing excessive service can stabilize the situation. In the lower-status restaurants, service providers can be more direct. Customers will treat service providers by patronizing them, ignoring them, and even treating them with deference. In addition, service roles are also influenced by the restaurant situation. In which case, that also carries its own set of normative expectations based on sexual differentiation.

Interestingly, a gender preference to serve also exists among servers. "The majority of the servers interviewed expressed a preference to wait on customers who were of the opposite sex, and claimed that servers and customers do flirt as part of the provider-customer interaction," but again that differed between restaurants of different status. In the lower-status restaurant, a more direct exchange of flirting and joking occurred between the service provider and customer; in the high-status restaurant, it was invisible and reserved. Hall (1993, p. 464) states that "flirting is something servers do, but harassment is something done to waitresses." It is not sexual flirting as in the real world, according to the service providers, but rather "a friendly flirt," a playing around, so to speak. Customers do badger service providers within the normative standards of the game, but female servers are more prone than male servers to receive this type of treatment.

Another way to control the interaction in a situation is through directive questioning. Ford (1998) states that prompting is a very common form of leading the conversation, asking the customer if they would like any other service, for example, "Would you like to see our wine menu?" However, service providers need to be careful not to exceed their authority leading to a disruption in the service goals, and to remain open and empathic to customers' needs and requests. The organization has to set limits on how far an employee is allowed to function and interact with the customer. But these processes cannot be smothering to the frontline initiative of those employees. For example, Furlong (1993, pp. 192–97) specifies more general employee norms about implementing role behavior with customers that increases customer retention by placing limits on the interaction process.

Box 5.2 Employee norms

- Let employees know they can't pass the buck.
- Don't let your people get hung up on job descriptions.
- Spell out in dollars and cents the value of satisfying customers.
- Don't let them (the employee) believe that money solves everything.
- Remind employers that they have a better finger on the customer pulse.
- Spread the responsibility, especially across the frontline personnel.

Carr (1990, pp. 263–65) also sets out commandments for achieving customer satisfaction for frontline providers that recognize the customer as a person through individual contact, whole verbal and nonverbal attention, a focus on the concerns of the customer, and concluding the contact "gracefully." Others in a similar vein, such as Weinzimer (1998, p. 88), Morgan (1999, p. 153), and

Cannie and Caplin (1991, p. 118), identify individual service provider behaviors that are positive interactive initiatives to be used with the customer. Such "explicit service standards clarify the service task and provide benchmark norms against which employees can judge their own performance and managers can judge the employees' … performance" (Berry, 1995, pp. 72–73). The Ritz-Carlton's basic list of 20 principles offers ways of dealing with the customer and representing the company. For example, any employee who receives a customer complaint owns the complaint (Michelli, 2008). The development of performance standards cannot remain solely at the level of mid- or upper management. The service employee must also be involved and free to operate within their situation.

Frontline jobs represent the interface between companies and their customers. Zornitsky (1995) studied 50,000 employees and found that job satisfaction and commitment are highly correlated. Nevertheless, building capability tends to focus on practical, work-related issues that pertain to empowerment, employee involvement, communication, teamwork, and consistency of priorities. A key approach to satisfying customers is educating and empowering employees on the importance of their roles in delivering a consistently high quality of service (Amenumey and Lockwood, 2008). Thus empowerment entails motivating employees to achieve goals and providing the necessary tools and environment to progress effectively toward those goals (Chernish, 2001). This can be accomplished most easily by sharing the results of an employee survey (Clarke, 1992). Such a recurring effort gives employees an opportunity to express their ideas and feelings about dealing with customers. Such surveys should be tailored to the specific situation, and all employees should be part of the process. However, firms should avoid being dogmatic in specifying guidelines for customer interactions. What a service firm doesn't need is a system that encourages conformity and discourages creative thinking, innovation, and problem solving (Jogaratnam and Tse, 2006). "You can't control or supervise each interaction with customers in any case" (Cannie and Caplin, 1991, p. 120).

There are norms controlling both server and customer behavior. "Because the provider is typically trained and authorized to deliver a very narrow service or range of goods, both provider and customer know it is a waste of the customer's time to ask the provider for something outside that scope" (Gutek, 1995, p. 41). Even seemingly simple requests may be difficult to fulfill. "As consumers, we are occasionally positively surprised by the service provider who goes above and beyond the call of duty, but more typically we are bitterly disappointed or angered by inane, unempowered, unmotivated, unintelligent, unyielding bureaucratic frontline workers" (Iacobucci, 1998, p. 516). Empowerment of the employee is based on a "service vision" and carrying out a "strategy" that sets limits (Connellan and Zemke, 1993, p. 20). In compensating a customer for a failure to provide satisfactory service, the Marriott Corporation lets its "employees decide on these limits largely on their own." Each staff member and supervisor decides on the limits the frontline staff are empowered to exercise. Most employees would like the chance to be asked about putting their ideas into action (Furlong, 1993, p. 90). Southwest Airlines empowers its employees to be fair with the customer, and no matter what decision the employees reach, just so long as they think it is right, the company will back up that decision (Wiersema, 1996, pp. 7, 13).

Tschohl and Franzmeier, (1991, p. 151) strongly suggest that managers accept four basic premises of empowerment: an employee at the lowest level in the organization (1) knows best how the job can be done, (2) can solve frontline problems, (3) will accomplish more if expectations are set higher, and (4) is "[t]he greatest untapped resource in the organization." The empowered employee is a valuable resource. Customer-contact people are a vital and frequently overlooked source of knowledge about customer requirements. That is, they often possess the most direct idea of what's going on, and they often have pragmatically grounded ideas for improving frontline systems (Cannie and Caplin, 1991). When exercising an empowerment option, employees need to ask themselves the following questions: "(1) How likely am I to face this situation again? (2) Would I say yes if it happened again? (3) Is it fair? (4) Will my company lose or gain in the long run if I say yes? (5) Can I say no in a way that the customer will understand? (6) Will my saying no say – I don't trust you?" (Broydrick, 1994, pp. 58–59). "When employees are empowered to pursue customer satisfaction, they are supercharged with enthusiasm" (Tschohl and Franzmeier, 1991, p. 149). "Giving people useful information can empower them, to a much greater degree than simply preaching at them or telling them what to do. In the early stages of quality effort, information can help people recognize the significance of customer value, understand what it means for their organization, and accept the commitment to quality. It can make the whole effort real for them on an individual, personal basis" (Albrecht, 1992, pp. 187–88). As demonstrated within the Ritz-Carlton Corporation, being armed with practical information and self-confidence, empowerment can lead to improved change and customer satisfaction (Michelli, 2008). "Empowerment is just a fancy word until you convince your employees it's not career threatening to make decisions and mistakes." A franchisee of seven Holiday Inns has used the limited and unlimited empowerment method. "Not only has unlimited power increased customer satisfaction, it has saved the company money – speeds service, increases repeat business, and develops employee self-confidence" (Broydrick, 1994, pp. 47, 49). When they used limited empowerment that would automatically key in credits if a person complained, they found that some customers would not accept a credit when they realized that the problem would be addressed and corrected for the next customer. If trust and commitment are important for the customer's loyalty, then the employee's trust and loyalty can be increased through empowerment, as cited in the studies of Liljander (2000, pp. 179–80). In an examination of service provider guidelines, "most companies have strict do's and don'ts about roles and responsibilities, many of which make no sense (Tisch, 2007). People therefore go outside the rules – as they should" (Geddes, 1993, p. 151). By addressing the needs of the situation, they keep and satisfy customers.

Employees must have the authority to do what is necessary to achieve customer satisfaction. Empowerment is a state of mind for service providers in which they (1) feel control over how the job is performed, (2) understand the big picture and context in which the work is performed, (3) accept accountability for work output, (4) share responsibility for the group's performance, and (5) expect rewards based on personal performance. Significant empowerment fosters a necessary foundation for sustained service excellence regardless of the nature of the business (Berry, 1995). They must be "*empowered and should help develop specifications for their own performance*" on the frontline (Tschohl and Franzmeier, 1991, p. 72). But role taking is only one part of interaction theory. There is also role making, where persons gradually formulate their perception of their role performance and identity. Modifications exist because there is "considerable leeway" (Albrecht *et al.*, 1987, pp. 156–57) between a person's performance and the role expectations chosen for action, and creating one's own personal style. Service firms should empower the frontline staff because both customer and employee are frustrated when noncomplex transactions have to be monitored by an authority figure (Liswood, 1990).

Nevertheless, it is prudent to note that empowerment is effective only in a climate of trust and shared leadership responsibilities (Berry, 1995). No top-down system; no chain of command; it only flourishes in an organizational atmosphere in which the overall goals, specific strategies, and supporting values are known and followed by the service providers. Organizational cultures with insufficient employee appreciation or empowerment provide little extrinsic incentive for solving customer problems creatively or responding to customer requests (Iacobucci, 1998). For example, a study conducted by Yoo *et al.* (2006) found that frontline restaurant workers delivered better service redress initiatives when appropriately rewarded for doing so. Trusting your staff provides them with assurance that management has faith in them. "If you tell people you don't trust them, they might as well cheat you" (Brown, 1989, p. 86). Employees need to be trusted as full partners in a service enterprise to ensure "a climate of full trust between management and employees," where management is not above "constructive criticism" and employees are "not afraid to speak out and generate ideas." A system exists in which employees receive feedback on their performance with customers; work areas and situations are increasingly administered and managed by employees; incentives are given to employees for generating satisfied, delighted, and loyal customers; and "discretion is given to these frontline employees to win back dissatisfied customers" (Bhote, 1996, pp. 77–78, 140–41).

Management also has an important stake in selecting and hiring employees who are sensitive to customer relations and have the ability to manage the actions of dissatisfied customers. Management needs to provide training to employees in those people skills, especially listening to and handling customers. Management also needs to compensate and recognize employees on their customer interaction, empower employees to make real decisions, and monitor morale among employees to ensure contentment. There is nothing worse for a customer than to have to deal with a malcontent employee who is more than willing to show you why you made a bad decision in choosing that tourist company. Frontline employee burnout may be dramatically decreased by service managers recognizing the needs of service providers as empowered personalities. Change should be monitored with the service providers, who may see it as being at variance with their needs. Empowerment works when the service providers perceive and feel that they are supported. Rewarding the frontline performance of the service provider should be assessed with understanding of the consequences for both employee and customer (Armistead and Clark, 1994, p. 117). Empowering employees is not just a recent fashionable approach to human relations. It really adds to the frontline staff's customer initiative. "To gain commitment and support, to integrate service quality goals, to teach service quality skills and principles, to convince employees that customer care is their job, to emphasize the importance, (particularly those of the frontline staff) of their roles, to increase participation, motivation and self esteem" (Cannie and Caplin, 1991, p. 163). The tourist institution's culture and social situations are dependent on how tightly they are defined normatively, and will be either more open or more closely restricted to role variations and personal styles. One of the most difficult norms for a service organization is to allow frontline staff to personalize and make decisions relative to the customer. However, hotels such as the Ritz-Carlton have succeeded through employee trust (Michelli, 2008). In that regard, Heil *et al.* (1997, p. 147–62) clearly specify that those in a serving capacity should be ready, willing, and able to serve. Moreover, the employer must grant the employee the authority, empower them, and trust them; and concomitantly the employee must show a spirit and enthusiasm about what they are doing. When service providers "demonstrate a love and interest for their work their spirit is infectious." It draws the customer into the service process, and provides emotional warmth that sometimes can be just as important as the service sought. Then the freedom of authority, empowerment, and trust given to the employee helps build that foundation for superior service.

Noting a caveat to empowerment, Hartline and Ferrell (1993, p. 35) also found that empowerment increases role ambiguity, meaning that employees are confused about how to perform their duties, which negatively affects service quality. "Our findings suggest that empowering employees may do little more than confuse them." Without established work guidelines, values, and clearly articulated service goals, managers should be cautious in empowering frontline personnel. Along these lines, Hartline and Ferrell (1993) contend that while empowerment is associated with a number of positive outcomes.

very little is known about its potential disadvantages. Empowerment and production-line approaches require different types of managers and employees. For empowerment to work, managers must think that their employees can act independently; and employees must feel a need to grow and test their abilities (Bowen and Lawler, 1992, p. 151). Blattberg *et al.* (2001, p. 180) believe the key organizational element in managing "customers with very similar needs, preferences, and behaviors," who are classified as a "market segment," is gained by the use of developing management teams where the sales, marketing, and service are pinpointed to meet the customer's needs. Empowerment and cooperation by the employees makes this approach work; rather than "traditional chains of authority, upper-level managers establish general strategies and objectives, while individual customer-facing employees or customer development management teams decide how to implement them for each customer or customer segment" (Blattberg *et al.*, 2001, p. 188). Following in that organizational vein, Macdonald and Sirianni (1996, p. 11) note that control over the frontline employee can be very subtle for the empowered employee who has personal control in contrast to the production-line service worker. "The paradox of empowerment in the service labor process is that while seeming unobtrusive, these forms of control are actually more invasive than direct means." Managers should not think that empowered employees have greater freedom, status, and control over how they function.

What types of service role perform most satisfactorily in the customer and service provider situation? Following the symbolic interactional–dramaturgical approach to hiring employees as cast members, Bell and Zemke (1992, pp. 5–6) identify three universal role requirements. First, "great service performers must be able to create a relationship with the audience [the customer]." Second, "great service performers must be able to handle pressure" and control themselves. Third, "great service performers must be able to learn new scripts" and implement them because expectations and situations are constantly changing. Based on these performance assumptions, the service provider has to be careful to implement measures to enhance the tourist customer's experience. The following list of actions on the part of the service provider is expected to produce positive reactions in the customer, leading to a satisfactory judgment about the tourist experience. This is far from a complete list, but provides an initial working list. It is based largely on qualitative evidence, but it is a start in examining the interaction process.

Service provider action – expected customer reaction

It is essential to recognize and always keep in mind that the locus of satisfaction resides between the service provider and customer (Noe and Uysal, 2003). The goal in describing the following interactions between the service provider and customer is to illustrate the importance of going beyond just satisfying the customer. As outlined by Berman (2005), the next step is to bring "delight" to the customer and create loyalty in the interaction process.

When you personalize, you increase self-worth

In this highly impersonal world, where many of us are mere numbers, we are delighted and highly satisfied when someone takes a personal interest in our tourist experience. To illustrate this point, Club Med, requires "providers that are able to interact with guests" to be responsive and organize activities that also involve the guest (Heskett *et al.*, 1990, pp. 67, 101). To illustrate, a charter flight from New York to Cancun Airport arrived ten hours late. For their 2 a.m. arrival time, the management and staff organized and prepared a "lavish welcoming banquet, complete with a mariachi band and champagne." That party lasted until dawn, with guests "commenting that it was the most fun they had since college." This kind of personalized service and attention avoided irate feelings and helped the guests recover their positive expectations for the remaining days of their stay. The positive self-worth of the guests was directly affected by such pre-emptive action. In essence, "relationships that add value for customers require some form of personalized interaction. They are built on the recognition that every relationship is different, that it is based on two-way communication, and that it should continue to build and change over time." Some hotels, such as the Ritz-Carlton, keep tabs on their customers' preferences so they can anticipate them without always asking (Day, 1999, p. 153).

When you know the customer, you clarify expectations

In determining the competence of an employee, it is crucial to know the expectations of the customers, then to match the skills of the employee to meet those customer expectations (Healy, 1996). More than likely, there will be very specific information requirements, and most likely, whatever the setting, accurate communication will be a necessity for satisfying the customer. Ritz Carlton has launched an approach to attract and build a following of loyal guests through frontline associates carrying preference pads in which guests' preferences can be recorded. They can track customer preferences for such things as pillows, snacks, and types of service preference to meet specific tastes (Michelli, 2008).

When you are friendly, you become close

"Hire people who want to be friendly and helpful" (Tschohl and Franzmeier, 1991, p. 109). The Marriott Corporation's focus in its Fairfield Inn division is clean rooms, a friendly atmosphere, and budget prices. This business model therefore focuses on the roles of the housekeeping and front desk staff (Berry, 1995, p. 166). Providing a socially welcoming situation sets a very positive tone for the services offered. This is obviously a basic service performance norm, probably learned from those who first cared for us. Willingham (1992, p. 51) lists some reactions that a service worker can engage to maximize their positive impact on a customer: (1) value them, (2) exert no pressure and make them comfortable, (3) give undivided attention, (4) do not judge their ability to buy, (5) focus on them not on your work tasks or schedule, and (6) don't ignore them in favor of someone else.

When you surprise, you bring joy

Wonder is a part of leisure and tourist experiences that are created through social interaction with the customer. It is the perceived freedom, intrinsic satisfaction, and positive reinforcement that result from being surprised in a free-time situation (Labone, 1996). The Walt Disney Company makes wonder intrinsic to its theme parks. Epcot schedules unannounced performances, including parades and appearances by Disney characters, that result in the customer feeling fortunate that they were in the right place at the right time to receive this extra value for their tourist dollar. In fact, it is this sort of "surprise" that distinguishes customer satisfaction from customer delight (Berman, 2005).

When you promise, you commit

What I can expect, and how I will be treated as a customer, is essential to the interaction experience. "A customer-contact role carries certain normative expectations, including display rules" (Ashforth and Humphrey, 1993, pp. 99–104). These rules identify with the positive impact of fulfilling the customer's expectations through positive interaction. For example, Ashforth and Humphrey (1993, pp. 99–104) cite one organization that had its service providers pin a dollar to their uniforms; customers were entitled to it if they did not receive "a friendly greeting or a sincere thank you." In a tourist situation, we would think friendly would be basic, and being sensitive to all reasonable requirements is guaranteed. In fact, this relates to all transactions, no matter how minimal, and grows with use; for example, there is the "role of a skier who makes use of the many services of a ski lodge," not just the slopes (Deighton, 1994, p. 135).

Box 5.3 Considering culture: language context

In certain cultures, the meaning of verbal communication relies heavily on the context in which statements are made. An example of such a high-context culture (also known as an implicit culture) is Japan, where the meaning of a statement depends on factors such as when and where it is made. At the other end of the spectrum are low-context (explicit) cultures, such as Germany and Switzerland, in which interpreting the meaning of spoken language is comparatively straightforward.

When you listen, you learn

Service providers on the team who can listen are essential to knowing the customer. "We hope you've hired people who are customer-focused, who can listen, understand, communicate with, and relate to customers as well as demonstrate ... knowledge" (Connellan and Zemke, 1993, p. 89). "Truly service-driven companies ... listen and they respond" to the customer. "They hold hands" with their customer, and adjust, improve, mend, abandon, and make right at every step in the service process. They strive to be characterized as "dependable" (Tschohl and Franzmeier, 1991, pp. 195–96). Most of us can recall those in the tourist sector who listened to our requests, questions, and tales of woe with compassion.

When you reward, you positively reinforce

Rewarding the loyal customer is top priority. For example, "the pricing strategies of many, if not most, companies shortchange loyal customers and reward the most disloyal ones." "So Southwest (Airlines) has one price for advance purchase and one for unrestricted purchase. Customers know that they are getting a fair deal" (Reichheld, 2001, pp. 142, 144). As an important point of reference for the customer, this kind of pricing strategy should be clearly linked to the benefits program. A more basic reward is making the customer a part of the corporate family. Zeithaml *et al.* (1990, p. 109) argue that treating customers as partial employees facilitates role clarity and produces quality service more effectively. Furthermore, customer co-creation of value not only benefits the customer, but also bolsters operational efficiency (Claycomb *et al.*, 2001). In such situations, "providing customers with realistic service previews, training customers how to perform, and providing visible rewards such as upgrading a customer to a first class seat" are excellent ways of creating stronger customer reinforcement. To illustrate, on a crowded flight, a stewardess sympathetically told two of their rushed passengers boarding last to stay in first class rather than struggle to the back. They relaxed, the plane was not delayed, and the customers were delighted.

When you recognize needs, you acknowledge importance

Social competence is "absolutely necessary" in face-to-face service contact, and customers must be made to "feel welcome and comfortable" because the service provider knows their needs and expectations (Petite, 1989, p. 111). It is in this way that "appreciation means actively acknowledging the value of a customer by recognizing his existence and by establishing knowledge of his particular needs and desires" (Vavra, 1992, p. 37). For example, it is becoming more commonplace for service providers to utilize data-mining software to identify patterns and trends in customer data, which results in an enhanced ability to serve them in ensuing interactions (Magnini *et al.*, 2003).

That action is central to the interaction process between service provider and customer.

When you solve a problem, you become special

The service providers on the frontline know where problems arise. Furlong (1993, p. 115) states that "studies by a U.S. research organization indicate that frontliners can predict almost 90 percent of cases where customers will have complaints." Given the frontliners' knowledge of problems, they have to be able to break down the interpersonal barriers that customers construct to protect themselves in problem service situations. They "should therefore be sensitive to critical contact situations; they should be able to quickly recognize the potential for escalation and then be able to reduce this potential by applying their finely honed communication and conflict solving skills" (Jeschke *et al.*, 2000, p. 207). The service provider gives a personal commitment upon which the customer may directly rely for solution to a service problem. At a well-known hotel, an employee dropped a guest's computer but immediately replaced it with a new one to avoid an even greater problem. Superb recovery efforts such as this can potentially catapult post-failure customer satisfaction levels above pre-failure levels (de Matos *et al.*, 2007).

When you are leisure-hearted, you bring a smile

A positive outlook toward life ensures life satisfaction. Such a disposition is reinforced by the psychological and social interactions of individuals that lead to personal happiness and contentment. It is the opposite of worry, depression, and sadness. Such employees do not hide in a social vacuum, but reach out to the guests around them. They joke, smile, and laugh, and it shows in their sincerity. If any service sector requires such an action, it is the tourist and leisure business, where a recreational seeker is expecting a little time off from the serious chores of work life and expects the service providers to respond in kind. As an illustration, Zeithaml and Bitner (2000, p. 76) report that the positive and negative emotions of river guides "had a strong effect on their customers' ... overall satisfaction." More importantly, the overall positive emotions of the guides produced a stronger effect than negative ones.

In closing, while we have laid stress on the positive, it is always necessary to remember the negative part of human interaction. When the rendered service cannot fulfill the tourists' expectations and the service provider is rude in their interaction, "you add to the fire" of insult, emotional pain (Gitomer, 2002, p. 28). Such action destroys the chance of future contact, and of many more patrons though word-of-month contact. Positive frontline employee interaction with the customer lies at the heart of ensuring satisfaction in a tourist situation.

6 Appealing to the travel and provider roles

Preview

This chapter illustrates how firms can appeal to their frontline providers and to travelers simultaneously. More specifically, if properly motivated, employees are more likely to participate in extra-role behavior in order to go the extra mile to please the customer. Hence devices for motivating employees, such as soliciting and implementing employee suggestions, are discussed. In addition, the chapter delves into the importance of designing top-rate service failure-recovery systems. Such failure-recovery systems have a marked influence on both customer and employee sentiments – when failures occur, customers have a heightened awareness of the service situation. Under the appropriate conditions, this heightened awareness allows an opportunity for the service provider to direct an excellent recovery effort and catapult customer post-failure satisfaction above its pre-failure level.

Rewarding the customer and provider

Positive and negative customer reinforcement

Rewarding the customer is the real challenge for the service provider. Brown (1989, p. 57) stresses the essential point that in developing a service process, it "must be customer driven, not company driven." Being customer friendly is the hallmark of the corporate giants in the travel and tourist industry. The practices of rewarding people, customer service, and turning customer information into insight produce four times the value of a profit-driven approach, on aggregate across industries (Dull, 2000). Good customer relations is more than just a warm, fuzzy communication message; it is demonstrated in a positive attitude toward customers and fellow employees. It shows in the professional appearance of the place and personnel for the customer. And finally, it resurfaces as a good neighbor in the community and in the professional peer groups that support the company's objectives in customer service (DeFrancesco, 1990). Being recognized is a reward, so "give servers closest to the work and to customers the chance to be heard by management to help themselves, customers, and the company" (Berry, 1995, p. 20). Personal awards and competition are good organizational methods for stimulating service quality. The Ritz-Carlton Corporation uses a Monday morning line-up of employees to share customer service stories. These employee-generated narratives serve as a source of employee recognition as well as a source of motivation and customer focus (George, 2000). This puts the major goal of the organization in front of everyone each week – what it takes to please and satisfy the customer. This strategy of bringing staff together at various scheduled times can be used to introduce customer service behaviors that are effective in an interactive situation. These meetings can encourage role play-ing as a means of reintroducing positive ways of communicating, reacting, and interacting with the customer.

Expecting the customer to articulate a new service strategy that would excite them and better serve their needs is too much to ask, but if you listen and encourage them, they will tell you what displeases them about the current service. Berry (1999, pp. 76, 98–99, 105) contends that being open to listening is required to assess what both the customer and employee are saying that can be used to improve the service strategy. According to research conducted by de Jong and Den Hartog (2007), it is important not only to evaluate the customer, but also to encourage employees to submit ideas for improvement as part of employee performance and reward evaluation programs. One pro-gram, for example, receives an average of ten ideas per employee per year, a total of 6000 ideas to improve the service.

In a large-scale survey evaluating service guarantees at Radisson Hotels worldwide, Hays *et al.* (2000) and Hays and Hill (2001) found that such pro-grams increased employee motivation, organizational learning, and improved service quality, customer satisfaction, and loyalty. The Radisson sought to achieve 100 percent satisfaction rating, so if a customer's dissatisfaction was not resolved, the customer did not pay. What is ingenious about this guaran-tee is the fact that the employee's job is focused on satisfying the customer, not on the routine practices of running a hotel. The company also reported increased profitability, and a reduction in labor turnover that results in important cost-saving measures. In fact, Hinkin and Tracey (2000) found that the average cost of replacing an hourly associate in the hotel industry is roughly 30 percent of that associate's yearly earnings

In building a personal relationship with your customer, it should be remembered that the social activities relating to the customer's personal lifestyle, be it their family or social activities, matter (Maister, 1989), very often defining expectations toward a trip. Every single customer at Southwest Airlines is thought of as being a family member. A survey conducted in 1994 demonstrated that the last five customers on an 80-passenger flight resulted in the company's profit margin. Losing just one customer per flight reduces profit by 20 percent. They practice one-on-one contact, using a unique custo-mer ID for every flight. They can track a customer's flights and automatically award a bonus flight for trips taken. They also can send birthday cards based on the age information available to them through this system. And finally, they track phone calls containing customer complaints, so they can inform the customer that they are not taken lightly as a no-name insignificant person (Wiersema, 1996, pp. 17–31). This customer complaint monitoring is a vital activity – a firm's failure-redress initiatives receive as much, if not more, customer attention than the original failure that sparked the complaint (Maxham and Netemeyer, 2002).

"Research indicates that about 25 percent of customers will switch to competitors every year. This can result in significant revenue and profit opportunities" (Weinzimer, 1998, p. 175). It also results in lost growth over the life of a company. Club Med is the innovator of the vacation concept that includes all amenities, paid for in advance (Horovitz and Panak, 1994, p. 6). This creates a special bond between the partner customer and provider friend. It has to, if they are to trust each other, for this kind of arrangement to be successful. In seeking customer input in the hospitality area, Marriott employs multiple data-gathering techniques that try to identify and highlight central customer service interests. Schaaf (1995, pp. 120–21) reports positive reinforcement activities such as speedy check-in, cleanliness, value, friendliness, and breakfast. The latter attribute might not seem so obvious until you put yourself in the position of a business traveler or tourist who has a schedule to meet: getting a quick breakfast provides fuel to help meet those planned objectives. Many hotels, especially in the upper price range, offer services that allow the frequent patron or flier to reduce their amount of luggage, ground waits, and loss of time. They provide clothing, toiletries, and basic essentials. Some hotels will even store clothing for an upcoming visit or have luggage, or large boxes, sent by FedEx or UPS shippers for customers (Emling, 2002). Meeting the special needs of a customer, requests concerning the adaptability of the service providers, and providing unsolicited surprises for the customer are ways in which the interaction process influences satisfaction (Zeithaml and Bitner, 2000) and even sparks customer delight (Berman, 2005).

"A customization strategy is to satisfy the demands of more customers by offering a choice of options, one of which meets their particular needs ... The major advantage of any customized approach for service is that it blocks out competition by meeting the needs of a wider variety of customers with only slight variations to the original product or service" (Horovitz and Panak, 1994, pp. 73, 76). The customer is rewarded with a tailored service.

The use of reward programs has also grown in the tourist industry as compensation to faithful and loyal customers. "The bigger the program, the better it is in the customer's eyes" (Brown, 1995, p. 187). In a frequent flyer program, the more ways a customer can earn awards, and the more ways of using them, the better. The magnitude of these programs should not be underestimated; for example, in 2003 the major carriers collectively had 8–9 trillion frequent flier miles in circulation (Johnston, 2003). Airlines have extended their awards program by teaming up with other corporations, such as banks, telephone providers, and hotels, to extend their commitment to the customer. In the case study reported by Blanchard and Bowles (1998, p. 138), people were rewarded through two major approaches: cash and congratulations. "One of the easiest ways to win customer share is to reward their best customers in the form of significant incentives" (Yeh *et al.*, 2000, p. 55). "Reward customer loyalty" with your own frequent-use program, and be alert to changing customer travel "attitudes, expectations, and behavior patterns" to anticipate trends, is sound advice from American Express Travel Services (Wiersema, 1996, pp. 142–43). Also, firms must be creative in how they design incentive programs. For instance, recent research conducted by Nunes and Dreze (2006) found that a customer reward provided after the completion of ten purchases (in which the customer is credited for three after their first purchase) produced more loyalty than a reward program designed for redemption after eight purchases.

In addition, firms should reward the customer for assisting in the delivery process. Benefits to the customer may include increased control over the delivery process, time savings, monetary savings, and psychological or physical advantages (Zeithaml and Bitner, 2000). Complimentary or value-added services can bolster loyalty by prolonging and intensifying the relationship and fueling satisfaction and barriers to exit (Meyer and Blumelhuber, 2000). These reward services can become habitual and expected by the customer, such as ground transportation between hotels and airline bookings for passengers. Other diversionary options, including magazines, videos, movies, and punctuality, may become expected in the transportation package. According to return-on-quality research, firms must realize that add-on services must be viewed with caution, for example, frill services may be considered as simply unwanted ornaments by some customers (Rust *et al.*, 2002). Southwest Airlines, with its no-frill service, on-time scheduling, and light-hearted spirit, is one example that takes honors in the travel sector.

There are other reward links to a company. Cross-selling deals such as lodging and food service add to an existing service. Add-on selling is broader, in that it brings in a new service, such as underwriting a credit card that links the tourist company to a billing activity. Such cross-selling gives bonus points for possession of the card to be used universally in other shopping situations. Cross-selling is related to customer "retention" and "lifetime profitability," but add-on selling needs more site work on determining customer needs and expectations, and involving other companies that also contribute to an improvement in "customer profitability" or "enhancing relationship duration." Stand-alone or teamed with other companies, customer benefit programs offer rewards. Certain airlines are linking up with rental car services, credit cards, and hotels that offer additional bonus miles. And units in the business and tourist service system are also building strong incentive programs. "According to Marriott corporate directors the Marriott Honoured Guest Programme, with 3.5 million members, is the largest, most popular incentive program in the hotel industry" (Gilpin, 1996, p. 153).

Positive and negative provider reinforcement

What defeats the service workers is not hard work. They are defeated by "work without personal growth, without teammates, without kindness, without meaning" (Berry, 1999, p. 51). Companies that often make the list of the top ten that employees like to work for in the USA, as reported by Heil *et al.* (1997, p. 178), also serve their workers well. This kind of company, if it "goes out of its way to treat its own people well will do the same for us [the customer]." Again, linking the worker's positive role experience to themselves is one way of reducing unexpected negative outcomes in anticipation of a service experience. In awarding pay in incentive systems to employees, Tschohl and Franzmeier (1991, pp. 128–27) maintain that employers should be timely with presentations and make them in a public forum, thus adding extra merit, while long-term tenure bonuses should be used to maintain stability in the workforce, especially where frontline service is threatened.

Turnover in the hospitality field for frontline employees can be so excessive that firms have received work permits for foreign nationals to cover these jobs. Econo Lodge of America also found that "respectful treatment of employees is one of the most effective means of reducing turnover" (Tschohl and Franzmeier, 1991, p. 157). A proper way to reward employees is by taking their direction and implementing their advice. "Encourage your employees and reward them for their ideas," which will enhance the customer care program. Also, "reward your employees for providing excellent customer care." "It can be as simple as saying 'thanks'" (Brown, 1999, p. 218). In this way, the customer is the central focus, not some organizational goal where monetary incentives drive the process. Let the customer drive the service process and reward employees for their innovative actions. Southwest Airlines recognizes its employees by identifying itself as a "great customer service organization that happens to be in the airline business" (Wiersema, 1996, p. 5). Rewarding an employee is basic psychology in winning and keeping their undivided support and allegiance. SAS (Scandinavian Airlines), after its big turnaround in customer service, held parties in three countries, gave gold watches, and sent employees home in private limousines. Marriott management finds shares in its stock to be motivational. Other firms use a bonus system, healthcare, and daycare centers for employees' children as incentives (Arthur, 2003). Rewarding the employee means more than financial rewards for acting positively with the customer. It also means "the rewards of celebration, status, strokes, and hoopla" (Maister, 1989, p. 263). It is worth repeating that employees are internal customers of a personnel department of a company, and how they are treated has a significant impact on the way they serve external customers (Zeithaml *et al.*, 1990). Techniques mentioned include employee recognition and appreciation programs, acknowledgement of new service ideas, employee newsletters, and communicating to employees in the same vein as if they were just another customer. The most effective reward systems combine financial compensation, career advancement, and nonfinancial recognition (Berry, 1995). In other words, employees must perceive adequate levels of distributive justice (such as pay), procedural justice (such as fair company policies), and interactional justice (such as inter-personal sensitivity of managers) (Narcisse and Harcourt, 2008).

To ensure effective employee interaction with the customer in terms of responding, being empathic, providing assurance, and offering reliable service, it is important to understand that motivating employees is based on classical and operant conditioning. To be effective, employees are rewarded for pursuing certain activities (operant) and for performing certain activities or behavior (classical). For the reward system to maximize responses, companies should match corporate and individual objectives and have sales incentives follow suit. Let the frontline staff set the compensation rules, steer clear of performance measures that can't be measured directly, and make sure rewards are related to real performance. Other factors relate to specifying the particular kinds of reward, whether related to dollars or stock options, but also "don't stop at cash as a means of motivating your people ... Consider the value of recognition" (Furlong, 1993, pp. 191–208). Employee incentives and rewards can "interfere with creating a highly flexible learning environment" when set goals are singularly tied to money (Heil *et al.*, 1997, pp. 217–18). Employees may cut corners and not provide the best service to meet these goals, and will not go out of their way to offer alternative service goals because of their concentration on meeting the demands at hand.

"Punishment almost never works in the long run. It fools us. It backfires." The employee retreats, slacks off, and stop taking risks (Connellan and Zemke, 1993, p. 112). Positive rewards work. "Economic monetary" rewards follow cash salary, bonus, or options benefit. "Economic nonmonetary" rewards involve receiving trips, dinners, or clothing credit benefits. "Noneconomic tangible" benefits, such as larger working area, a window, parking privileges; and finally, "noneconomic intangibles," such as compliments, smiles, or letters of recognition are other reinforcement possibilities (Connellan and Zemke, 1993, pp. 118–19). In general, noneconomic reinforcement differs from economic reinforcement in three key ways. Economic reinforcement has a relatively high cost, is difficult to bestow immediately, and focuses the individual on service *results*; noneconomic reinforcement is relatively low cost, can be given immediately, and has the potential to focus the individual on service *behavior* as well as service results (Connellan and Zemke, 1993, p. 141).

Certain reward programs requiring the service provider to help implement the frontline are often necessary to increase retention equity. Rust *et al.* (2000, pp. 97, 99–105) list such common approaches. First, through greater "understanding of the customer," "customizing the purchase" and "ultimately through on-going dialogue," customer bonds can be strengthened. Second, through "reward behaviors that enhance the retention connection and special recognition and treatment programs." Third, "through emotional ties", having formed bonds, being concerned about what matters to customers in their life and social ties with the community. The single program involving probably the greatest allocation of service provider need, care, and commitment is when the customer has a lifestyle affinity and emotional link with the company. There is a natural prejudice to downplay the emotional and attitudinal customer factor in tourist relations. It is easier to focus on schedules, timetables, and other tangible service attributes, such as rooms and modes of transportation. "All across the corporate landscape, performance measurement systems reward employees for functional goals rather than enterprise goals" (Weinzimer, 1998, p. 149). In that regard, Horovitz and Panak (1994, p. 16) cite a company that places customer service as a criterion for performance evaluation and pay. Management-promoted employee-based rewards play a role in customer performance by directly influencing the actions of the employee.

Not all kinds of reward system enhance employee satisfaction and performance, however. Behavior-based rewards that are tied to how the service process is carried out and performed positively affect employee job satisfaction and innovativeness (Hartline and Ferrell, 1993, pp. 34, 40). But goal-oriented rewards associated with trying to achieve an outcome can be counter-productive. These reward systems are usually part of the numbers game, where frequency and quantity take precedence over the quality process of interacting with the customer. The service provider, in trying to achieve a goal, handles the customer in a speedy and often unrefined manner. The provider may achieve the goal of filling rooms, moving baggage, or scheduling, but the service outcome is not smoothly elegant or refined. Customers notice when they are treated as a number on an assembly line. One of the worst mistakes a manager can make is to pay lip-service to customer-oriented behavior, yet evaluate and reward employees on the basis of outcome-based measures. Behavior-based rewards, on the other hand, give employees control over the interaction process and the day-to-day conditions through increasing self-knowledge and personable encounters or relationships that promote the company's goal of service quality. It is common sense that if people are treated as machines, not as individuals, they are unlikely to have loyalty and trust – they will not give of their best.

It is plausible for people to be valued for themselves in the workplace, not just their functions; for people's souls to be nurtured and allowed to emerge where they work. In short, it is possible for work to be more than just a job. Work can be fulfilling and a life-enhancing experience, with all its trials, tribulations, and thrills. This is what Lewin and Regine (2000, pp. 23–24) observed in discussions with very successful companies on how they related to people. Performance standards are not to be totally ignored for nondirect contract personnel in the tourist industry. As an element of employee reward or enfranchisement, Pickard (1993, pp. 165, 172) uses an example from Fairfield Inn, where room attendants can receive a full day's salary if they finish a certain number of rooms, and they can bid on extra rooms and receive cash when finished. Each Inn also establishes an employee-of-the-month fund and a second monthly fund managed by the employees as they see fit. Employees are rewarded with a day off for learning accurate responses to the 15 to 20 questions most asked by customers (Connellan and Zemke, 1993). These practices can add to customer satisfaction directly or indirectly.

Dealing with customer problems

Customer care

By definition, a problem is "a situation for which there is a solution" (Carr. 1990, p. 63). "A problem is the difference between what we want to happen and what actually happens" (Willingham. 1992, p. 122). Expectations of reality do not always match the reality of what really happens. Cooley posits two reasons why problems of action arise in social situations: "either we are mistaken about the expectations and prognoses derived from our reservoir of images concerning the actions of our partners; or we are mistaken about the presupposed communality of meaning of those images" (Cooley, 1998, p. 21). An essential of a customer care program is the front desk. "All customer interactions ... take place through the front desk of a customer service center, where incoming complaints, questions, ideas or emergency calls (are) received" (Ahlert, 2000, pp. 258–59). All manner of information relating to the customer is necessary for meeting their demands. This includes health needs, hobby interests. dinning tastes, reading material, etc. In reviewing ten problems commonly associated with service companies, Edvardsson *et al.* (1994, p. 126) note that they can be summarized around the "relationship" to the service, communication, information, and accessibility of the service system and process to the customer.

Unfortunately, frontline problem solvers have no incentive to communicate with management. "In most organizations, frontline contact people – who handle the complaints, hear the requests for new services, cope with lead users, or lose sales due to competitor initiatives – are seldom motivated to inform management on a systematic basis" (Day, 1999, p. 88). Management needs to request systematic input from frontline workers and then give them the means and materials to resolve problems. "The frontline is where your customer's experience can be most dramatically affected. And in most firms, it is frontline compensation that seems to have drifted furthest" from consideration (Reichheld, 2001, p. 141). According to Gitomer (2002, p. 28), "we are living in an era of responsibility shirkers and blamers." Thus firms should see to it that they reward employees for exceptional complaint hand-ling (Yoo *et al.*, 2006).

Harris (1991, p. 4) sees an opportunity for irate customers to be turned into profit outcomes by changing their negative perceptions. Customer complaints can open channels of communication for positive change. At Ritz-Carlton hotels, all frontline service providers feel respected, which is a fine tribute to the CEO since, as reported by Berry (1999, p. 31), they typically do not hear the most common customer complaints. These include using dishonest or unfair practices, assuming customers are stupid or dishonest and treating them harshly, breaking promises, dealing with powerless employees who cannot act, long waits for service, impersonal motionless responses, not communicating with customers about solving a problem, employees not going out of their way, lack of knowledge, and being too busy with their personal exchanges rather than the customers. Firms should view customer complaints as an opportunity to build customer loyalty by turning lemons into lemonade. The moment of truth in the service encounter is when the customer interacts with the service firm. Zeithaml and Bitner (2000, p. 860) go on to report that the Walt Disney Company estimates about 74 encounters per visit and that "a negative experience in any one of them can lead to a negative overall evaluation." Although "dissatisfied customers may be a minority, they may be knowledgeable, they may be heavy users, and they may be highly profitable to the organization, and there is also the possibility that discontent may spread" (Chakrapani, 1998, p. 223). Research indicates that if the product is of high quality, customers tend to voice fewer complaints, which in turn leads to employees having fewer problems with dissatisfied customers (Liljander, 2000).

According to Timm (1998, p. 7) the average American company will lose 10–30 percent of its customers because of poor service. Conversely, companies that have strong service programs and realize the benefits of holding on to customers, see their profits typically jump 25–100 percent. Timm (1998, p. 9) also reports on studies that show that a dissatisfied customer tells ten to twenty other persons about their unhappy experience, and in turn they tell five to ten others. Word-of-mouth advertising is a powerful force to recognize, and should be regarded with the utmost respect because it is thought to be more sincere than other marketing communications (Kaikati and Kaikati, 2004). Opinion-leaders in our society are regarded as major role communicators who shape innovative acceptance of services or their rejection (Shoham and Ruvio, 2008).

Service failure was reported most among customers. suggesting that "in face-to-face service encounters, inattentive service ... directly attributable to the behavior of frontline employers, may detract more from satisfaction" and receive more "attention from customers" (Smith *et al.*, 1998, pp. 29–30). There is another problem in dealing with service complaints. "In encounters, glitches, problems, and mistakes can be more difficult for customers to deal with ... feedback about problems encountered by a customer is of little use unless the organization knows which provider(s) handled the aggrieved customers" (Gutek, 1995, pp. 50–51). Often the lag time is too long, so that memories fade, even if the provider is identified. The customer is not always right, and one-way perceptions represent only one side of the truth. In fact, research indicates that illegitimate customer complaints routinely occur in service settings (Reynolds and Harris, 2005). To judge a service provider on a single "glitch" is not very astute management. In this sense, firms should protect their customer contact employees from abuse (Carr, 1990). In problem situations, firms should not leave them alone, but rather should move quickly to help them control the situation. Southwest Airlines never expects its employees to endure verbal abuse, cussing, or hostile confrontations from a customer; "we say goodbye and good riddance" (Wiersema, 1996, p. 20). There are situations that make encounters and relationships between custo- mers very difficult and problematic to handle due to heightened customer and provider emotion during failure situations (Mattila, 2004). Customer behavior that is "rude, abusive, overly controlling," and makes "unreasonable demands, requests, changes" in a service situation needs to be recognized as excessive (Bly, 1993, p. 235). Moreover, cross-cultural differences in the expression and interpretation of these emotions further complicates such failure situations (Yuksel *et al.*, 2006).

Care must be taken in every step of an interactive exchange. "Perhaps most important of all, we must note that a false impression maintained by an individual in any one of his routines may be a threat to the whole relationship or role of which the routine is only part, for discreditable disclosure in one area of an individual's activity will throw doubt on the many areas of activity in which he may have nothing to conceal" (Goffman, 1966, p. 206). When a service breaks down "the content or form of the employee's response is what causes the customer to remember the event favorably or unfavorably," or how the "response to problem customers" is handled by the service provider (Zeithaml and Bitner, 2000, pp. 90–91). A double deviation, for example, is said to transpire when a complaint is handled so poorly that the redress is viewed as a second failure in the eyes of the customer (Maxham and Netemeyer, 2002).

In dealing with complaints in general, Vavra (1992, pp. 128–29) states that the service provider needs to recognize the customer as a human being with feelings, anxieties, even nerves; and acknowledge the contact without vali- dating its accuracy. Next, without interruption, the provider should express a sincere concern, clearly identify that concern, offer a skilled correspondence not a form response, offer a solution with the customer's agreement, end with a sincere apology and ask for their future business, and finally follow up in a week to see if the problem was handled effectively. When Marriott has a customer problem, it deals not with formal responses, but with direct contacts with the customer, and has the resolution decided upon by them. "In this way, Marriott maximizes the ultimate satisfaction of each problem" (Vavra, 1992, p. 149). In fact, recent research conducted by Karande *et al.* (2007) indicates that customers typically prefer to help participate in formulating their redress initiative. Removing negative emotions from the process of interaction is the key to resolving problems. Willingham (1992, pp. 126, 131) recommends reacting and not "ducking the problem," or pushing the "blame on others," "reacting to customers' anger or negative actions by automatically demon- strating the same behavior," and "patiently and calmly getting people talking, venting and us listening." To be outstanding at understanding problem situations: "get the facts, listen, and repeat back the problem." Travelers are facing an electronic world, according to Forrester Research, a company that analyses changes in technological use. Given the present data, 9 percent of consumers still use the telephone to complain about travel problems; 15 percent use email; and the remainder turn to faxes and letters. Companies are emerging to take up the case of aggrieved customers for a fee. Airlines are seeing the emergence of these new intermediaries, who can be quite successful in handling customers. Companies should eliminate the middle-man before this becomes a practice that will cost everyone – the customer and the service provider – more time and money.

Research indicates that for every dissatisfied customer who complains to an organization, there are 26 other customers who are equally dissatisfied, but do not voice their complaint to the firm (Scheuing, 1999). "On average across all industries, the Technical Assistance Research Program has found that 50 percent of all customers and 25 percent of all business customers with problems never complain to anyone." Rather than complaining, they defect to other service providers (Goodman, 1999). The damage done to a customer by not following up or resolving the problem is extremely costly. The service situation is not always under the direct control of the service provider, so care has to be taken in understanding the scope of their role. "The problem manifested (symbolized) by an employee could be the result of a number of factors that are not under the direct control of the employee – such as policies, procedures, people, and equipment already in place – and may have little to do with factors under his or her control" (Chakrapani, 1998, p. 40).

DeWitt and Martin (2009) suggest that written responses to "form letters" of complaint should include a combination of distributive, procedural, and interactional justice. In the business of handling a customer complaint, the customer expects a fair, tangible outcome (distributive justice) and would like to understand and perceive if policies and procedures, and criteria used by decision makers, are fair (procedural justice). The provider should also create an environment in which the customer feels they are treated fairly and that they can trust the provider (interactional justice). Effective resolution of customers' complaints and dissatisfaction leads to greater trust and stronger organizational loyalty (Tax *et al.*, 1998). In summary, in responding to a complaint, it must be communicated to the customer that the problem is not a stable one and is not likely to reoccur (Magnini *et al.*, 2007).

A customer care program ideally should be administered by someone "in the flesh," but if that is not feasible, the "customer should not have to languish in a vacuum" (Harris, 1991, p. 109); communication is essential in both situations to resolve any differences and problems to the customer's satisfaction. Southwest Airlines' policy of taking care of a problem at point of occurrence and not passing the buck is direct and effective, not unlike the policies of similar successful companies (Wiersema, 1996, p. 23). "There is a clear understanding that the best time to deal with the complaint is while the complaint is happening" (Nucifora, 2000). Generally, if the complaint is handled in the customer's favor, 70 percent will reuse the service, but this figure soars to 95 percent if the complaint is resolved at the time and at the point of contact. Problem discovery needs a proactive company orientation to avoid a service loss, and the window of opportunity in which to orchestrate a successful redress effort may be very short (Berry, 1995).

Service recovery should be personalized, hopefully during the service interaction. The process should begin at the "first point of contact," dealing with only one service provider if possible, and "should be quick," emphasizing a fair-play solution. Inform the customer how the problem arose, communicate an acceptable solution, and inform management where service is breaking down. Marriott's Camelback Inn has a clearly stated mission: "no guest leaves unhappy – means we resolve any and all problems before the guest leaves" (Cannie, 1994, pp. 100–101). It is the only five-star facility in Arizona, and the only one of six in the USA – evidence of the effectiveness of Marriott philosophy. Adding service value is effectively premised on the following responses, as outlined by Carr (1990, pp. 155, 161): focus first on the customer; be clear and relevant; respond sincerely and spontaneously, as a further opportunity to cement a relationship.

A problem situation offers no choices. Value-added is a must and absolute, without compromise. Therefore, firms should see to it that the customer is told about the extra value being added to compensate for the inconvenience. Griffin (1994, pp. 192–98) has identified certain effective procedures for safeguarding and keeping customers from leaving. These include providing easy means for customers to give feedback, providing help when customers need it in a fast and responsive way, reducing guarantee and refund hassles, and comforting angry customers. This can be done by letting them blow off steam, showing them you understand their problem, learning what they want, suggesting a solution, and determining what they think is a fair resolution, concluding with a follow-up to show you still care for them. A stay in a room that is not clean, quiet, or comfortable, coupled with ineffective maid and room service, needs immediate attention. Acceptable offers to travelers include dinner, a free weekend, no charge for the previous stay, flowers, wine, candy, etc. Kyi (1989, p. 7) found in a study of service organizations that those with a written policy are more likely to use "customer service as a competitive tool." In evaluating differences between organizations with and without a written policy, it appears that having a "definite person handling complaints" was the most significant attribute. This again calls attention to the need for prompt handling of customer problems. A written policy statement "serves as an operational definition to orient the entire firm to the demands of fulfilling customer service needs."

In guaranteeing customer satisfaction, companies have generally found that customers do not take advantage of the practice, nor are employees making inappropriate decisions and affecting cash profits. In one year, "Embassy Suite's guests invoked the guarantee 4,986 times out of 502,958 stays ... But that amounted to 0.2 percent of Suite revenues, a small price to pay for happier customers and rapid feedback on problems" (Schaaf, 1995, p. 298).

As previously stated, studies have shown that customers for whom a problem is quickly and satisfactorily resolved are more likely to remain loyal to a company than customers who never experience a problem (de Matos *et al.*, 2007). Problems may present an opportunity to gain a customer's loyalty if, in the recovery phase, the service providers "make it fast, involve everyone, make it distinctive, be proactive, keep us (the customer) informed, and don't make the same mistake twice" (Heil *et al.*, 1997, pp. 90–99). Using longitudinal data, Maxham and Netemeyer (2002) demonstrate that excellent recovery initiatives typically do not spawn paradoxical satisfaction ratings after a second failure. The service provider on the frontline must remember that "the complaint process is essential to the growth of your company. ... If complaints are heard graciously and handled effectively, customers will stay with you" (Petite, 1989, p. 22). In essence "treat customer complaints as opportunities to do better" rather than as threats (Liswood, 1990, p. 65).

In their article for improving service, Berry *et al.* (1990) suggest three ways of dealing with customer problems in an attempt to resolve them. Each of the three suggestions involves role responses and interaction on the part of the customer and employee. The first is making it easy for customers to complain about what they perceive as poor service. This is a difficult role for customers to play because, on average, only about 4 percent of customers now complain; most walk away from slipshod service, never to return. The customer has to perceive complaining as a positive, helpful aid to improving their service, and they should be rewarded for it. The second suggestion is being aware that timely personal communication with the customer is an essential part of the service program in order to resolve any problem. It should be resolved on the spot, not passed on for second- and third-party review. And third, employees should be encouraged to respond effectively to customer problems – no organization is perfect, and mistakes, oversights, accidents, delays, and miscommunication will happen. These employees have to possess the resources and the empowerment to resolve the problem. In handling customer complaints and problems, the service organization needs to support the frontline service provider.

In defining the limits of a service role, regarding problem situations with a customer, Nuclfora (2000, p. 20) identifies four role actions that need to be considered. First, give the employee the authority to break the rules and the resources personally to decide how to resolve a problem. Second, employees should not pass the buck – encourage them to resolve the problem to the customer's satisfaction at the time it is taking place. Third, watch the body language of the customer who shows signs of exasperation and disgust with a service situation. It is not always a verbal cue that is a tip-off that something is not working for the customer. Fourth, encourage feedback from the customer, and mean it by having the frontline provider demonstrate how they can improve their service. No-one is above that call and goal. Finding out first-hand may be a cheap way of improving and changing how the role providers function. The goal of any "customer centered organizations should be to make every employee a quality strategist, i.e. who can take ownership of customer problems or quality issues and has the capability and freedom of action to solve them" (Albrecht, 1992, p. 145). Carr (1990, pp. 98) also describes a number of similar steps for problem resolution. Listen to what the customer has to say about the problem. Do not make any assumptions. Ask the customer what would satisfy him/her and resolve the problem. If the customer's solution is within your means, then follow the customer's suggestion. If the solution suggested is not practical, not good taste, or against policy, negotiate by working on other alternatives. If the solution suggested by the customer will not solve the problem, come up with a better alternative. "Remember that a satisfactory solution not only takes care of the immediate problem but also increases the customer's expectations of the value of future dealings with you."

The customer may actually anticipate a sequence of interactions to follow in the wake of a problem. Zemke (1999, pp. 282–83) reports that when a service transaction breaks down, the customer expects certain events to take place to ensure a recovery of the service act: first, an apology and an acknowledgement of their inconvenience; second, listening, empathizing, and asking open questions; third, offering an equitable remedy to the problem; fourth, the offer of some value-added atonement for the inconvenience; five, keeping your promises; and sixth, following up to ensure success of the remedy and obtaining customer input for service improvement in the future. To accomplish these tasks, a service provider will need skills. Those include empathizing with an unhappy customer as a valued person, identifying and rectifying customer problems, and using commonsense and practical understanding to resolve them (Carr, 1990). This is far from a perfect world, and problems and errors occur to remind us that we are fallible. If apologies are necessary – and they will be perceived as so – everyone interacting with the customer, whether directly or indirectly, should be sure that they are "sincere," "personal," and "timely" (Anderson and Zemke, 1991, p. 94). The bottom line is that "People get most irate when they aren't greeted with a smile or with concern about their problems" (Tschohl and Franzmeier, 1991, pp. 246–47). To avoid this situation, accept responsibility, show your concern, stay calm, be sure you understand the problem, and solve it. In this regard, Jeschke *et al.* (2000, pp. 202–3) investigated a number of researchers' findings and observations, and concluded that employee–customer relations should be as conflict-free as possible when dealing with problems and complaints. In reaching this goal, the service provider needs to avoid accusatory language, power or status plays, and over-acting, and providers must "control their behavior, maintain contact with the customer," and "build a constructive interaction centered on the complaint."

In service recovery and restoration, Cannie (1994, pp. 100–1) feels a five-step process is critical, beginning with an apology, followed by a good-faith effort so that the customer sees things are being done, being empathic to the needs of the customer, compensating the customer for their inconvenience, and following up with them to get closure of the problem and cement future ties. This is not unlike other steps in problem resolution already noted above. Very similarly, Hartley (1999, pp. 291–92) feels that cooling off the customer when problems occur in the service transaction is done by applying HEAT (hear, empathize, apologize, take ownership on the spot). The guidelines and prescriptions cited above are universally recognized.

There is a phase called "complaint management (that) means satisfying the customer," and the "enterprise stands to benefit if the personnel in contact with the dissatisfied customer handle the process skillfully" (Jeschke *et al.*, 2000, p. 194). But in this process from beginning to end, the authors note that the "Psycho-sociological competence of front office staff" and those employees obtaining feedback information is "required of those employees who collect such information in face-to-face contacts" (Jeschke *et al.*, 2000, p. 197). Steps should be taken to resolve all problems in the service interaction process, no matter how small or insignificant. This can be accomplished by bringing the "dissatisfaction out in the open," removing blame and focusing on "what can be done about the problem." As a service provider, take the "blame" for the problem. Get the customer to "commit" to resolve the problem with the service provider, and finally "solve" the problem despite the time and effort it may take on the service providers' part (Bly, 1993, p. 253).

An empathic response gets to the heart of the problem. Empathy represents the difference between a lost customer with a problem and a saved one without a problem. The customer's perception of a situation and a problem is always the basis for beginning a resolution to that problem. It is important to note that a service failure can be defined as any problem – real or perceived – by the customer (Maxham, 2001). Therefore understanding how the customer sees and views the situation requires empathy on the part of frontline staff. Empathic discourse helps pinpoint the problem by playing it back to the customer in order to verify what the causes are and to determine what it will take to correct the problem to the customer's satisfaction (Denalli, 1989). Empathy helps buy precise moments and minutes for the frontline staff to determine what actually happened, and what it will take to make a customer happy, and hopefully delighted.

Monitoring of customer usage is essential for maintaining a stable customer base and clientele. This part is especially important: Liljander (2000) suggests that companies can improve by learning from customers. This kind of effort takes commitment and the willingness to communicate with those customers who are likely to abandon a service. The time in personal interviews may well be worth the effort to construct a more effective survey polling design that would determine advance problems or underlying weakness in a service system. "We rush to wait," only to wait again (Collier, 1994, pp. 125–27). Empathy is best built upon a foundation of information. World-class service process managers learn when, where, how, and why the customer waits, and in some cases the customer feels so abused that a "social justice has been committed by the service delivery process." Service representatives of the United Services Automobile Association (USSA), for example, use an ECHO (every contact has opportunity) system that records customer service comments in about 30 seconds and content-analyzes some 1500 calls a week. This database is used to sort the causes found among categories of complaints. "This new way of dealing with customers is about responsiveness" (Wiersema, 1996, pp. 190–94). And empathic responsiveness is one of the ultimate building blocks of a successful customer service program. In summary, top-rate service failure recovery programs can yield the immediate outcome of increased customer satisfaction and the long-term outcomes of favorable word-of-mouth behavior and customer loyalty (Sparks, 2001).

7 Nuances of interpersonal interactions

Preview

This chapter describes the role model for the service provider – how they should react, project, and promote a positive posture or attitude when interacting with the customer. It therefore places heavy emphasis on the verbal and nonverbal communication skills needed to excel on the frontline. Specific, less obvious aspects of verbal communication are considered, including how a service provider can create a rapport with customers by using phrases that foster verbal immediacy. In terms of nonverbal communication, this chapter illustrates how gestures form a basis for messages of communication and need to be actively managed in a service environment. Moreover, because most gestures occur with little or no conscious effort, this chapter explains that frontline personnel benefit from specifically designed body-language training. In a similar vein, a discussion of the literature surrounding proper listening skills is also offered. This discussion is germane to customer–provider interactions because a provider's listening skills, as perceived by the customer, are a critical component of customer satisfaction sentiment.

Communication messages

Message content

After ·the target customer is identified, a service concept is in place, and an operating and delivery system has been defined, it is then time to communicate to the potential customer (Heskett *et al.*, 1990, p. 60). The content of the message makes a big difference, and it is what the words denote that characterizes the tourist's anticipated experience (Magnini and Karande, 2010). "It is not possible to package and display an entertainment or transportation service in the same way Kodak packages and displays film … A strong service brand is essentially a promise of future satisfaction. It is a blend of what the company says the brand is, what others say, and how the company performs the service – all from the customer's point of view" (Berry, 2000, pp. 128–29). The customer seeks specific details within the communication content concerning a planned tourist experience. Customer confirmation is a powerful source of communication for internalizing the brand image of a company for both customer and service providers.

In a study of communication needs of tourists taking short overnight trips in the mid-west region of the USA, Vogt *et al.* (1993) find that the main travel information need in the context of getaway trips is to identify sites that might be visited. Along these lines, getaway travelers experience a need to use their own vacation time more effectively, or to select a place that actually achieves what they had intended. As a result of these findings, the researchers suggest that communication messages must sell a destination site, and also provide details about a site in terms of where to stay and what to do. Marketing communications, such as coupon books, events calendars, and lodging guides, appear to serve these types of information needs. Customers typically respond to messages that reinforce their attitudes, but they are most effective with the proper use of symbols (Labroo *et al.*, 2008). Noe *et al.* (1993, pp. 149, 164) sought to determine "which symbols in the presentations of the content of the message would evoke a positive response" among park recreational users; how to manage communication messages more effectively; and how their attitudes related and reinforced these messages. Different messages were crafted to represent how a recreational resource is to be managed or controlled, either from a more natural perspective or on a more man-made theme. The study found that the more environmental dimension of the attitude scale was positively associated with protecting and living in harmony with the environment; whereas the more human control dimension had no association. But personal attitudes are only one part of a message's content.

The inherent intangibility associated with a tourism experience makes it difficult for individuals to develop refined expectations of a planned experience (Laws, 2004). Therefore firms should shape expectations through the use of advertising and promotional campaigns, because satisfaction is based in part upon the delivery of what was marketed about the destination (Uysal, 1998). Often destinations that provide more relevant information about their vacation products produce the highest guest satisfaction ratings (Moutinho, 1987). For example, Magnini and Karande (2010) found that ecotourism ads that incorporate a written smell reference (such as "enjoy the fragrant mountain air") have a greater influence on individuals' affective responses than do the same ads with no smell reference. That is precisely why it is so important to provide relevant defining and realistic advertisements. "If customers' service experiences differ from the advertising message, customers will believe their experiences and not the advertising" (Berry, 2000, p. 130). No brand name can offset poor service and negative word-of-mouth messages from dissatisfied customers that will only serve to undermine future use. Indirect communication, where advertising, brochures, media blurbs, and other techniques are used to communicate a message, should be focused on how different you are in providing a unique service that separates your company from others (Ries and Trout, 1994). Conveying an image is important in the mind of the customer and should be thought out and tested very carefully. Sometimes messages produce negative rather than the desired positive results. For example, a world-class hotel advertised a weekend rate for shoppers with a young lady lying on a bed with her shoes resting on the wall over the bed's headboard, clearly not an inviting image of cleanliness and neatness. Such images can erode the work of direct face-to-face communication and situational interaction between staff and customer.

Communicating on a personal level

After marketing the tourist package, then the more intensive face-to-face interaction from the service provider takes precedence. The ability to create a forum for meaningful dialogue is necessary in determining the tourist's expectations. Relationships are labor-intensive. Generally, providers interact with only one customer at a time. Due to the more intense process of interaction between provider and customer, there sometimes exists an automatic feedback loop between customer and provider (Gutek, 1995). "Face is defined as the positive public image that a person claims for him/herself," and "fellowship-face is a person's image that they are worthy companions" (Lim, 1994, p. 217). He emphasizes the important similarities between the self and other, and promotes using an informal style in interacting, agreeing with the other, appreciating the other, and using a cooperative, empathic, and affirmative manner when neither party knows the other. These positive tactics of communication draw the service provider and customer closer together. Verbal behaviors discriminate between properties, objects, and people in the world.

Once in a customer relationship, Timm (1998) observes that customers routinely gauge the relative equity or fairness of their involvement. Expectations are the measuring criteria and an effective service provider will prompt the customer by asking how their experience can be made more enjoyable, pleasant, and rewarding. Certain attributes are identified by Timm (1998, pp. 71–79), including stressing the value of a service by explaining its superiority; providing better and clearer information; and speeding up the service process with more efficient, friendlier, knowledgeable service providers. Both expectations and informational content interact in a situation resulting in social judgment and action on the part of the customer and service provider. It is the relative strength of both the expectations and the information available to a person in the situation that "determines the nature of the perceptual processing and resulting social judgments" (Smith, 1995, p. 94).

Often, however, personal expectations may be weak, and available information to form a judgment about how to act and respond in a situation may be absent. Sometimes neither expectations nor information are clearly defined, or they may present diametrically opposite behavioral outcomes. In this case, when perceivers experienced cognitive dilemma from the incongruence between prior expectation and current situational information, social judgments were strongly affected by current situational information. That is why it is so important to design situations that speak to the customer – for example, walkways, signage, and strategically placed service providers that assist in the customer's experience. In Zeithaml *et al.*'s (1993, p. 9) study on different levels of expectation, the researchers find that explicit and implicit service promises affect the level of expectation anticipated. The researchers point out that "a hotel customer describes the impact of those promises on his expectations: They get you real pumped up with the beautiful ad. When you go in you expect the bells and whistles to go off. Usually they don't." While another hotel guest says: "You expect the service to be better in a nice-looking hotel," but that may not always be the case. Symbols are powerful communicators, either explicitly or implicitly, so care is always the watchword when intentions are being communicated. In passing out snacks on an airline near the dinner hour, a passenger kindly declined the offer from the flight attendant saying they would have dinner upon arriving in their destination. The flight attendant apologized, and commented "what do you expect from this airline?" (Donnelly, 1992, p. 35). Upon arriving, that passenger's luggage did not make the connecting flight, and he thought the same verbatim phrase that the flight attendant previously uttered in frustration. This passenger was not endeared to this airline, and would probably book on a competitor in the future, not because his bags were delayed, but because his expectations were shattered.

The numbers game is an easy trap to fall into, rather than the awareness of how customers' expectations are being negated. "Most organizations find the move from countability to accountability difficult." That is, both managers and frontline service providers tend to resist setting or formalizing standards of human interaction (Anderson, 1999). Donnelly (1992, p. 35) relates an incident involving an elderly women on a national airline struggling with her bags in full view of three attendants, busily chatting among themselves with no offers of help. This not only dismayed the woman, but was witnessed by several fellow passengers. Examples like this are more common than they should be in the service arena. On the other hand, Carr (1990, pp. 55–56) reports on a customer approaching the front desk of a Marriott Courtyard in Andover, Massachusetts while two employees are engaged in an exchange. Instead of continuing the exchange, they turn to recognize the customer. Carr concedes, however, that this kind of conduct occurs among only 1 percent of service personnel. That number is very low and sends a signal that service personnel have their priorities misplaced if they do not drop everything and attend to the customer.

Sending signals requires both verbal and nonverbal channels of communication. Verbal behavior provides cues about a person. By what and how we speak, we can draw conclusions from word selection and usage. Gestures also form a basis for messages of communication and are maintained by a sophisticated system of signs that we generally agree upon (Guerin, 1994, pp. 91, 97). However, "gestures are limited because there are only so many ways in which we can re-arrange our faces and postures" (Guerin, 1994, p. 98). Smiling rearranges our face, but its meaning is dependent on the social circumstances (Hennig-Thurau *et al.*, 2006). The smile of a thief is not the same as one coming from a customer service representative. "In this sense the 'Link' between a gesture and its typical consequences is actually *in the environment*, not innately sitting inside our nervous system" (Guerin, 1994, p. 99).

Nonverbal channels of communication

The service provider has open personal communication channels to the customer. Face engagements are both verbal and nonverbal, and the cues displayed are paramount in signaling the nature of the relationship as well as a mutual definition of the given scenario (Littlejohn, 1983). Canary and Cody (1994, pp. 75, 79) claim that it is difficult to read facial expressions as representing an emotional feeling, since most of our gestures and expressions are blends of a human emotion, whether surprise, anger, fear, sadness, disgust, or happiness. They are well blended and are not one-dimensional. Also, it is sometimes difficult to read facial expressions because of cultural differences in the masking and inhibiting of facial affect (Hodgson *et al.*, 2000). Further, people can differ dramatically in their style of expressing emotions. "If a person acts outside his PGM (postural gesture motion) pattern," he is judged to be acting not only in a contrived manner, but also uncharacteristically. "We all behave characteristically, when our PGM patterns are in spontaneous action, and this behavior reveals who we are" (Lamb and Watson, 1979, p. 107). Postural norms change with the times. At the turn of century, a more dignified rigid form was required for public appearances, while today, in a more relaxed society, a loose, unstructured form is seen as more acceptable (ibid., p. 30).

Gestures or expressions can be used to influence customers – a smile, a handshake, a pat on the arm – within limits and always being cognizant of the customer's personal private space (Pease and Pease, 2004). But public hugging of strangers may not be looked upon too kindly for fear of stepping outside the norm and being too familiar or intimate. Tansik and Smith (2000, p. 244) cite Erving Goffman, the symbolic interactionalist, who suggests that public expressions gleaned by an observer to improve an interaction situation are highly likely to be valued and sanctioned. Intimacy is obviously to be discouraged and the opposite encouraged for the service provider. Body language is part of the communication and social interaction process that conveys meaning and intentions (Sundaram and Webster, 2000). Knowing what kind of body language to use and not use is basic to how we would expect a service provider to react and project themselves to the customer. As Smith's (1995, p. 97) research on the literature indicates, persons have certain expectations concerning specific nonverbal behaviors. Gestures, expressions, and intonations tending toward greater intimacy that can be used with care in a service situation include such actions as: "(a) more smiling and positive facial expression; (b) contact, including frequent and longer mutual gaze; (c) more gesturing; (d) forward body lean; (e) direct body orientation and more open body position; (f) more head nods; (g) closer distance or proximity; (h) frequent touch (used with caution); (i) moderate relaxation; (j) less random body movement; and (k) warmer vocal tones." These gestural dimensions of behavior are obviously a matter of degree, with the service provider scaling toward the less intimate. These are not nominal distinctions (yes or no), but are interval in nature (more or less). Understanding the role gender plays in these exchanges is also important (Pease and Pease, 2004). Moreover, knowing the limits is even more important and is the ultimate key to a successful encounter.

Box 7.1 Considering culture: nonverbal gestures

The meanings and interpretations of certain nonverbal gestures can differ between cultures. An illustration can be seen in the interpretation of the hand gesture made by connecting the thumb and forefinger into a circle and holding the other fingers straight or relaxed in the air. In Australia this can mean either okay or zero; in Japan it can mean zero or money; in India it denotes something paradoxical or incredible; in most Mediterranean and South American countries it is a vulgar and offensive expression.

In winning over customers and having them become loyal, there are also some winning behaviors that are needed in the interpersonal exchange process. Simply defined, "Behavior is, of course, what people do. It is conveyed to others via both verbal and nonverbal communication" (Timm, 1998, p. 90). Behavioral actions are not always obvious. Chakrapani (1998, pp. 29–30) discusses the need for, and difficulty of, measuring latent customer attributes. "Personal service attributes, such as competence and concern for the customer, are abstractions (latent variables)" whose attributes are displayed symbolically through verbal and nonverbal interaction between customer and provider. It is not necessarily what a service provider says, but also how it is said, and how it is acted out through body language and gestures. A smile, a quick glance, a frown help convey the meaning of a message (Pease and Pease, 2004).

Since it has been estimated that up to 80 percent of the meaning of a social encounter is transmitted on nonverbal channels, Solomon (1998) argues for an understanding of this part of the interaction process. Cannie (1994, p. 84) goes so far as to estimate that "over 90 percent of all communication occurs nonverbally. This means that the real message we communicate is in our body language, tone of voice, and gestures." Care is needed in controlling body language, realizing that verbal communication is only a small part of the interaction process (Willingham, 1992, p. 66; Petite, 1989, p. 111).

In face-to-face interaction, Anderson and Zemke (1991, pp. 61–63) posit that 70 percent of interpersonal communication is nonverbal, and suggest nine factors that play a major role in that exchange process. (1) Proximity: North Americans feel comfortable between one and two feet apart. (2) Eye contact: by making eye contact, you acknowledge the customer. (3) Silence: listening and nodding while your customer is talking, and "uh-huhs," positively reinforce their concerns and needs. (4) Gestures: open gestures convey that you are open to the customer and invite them in. (5) Posture: standing up straight communicates confidence, and leaning toward the customer says that what they are saying is important. (6) Facial expressions: open expressions of the month and eyes signal friendliness. (7) Physical contact: less is better. A handshake is ok, but a touch on the arm or shoulder may offend. (8) Smell: a neutral smell is preferred. Strong perfumes, colognes, and tobacco may be offensive. (9) Overall appearance: cleanliness and neatness communicate competence. These facets largely communicate the general content and meaning of an exchange, not its specificity.

> ### Box 7.2 Considering culture: personal space
>
> While the quantity of personal space between two individuals depends upon factors such as the context of the interaction and the closeness of their relationship, country culture also plays a role in determining personal distances. South Americans, for instance, are known typically to allow for less personal space than do North Americans. Interestingly, a country's power distance norms also moderate the sizes of personal space. That is, in a high-power-distance society such as South Korea, the boss is afforded more personal space in work settings than in lower-power-distance societies such as Finland.

In the social interaction process, some nonverbal behaviors are presumably difficult if not impossible for most people to regulate. Also, attitudes toward individuals are also represented in how a person displays friendliness and interest. Individuals' implicit beliefs about themselves and their social interactions are critical in shaping their reactions to important interpersonal experiences (Pelham and Hetts, 1999). Although change is a possibility for all, a lifetime of experiences may be very difficult to change. Training can make them more explicit and controllable, especially those that are of a prejudicial manner. As noted earlier, nonverbal communication employs multiple channels in conveying a message. The confluence of cues from different channels (face, body, tone of voice) are used to communicate a message (Canary and Cody, 1994). Pinker (2002, pp. 435–39) lists those human commonalties of interest to us as customary greetings, facial expressions of communication, disgust, happiness, surprise, masking, standing close as distinguished from being distant when facing each other, and the judging of others. As Darwin recognized, some forms of body communication are innate, such as crying and smiling, while others are learned. The learning part takes place in specific cultures and social situations, where different bodily acts are done and timed in an interpersonal interaction to mean and convey the message content.

Axtell (1991, pp. 219–21) examines common universal gestures and the various interpretations they have according to different cultures. He deals with all parts of the body that can produce a gesture, including the eyes, face, lips, arms, hands, etc. In the USA, for example, direct eye contact is basic, along with firm handshakes, no touching between parties, and conversing about an arm's length from one another. Prolonged silence makes Americans uncomfortable, using the index finger to point to objects is acceptable, and beckoning can be done with the index finger held up and moved in, or the palm held up waving the fingers. These are the more prevalent positive gestures that would apply in a tourist interaction situation, and are worth noting. "Cooked communication" (Tschohl and Franzmeier, 1991, pp. 193–94), uttered in contrast to body language, or delivered as a mechanical robot, is insulting and demeaning to the intelligence and dignity of the customer. There are the classic cases of: "I'll be right with you" – or the smile that goes nowhere. Ford (1998) reports on the findings of a nonverbal study that signaled customer discomfort. Actions such as side-to-side movement, fidgeting, extraneous foot movement, and postural shifts are all indicators that something is amiss in the interactive exchange. "We also communicate interpersonal attitudes through body language. There are clear signals for friendliness and hostility" (Furnham, 1999, pp. 56–57). Bodily communication can substitute effectively for words and can signal either positive or negative attitudes toward the situation. Furnham (1999, pp. 1–3, 7) lists such examples as hands in pockets meaning being cold and withdrawn, folded arms being cold, and yawning indicating a preference to avoid a situation.

Box 7.3 Considering culture: silent periods

Usage of, and comfort level with, silent periods during conversations varies between cultures. Relative to other cultures, the French and Spanish, for example, often have very few silent periods (measured as a gap of ten seconds or longer) in business dialogues. At the other end of the continuum, Russians are known to employ more silent periods than others in their business-related conversations. Americans typically reside in the middle ground of the continuum.

Attitudes can also be inferred from gestures and posture. For example, Feyereisen and de Lannoy (1991) observe that in western societies, closed postures where arms and legs are held close to the body convey an impression of passivity and coldness. A service provider playing the role of a listener may be judged to agree or disagree by how they position their head, and the orientation of torso, arm, and leg positions. It is not just what is verbally exchanged, but how it is transmitted from the person. Gestures too are part of the communication system (Preston, 2005). Again, emphasizing the positive connotation in human exchanges, "brief self-touching of the face and palm presentation movements give higher impressions of warmth and naturalness than does immobility." Just as "Closed gestures often mean that people are protecting themselves from you, screening you out, or feeling uncomfortable in the situation … The opposite such as laughing or widening their arms and hands signal comfort and joy" (Willingham, 1992, p. 62). Briton and Hall (1995, pp. 83, 89) sampled male and female students to see how they responded to a scale of 20 nonverbal signals used by either a male or female speaker. The perceptions of these participants indicate that they "rated women significantly higher than hypothetical men on the following variables: interacting with other people at close distances; recognizing faces; smiling; gazing; having an expressive face; paying attention to others' nonverbal cues; using the hands to communicate; laughing; and having an expressive voice." In fact, psychological research indicates that females are better than males at recognizing faces (Everhart *et al.*, 2001). Women were also perceived by our participants as having better encoding and decoding skills than men. Men were rated significantly higher than women on the following variables: using speech dysfluencies such as stammers and false starts; interrupting others; having restless feet and legs; interspersing speech with "um" and "ah"; speaking loudly; and touching themselves during interactions.

The above research suggests that gender differences in nonverbal behaviors and skills are not unlike gender stereotypes for other forms of communication. Women are believed to possess greater skill and involvement in nonverbal communication. This enhanced ability is consistent with general sex-role stereotypes of women as being more concerned with interpersonal relationships and the affiliative needs of others (McColl-Kennedy *et al.*, 2003). However, Briton and Hall (1995) do point out that their research design did not take into account situational contexts that are relevant in interpreting the meanings of nonverbal communication. Situational consideration must be given to the verbal and nonverbal behavior of either sex in various service situations, such as a resort entrance, front desk, recreational facility, restaurant, and transitional spaces. Hall (1993, pp. 455–56) reports on a qualitative study of waiters and waitresses performing customer provider scripts. The term "gender organization" was used to define those situations where service was characterized as being more female or more male in orientation. "Most service jobs are considered an extension of women's roles in the home and an expression of women's supposed feminine nature," despite the common existence of both male and female service providers. They are expected to display "an image of a deferential servant," by accepting their subordinate place or "showing deference, particularly by smiling to show they take pleasure in serving," and being invisible regarding their own human activity: sitting, talking, eating, or drinking. In some cases, restaurants hire one gender over the other, often to display an ornamental role, such as young attractive women playing a "cocktail waitress" script.

Canary and Cody (1994, p. 82) summarize three decades of Hall's work on the nonverbal differences between men and women. Their findings include the perception of female behavior as judging and sending emotions, smiling and gazing more, body directness, touching, involvement, expressive, and being self-conscious. Males were seen more as being distant, restless, relaxed, expansive, interrupting, filling pauses, making speech errors, and speaking more loudly. It becomes evident that gender perceptions play a vital role in a customer's expectations of service.

Communication is the beginning of any relationship, especially through nonverbal actions: gestures, movement of limbs, eyes, and posture can convey important meanings about how you feel. Duck (1991, pp. 54–56) reports that when we like someone our pupils dilate and we look more at their eyes. If we appear relaxed, smile, and nod in reaction to another, "they will enjoy that and like us more." For example, "airline cabin staff are trained to smile when talking to passengers; call-center operators are sometimes given mirrors to ensure that they are smiling when talking on the telephone; and clients in therapy can be trained to look at people when they talk to them: anyone can be encouraged to use such behaviors satisfactorily" in an exchange. Language appropriate to the situation and paying attention to nonverbal cues help facilitate a relationship, but the most important element is that the transacting individuals enjoy conversations and focus on the other person rather than on themselves (Duck, 1991).

How do you recognize the customer as a person? Carr (1990, pp. 61–64) identifies points of social interaction that begin by making eye contact, clearly attending to the customers' requests, and demonstrating with body language: "smiling, shaking hands, looking concerned" that you are there for the customer. Tschohl and Franzmeier (1991, p. 189) also assert the need for eye contact, a smile, and total attention to the customer. Conrad Hilton (1987, p. 114) pointed out to his staff of frontline employees that they were the only ones who could give smiling service. "A smile, for example, is one of the most powerful expressions of empathy available to us, for when we smile other people experience an automatic, almost irresistible desire to smile, too; and when our facial muscles move into a smiling position, physical changes occur that improve our mood" (Ciaramicoli and Ketcham, 2000, pp. 55–56).

Service personnel jokingly talk about going to smile school. The fake smile, however, can be easily detected (Furnham, 1999, p. 18). It usually "spreads across the face more slowly and seems to last longer; the eyes are not as narrowed or closed as in a real smile; the upper lip is often exaggerated in movement, while the lower lip is less mobile." Transactional service standards are not about "a smile 2.75 inches in length. Rather, they are about the *manner* in which the customer service provider and the customer interact" (Anderson, 1999, p. 91). Companies that offer smile training have "no chance to be great" (Berry, 1995, p. 90). Only firms in which frontline providers want to smile have a chance to be great. Some of the least effective of the customer care programs are the "smile campaigns, ineffective because you can't make silk purses out of sows' ears." Some staff should never be given jobs that entail a significant degree of customer contact because their personality is such that no amount of training will make them appear friendly and sympathetic (Armistead and Clark, 1994, p. 80). In a study by Ford (1998, pp. 111–12), communication provider behavior and customer response is tested employing the RATER service model (reliability, assurance, tangibles, empathy, responsiveness; see Chapter 4). The RATER variables of responsiveness, assurance and empathy guided the testing, and results showed that those displaying more eye contact and head nods, stood closer to customers, and ended the interaction with bigger smiles were more likely have to positive customer-related outcomes, such as reinforcing assurance and empathy with the customer. Also, a provider "hustle" in responding to expectations shows respect for the customer and their value (Tschohl and Franzmeier, 1991, p. 194).

The eye is a powerful tool of communication; Furnham (1999, pp. 13–16) says that when we gaze, we signal greater power and also greater liking for that particular person. Not only the eye, but also the whole face, mouth, and eyebrows are able to move independently, communicating various meanings. To improve the act of greeting people, Willingham (1992, p. 17) suggests making eye contact by looking into another person's eyes to signal attention and thanking them for coming in, contacting you, or seeing you. "Drifting eyes mean a drifting mind." Service personnel who are actually listening look into the eyes, signaling increased attention, which transpires on a deep, emotional, and unconscious level (Willingham 1992). "The smallest twitch of an eyebrow is, in fact, only significant in relation to the body posture on which it takes place." "Gesture is dependent on, and derives from, posture" (Lamb and Watson, 1979, pp. 21–22). It is natural to the person and something that we live with, without any thought, except when we consciously attempt to modify it. And then we are limited by physiognomy and bodily tendencies. Eye semaphoring can be a glance, a look, a signal of sorts, a wink that means in jest, disdain, or agreement that you are in the know with the party you are interacting with. Such gestures are probably best used with caution – not every customer has been exposed to the same standard gestures. And finally, where touching is involved with a customer, and since such contacts are considered intimate and "the closest by consumers" (Barnes, 2000, p. 93), less is often better and sanitized versions are more effective.

Illustrators are movements that can be used to emphasize a point that the speaker is making, and can also be used to demonstrate that we are highly involved and interested in the conversation (Canary and Cody, 1994). These include pointing, waving, flagging, stopping, and other more complicated signs, such as those that indicate you do not know, palms and two hands raised up; or disgust, palms turned down and hands sharply moved to the right and left simultaneously (Pease and Pease, 2004). These signs represent a more intense interaction between persons. "While most customers in encounters appreciate an attentive and pleasant provider, they may be put off by a display of emotion that they perceive to be superficial and inconsistent with felt emotion" (Gutek, 1995, p. 82). These nonverbal movements are a large part of the communication process and need to be applied realistically in particular tourist situations.

Customer provider attractiveness

Solomon (1998, pp. 85–86) reported that 68 percent of customers stop purchasing a product or service due to dissatisfaction with an employee. A variety of characteristics, such as "physiognomy, verbal abilities, apparel, grooming, attractiveness, and so on." to mention just a few, can have direct effects on customers' evaluation of a service. Given the centrality of employees in many service situations, it is essential to know and gauge their influence. Czepiel (1990, p. 14) recognizes the central role of the service provider. "All acknowledge that the personal characteristics of service providers have an important effect on their attractiveness" to the real and potential customer. When a high-end casino and entertainment complex was build on the Mississippi Gulf Coast, management sent out scouts to recruit employees by observing them working in actual service situations. Their manner and appearance were two essential criteria that were used to distinguish between acceptable and unacceptable employees. A person's assessments of others are significantly influenced by the other's degree of physical attractiveness. A corpus of research spanning more than a 20-year period has generally supported this belief (Solomon, 1998, p. 90). In this regard, Myers (2005, p. 432) summarized extant physical attractiveness research by stating that "Good looks are a great asset." In that regard, "we like attractive people, we attribute positive qualities to them and find it rewarding when they appear to like us" (Canary and Cody, 1994, p. 72). "We are more likely to comply to requests from likable, good-looking people than from people who are unlikable and unattractive" (Canary and Cody, 1994, p. 301).

The question of physical attractiveness affecting social interaction is raised by Mulford *et al.* (1998, pp. 1580–87). The subjects in the study, one-time strangers in a laboratory setting, were found to be more likely to cooperate with others they found attractive. They found that "men who saw themselves as highly attractive were more likely to cooperate than men who saw themselves as low in attractiveness (43 percent vs. 26 percent)." While just the opposite occurred for women: 36 percent of decisions by women who saw themselves as "highly" attractive were to cooperate, while 51 percent of decisions by those who saw themselves "low" in attractiveness were to cooperate. In addition, 59 percent of highly attractive individuals would interact with other highly attractive persons, while only 27 percent would interact with others low in attractiveness. The tendency to be least cooperative toward others seen as low in attractiveness remained across all levels of self-rating "including those of low attractiveness."

Expectations followed a similar pattern, where subjects who saw themselves as high in attractiveness expected higher levels of cooperation from others, while those lower in self-definitions of attractiveness expected lower levels of cooperation. "Both male and female subjects more often cooperate with others they think will cooperate with them, but also cooperate more often with others they rate as highly attractive *independent of their expectations about how those attractive people will behave.*" Recognized beauty in transactions with "employees and customers" plays a role in how service is perceived, and by those delivering that service, and is one of the cues customers and service providers use in the interactive process. However, since perceptions of beauty are associated with the expectation of cooperative behavior, that affect can be "compounded" by those who just like interacting with others they see as attractive. Physique alone cannot be used to associate meaning with a posture.

Dress is another outward display. Clothing cues are among the most visible and most utilized information source used in impression formation (Solomon, 1998). Toward that end, the legality of enforcing a dress code is possible if it meets three criteria: "(1) it is not discriminatory, (2) is reasonable, and (3) based on business necessity" (Solomon, 1998, pp. 100–101). Clothing helps to set off the service worker. The service worker also might derive a benefit from wearing a uniform, which can instill a sense of belonging and sometimes even responsibility in the service provider (Tansik and Smith, 2000). The service provider's exterior projection symbolizes another layer on which verbal and nonverbal communication rests.

Outstanding service workers display and project goodwill toward their customers and clients: (1) they see it as an opportunity to serve people; (2) they enjoy it; (3) they make people feel comfortable; (4) they can offer the customer more than they expected; (5) they can share their knowledge relative to the situation; and (6) they make the brief contact on the front-line entertaining (Willingham, 1992, p. 7). The actual behavioral process, while requiring many behavioral actions, reactions, and responses, is for the most part "casual" in terms of the level of involvement required (Solomon *et al.*, 1985, p. 107). Smiling and being friendly and responsive can cover many brief encounters. "Genuine caring about customers and excellence – and the authority and confidence to exercise it – create emotional bonds with customers" (Berry, 1995, p. 90). To illustrate, in a Cornelia Street restaurant in Greenwich Village, the owners nurture a creative atmosphere for their workers and a relaxed, welcoming place for customers. The plastic grin and "hello, I am your waiter or waitress for the evening" does not cut it because "it is not genuine and the customers know it. We try to teach our staff to be real, and the best way to do that is to be real yourself. It has to come from you. These principles can be very effective, but it is difficult, and we are still figuring out how to do things" (Lewin and Regine, 2000, p. 140). In this example, the owners would rather err on the side of the heart than with a patented, automated response to life. Their restaurants, cafes, and supporting specialty food stores share this belief in customer care, and as a result, a community ethic and set of values has emerged that is intent on providing a first-class experience. All benefit, from the internal customer (the worker) to the external customer, and the patron, as a result of this shared value and belief. If you are interested in appealing to the soul of the worker and customer, you will be operating at times on an act of faith, because each person brings their uniqueness to the interaction situation. In the highly acclaimed River Café in London, Lewin and Regine (2000, pp. 144–45) found the same atmosphere. "It had a *feeling* about it, a sense of community and connection"; "Yes, you're right, our waiter told us ... this place is different. There's respect here for everybody – the chefs, the wait staff, the dishwashers, everybody." But the manager observed that "best of all, it's *fun* working here. Listen to that." At the time waiters and other personnel were checking in, their interaction resounding with joking, singing, laughter, and joyful exchanges.

Fifteen behaviors are outlined by Timm (1998, pp. 92–103) that make the service provider more aware of the external customer. (1) Greet the customer like a guest and do so promptly without delay. A smile and pleasant attitude convey a sense of openness and a friendly atmosphere that welcomes the customer's patronage. (2) Break the impersonal barrier by making small talk about the weather, local events, traffic, and be responsive about helping them by focusing on their needs and requests. (3) Make it a habit to compliment your customers on their dress, luggage, or arrival time that differentiates them from the masses. (4) Address people by their family name, as Mr., Mrs., Ms., creating a sense of identity. (5) Look at your customers when you talk to them – making eye contact means that you are willing to serve them. (6) Ask the customer how you are doing and how you can do better to make their experience more pleasant. (7) Listen attentively to what people are saying, not how they are saying it. (8) Be polite and use "thank you" and other phrases to convey your respect for the customer. (9) Reassure the customer that they made the correct decision about using your service. (10) Smile from the eyes and mouth, which is a universal gesture and symbol of goodwill. (11) Use practiced but personal communication techniques, especially when using the telephone, by zeroing in on customers' requests and needs. (12) Exercise good timing by always following up on a request to see that the customer is getting what they desire. (13) A handshake or a pat on the arm helps to convey a personal response – but respect the customer's personal space by not getting too "touchy-feely." (14) Enjoy the customer for their diversity and uniqueness and avoid saying or thinking anything negative about who and what they represent as a culture: they are your diplomats, to be treated with the utmost regard. (15) Maintain a positive attitude about the kind of service you are providing and take joy in serving. If you don't sincerely feel that way, then find a new career. These personal behavioral attributes can be found in a service guide checklist that Timm (1998, pp. 114–16) has constructed as a reminder to the service provider when dealing with customers on a daily basis. A customer who builds a relationship with a provider comes to trust and depend on that provider (Gutek, 1995, p. 17). Interpersonal trust results only from repeated incidences of experiencing a reliable service procedure.

Verbal channels of communication

The role of verbal communication in the exchange process directs attention to obtaining specific information from the service provider for the customer. "As an employee you work with and through other people. This means that your success as an employee – and I am talking of much more here than getting promoted – will depend upon your ability to communicate with people" (Drucker, 1977, p. 262). Communication with customers tells us about whether they are satisfied: we learn what they did or didn't purchase, what they were expecting to buy, and finally we learn more about their preferences and changes over time (Tschohl and Franzmeier, 1991). According to the work reviewed by Ford (1998), different messages from customers mandate different types of response from providers. The provider needs to learn when to use restatement to show that the customer message was understood; to reflect on what the customer said to understand the implications, to clarify by asking the customer questions, and finally to interpret the customer's intent. "Words are … the most important glue of social behavior," which Semin (1997, p. 302) believes we must understand better "if we are to understand what it means to be social." And part of that glue is how individuals use words better to offer a service. "Every employee on the frontlines … should be able to direct customers to the right place and give them basic information in a courteous fashion … Some of the best informed employees at Disneyland are the street sweepers" since they get around more than most of the employee representatives (Liswood, 1990, p. 56). In exchanging responses in social situations such as in a restaurant, a waiter will ask "how is everything?" to reinforce the effect of the experience (Deighton, 1994, p. 135). Customer feedback is essential to the running of a service operation. "Every frontline person should understand this and should act on it. … Most of all, it takes an atmosphere that makes it clear to frontline people that their input is wanted and will be used" (Carr, 1990, p. 68). The people in your organization who interact with customers on a daily basis comprise your staff of communication providers (Gitomer, 2002, p. 28). They are the keys to success in your business and the bottom line. These employees, despite their organizational titles, need to have an understanding of the company's service goals, values, and principles of conduct. "Internal systems and interpersonal relationships are being forced to change if we're to effectively handle the ever-increasing levels of customer-critical knowledge coursing between the frontlines and the nerve centers of our organizations" (Schaaf, 1995, p. 5). The process needs words.

A number of behaviors maintained by very general verbal communications can be used to signal impersonal trust (Guerin, 1994). The promotion of professional or certified "experts" also leads to increased trust, as do past experiences with similar institutions. There is also the beneficial experience of dealing with the strong personal reputation of an institution and its service people, who are recognized and known to be credible and trustworthy. All such interpersonal interaction reinforces trust with service providers of that often-large impersonal organization. "Genuine communicative understanding, and hence the competency of the user of language, depends on three assumptions" (Malhotra, 1980, p. 13). The first depends on whether "what is being said is comprehensible (can be understood), truthful (that it can be believed in) and correct or right in light of existing norms. Responsible communication presupposes all three." There are two skills necessary for empathic contact between individuals, including the accurate perception of another's behavior and the ability to communicate (Holm, 1997, p. 680). Sometimes a service provider would be far better off not being so forthright, and to be glib in their conversation with clients. Diners "were in one of the finest restaurants in town, paying premium prices for the food, and the couple is listening to an employee inform everyone that she had never before prepared what they were about to eat" (Donnelly, 1992, p. 34). Obviously, this kind of message blemishes the expectations of the client. Language and delivery are also a big part of the script of the service provider. "A cheerful greeting, a sincere 'thank you,' and along with a happy smile will please customers and bring them back ... (and note), that these employees are not being told how to feel; rather, they are being told how to act in their work roles" (Tansik and Smith (2000, pp. 244–45).

Box 7.4 Considering culture: meanings of phrases

Even among English-speaking nations, the meanings derived from the use of certain phrases can vary considerably. While "keeping your pecker up" is associated with vulgarity in the USA, a Brit might dispense the advice with the intent of communicating "keep your chin up." Likewise, while "please knock me up" usually carries sexual connotations in the USA, a Brit or an Australian might say the phrase when requesting a wake-up call at a hotel.

In nearly all circumstances, it is imperative that the service provider initiates conversation promptly (Timm, 2005). Small talk is helpful because it relaxes, but it may also relax the service provider's mind where they may say the wrong thing. Thus, small talk is acceptable, but keep it to consciously monitored (Bly, 1993). When making small talk, avoid areas that are unsafe or controversial. "Avoid sex, money, politics, or any other area where people who have conflicting views are likely to argue and fight passionately to defend their side" (Bly, 1993, p. 97).

Obtaining information remains the major function of a verbal exchange. Willingham (1992, p. 50) suggests that when you suspect that a customer is seeking help, first ask "how may I help you?," "Find out why they came in or contacted you," and finally, "ask open-ended questions to further understand their needs." Tschohl and Franzmeier (1991, p. 190) point out that being friendly with the customer works toward promoting positive feedback from them when service providers give them personal treatment or use their name. Authentic ingratiating is an interactive tactic legitimately employed by the service provider to compliment a customer on their good taste, not to patronize them, but to assist them. By helping others, we render favors by communicating "to others that we respect them and are willing to help them pursue their goals. Like offering compliments, rendering favors is based on the principle that we reciprocate liking for people who like us. One of the ways to avoid suspicion of ulterior motives is to do only favors that are considered appropriate for a given situation" (Canary and Cody, 1994, pp. 116–17). One customer service program encourages paying compliments, which it calls positive feedback, and discourages negative feedback and "plastic" (phony) language (Tschohl and Franzmeier, 1991).

In a study conducted within the hotel industry, Kim *et al.* (2001) found that effective communication is a driving determinant of the quality of customer relationships. In this vein, customer-contact personnel should be advised to "Speak English – Not companyese" (Liswood, 1990, p. 63). "Your reservation was oh-op-ed by our central processing oversight formulator with a reconciling terminal." In other words, we lost your reservation. Anderson and Zemke (1991, p. 58) list five phrases that should be avoided because they all contain a negative connotation that correspondingly brings out the same response from the customer: "I don't know; We can't do that; You'll have to; Hang on a second: I'll be right back; and *No* when used at the beginning of any sentence." Okun (2002, p. D4) also points out that the phrase "no problem" can be substituted with the simple phrase "certainly," with more positive implications.

Verbal courtesy and respect

Both surface and deep acting are used by the service provider in expressing emotional interaction (Ashforth and Humphrey, 1993, pp. 93, 95). Surface acting focuses directly on one's outward behavior, while deep acting entails one's inner feelings. While the range of behavior in a service situation is controlled, there are personal limits where a sense of self, or who one is, can be projected. "Use good manners in all interactions with your clients" (Bly, 1993, p. 153). Survey and observational data, although it may bring little to measuring the effectiveness of "courteous service," must still be considered as part of providing a positive relation with a customer. Ford (1998, pp. 11–21) identifies three types of courteous service: "phatic speech, nonverbal immediacy and verbal immediacy." Phatic speech is the use of simple words to create a warm and inviting service climate. Short phrases, such as "how are you?," "things going okay?", "what do we need to do?," establish a base on which to build in an interaction exchange. And of course, the nonverbal immediacy refers to the directness and intensity of the social interaction such as eye contact, a smile, an open gesture signaling that the customer is part of the enterprise, not just a passive receiver.

Like the above, verbal immediacy ties a personal set of words, such as "we" or "you," and the use of personal role references, like "mom" or "dad," to the provider. Verbal immediacy is also increased by "temporal and spatial closeness – using phrases like I am doing it, and here it is." Topic immediacy refers to subjects without avoiding them or being evasive, just being honest and expressing your attitude or opinion as such. Another strategy uses language that accepts responsibility for your actions with emotional words such as "terrific," "great," "what a ball," etc. Or more personal social interaction references can link one's self with the customer – such as humor, taste in food, the arts, and sports, and other cultural attributes and topics. But the first step is to greet your customers and ask how you may assist them (Smith, 1999, p. 64). Very simply, use praise, be sincere, and thank your customer (Tschohl and Franzmeier, 1991, p. 145). "Fulfill requests promptly and politely and correct problems promptly and politely" (Bly, 1993, pp. 92–93). By exhibiting courtesy and respect to one another, individuals demonstrate an understanding of the basic elements of social skills. For instance, they possess the ability to exude appropriate behavior in personal and business situations regardless of their private feelings (Petite, 1989).

There are service breakdowns in an imperfect world. That is, sometimes effective service involves delivering apologies (Donnelly, 1992). It is unwise to invent silly explanations when there is a breakdown in service; rather, well-thought-out explanations should be offered (Choi and Mattila, 2008). In an incident where a message was not posted for a guest on his phone, the desk person explained that there was a change of shift and the new crew was not in to handle the message. The guest explained that they were there later and the message was not posted, whereupon the front desk manager explained that the guest probably did not see the phone light with the new morning sun shining so brightly. A simple acknowledgement of the error by the hotel staff or the manager would have saved a future client and customer, but instead they played the status game of "we're in charge and we are perfect and do not make mistakes." A simple apology would have solved the problem. It is bad enough for a customer to hear, "that's not my job," but it is even worse to be told that "it is your job and you failed." That is downright insulting and uncaring, and certainly far from being a model performance by a service provider. The moral of this incident is starkly evident to even the most shortsighted: "the delivery of quality service is never the customer's job," no matter how the tourist situation has been defined by management. An apology often has a significant influence on customers' perceptions of interactional justice (Smith *et al.*, 1998).

A full-blown apology (as opposed to a perfunctory one) entails an admission, your corrections, and avoidance of doing the same in the future. Expressed in attitudinal terms, service is; "thoughtfulness, courtesy, integrity, reliability, helpfulness, and friendliness" (Tschohl and Franzmeier, 1991, pp. 8–10). Frontline providers need to train customers to expect that they will: (1) receive "reliable, courteous and effective responses to their problems," (2) receive value for what they pay for, "no matter what," and (3) recognize there are "some situations that you cannot remedy" (Carr, 1990, pp. 92–93). A tenet of a restaurant in a Marriott Hotel in Maryland states that their "service staff will be friendly and courteous evidenced by their smiles and cheerful attitudes" (Heskett *et al.*, 1990, p. 91).

Vandergriff (1999, pp. 73–74) identifies certain role characteristics that service providers ought to embody and exhibit. They should be courteous in their exchanges, flexible in how they approach each situation, knowledgeable about the range of services offered, empowered to act, have the authority to make decisions, be trained to handle all relevant situations, possess sufficient peripheral information that may be requested of the customer, and finally be adequately rewarded. Manners or courtesy is also a process through which inattention is overcome and love toward one's fellow man is prized. In the service sector that means manners – the "thank you, please, good morning and night" greetings. At the maximal level, the use of "sir, madam" greetings, while looking for ways to assist the customer and listening to what they have to say, demonstrates a more personal level of achievement in one's level of courtesy recognition (DiBenedetto, 2001, p. 14). Be "appreciative" and thank the customer for their patronage, because in a free and open society there are competitors who are more than willing to cash in on your lack of courtesy (Tschohl and Franzmeier, 1991, p. 194). Research shows that courtesy, empathy, and responsiveness affect customers' perceptions of good service, and when employees feel that management is attending adequately to their needs, the above feelings also spill over to the customer (Bowen and Lawler, 1992). This spill-over of positive outcomes is particularly germane to service failure recovery situations, because such situations often mandate employees' extra-role performance (Maxham and Netemeyer, 2003).

Greater attention is necessary to detailing what works positively in these situations. There are stages in the perception process that Bower (1992, p. 201) has summarized based on the work of Gilbert and Malone, who see social judgments proceeding through three basic stages. "First, observers categorize a behavior (polite, rude, or bizarre) then characterize corresponding traits of the actor (pleasant, unpleasant) and finally correct those inferences with information about the situation." What can get things off to a confused start and "mire" the interaction process is "blurry words and fuzzy deeds." Attention to detail is imperative in the interaction process to be able to reproduce consistent and reliable results. In three different areas of conceptualizing service encounter interactions, Walker (1995) emphasizes the need for efficiency and pleasantness of the service provider's personality.

In dealing with hotel customers, a pleasant desk clerk is a key part of the service, and personnel being trained to take pride in serving customers efficiently during their inevitable interactions bolsters customer satisfaction. Yet some customers expect more than the efficient completion of a transaction from a provider; they want service with a smile, and are resentful if they do not feel they have received it. Other customers couldn't care less, and just want to complete the transaction. Nevertheless, it is the provider's responsibility to "interpret the customer's wishes without any prior experience with that customer" (Gutek, 1995, pp. 82–83). Making such an interpretation is a difficult task in a brief exchange. In interpreting the expectations of the customer, however, the provider will be credited or condemned for their action, not that of the situation or company policy, which may be directing the outcome through its service design. Gutek (1995, pp. 84–89) finds this practice normal in the attribution process. "Because in the absence of other information people tend to make actor attribution – that is, make the fundamental attribution error – customers and providers who behave less than ideally will probably be seen by the other (the observer) as inherently rude or uncivil." Pleasant behaviors will not "automatically" be attributed to the provider; however, they may well be attributed to the company's service policy. Singapore Airlines took advantage of the attribution process by "exploiting the image of Asian women as inherently courteous and eager to please," while most other airlines focus on the friendliness rather than the intrinsic pleasantness of the provider (Gutek, 1995, p. 86). The medium in this case, the female flight attendants, became the satisfaction message.

In changing service to a more positive perception, complaints can be used as a valuable source of proactive change (Naylor, 2003). Analyzing failure points in a service process is another way in which important information can be obtained to improve a program. And finally, designing appropriate responses to the customer in advance of a problem is necessary planning. Nevertheless, perhaps most critical of all is the personal manner in which the redress process is carried out. This requires assigning associates with the best listening and interpersonal skills to the recovery process (Heskett *et al.*, 1990). Service providers must have a detailed knowledge and understanding of what is acceptable behavior on their part to resolve customer problems. In an example of poor manners and not taking responsibility for the loss of a reservation, a hotel receptionist launched into a five-minute diatribe explaining why it was the fault of the operator at the 800-number, made no effort to find an alternative solution, and left the customer hanging (Martin, 2002). Passing the buck is never acceptable behavior.

Verbal listening

It is very common for customers to make overly expectant assumptions about the level of their purchased service. To avoid unnecessary problems in the future, sales personnel need to be really good listeners (Justice, 1984) to be sure that the customer really understands what they contracted for and what they are not getting. Just listening, however, is not enough for future planning or visionary innovative moves in a competitive marketplace, if that is all a service provider is relying upon as a substitute for strategic planning (Percy, 1998). As a public relations program, obvious benefits from listening to customers are assured, but care must be taken to indicate what a company can provide up-front in its advertising and promotion. An open-ended listening venue is unrealistic for any service provider, since it will risk quickly being taken beyond the level of expectations that it can deal with in a practical manner. Just listening, without active probing to determine if the customer will do what they are saying when given a choice, needs further inquiry. Listening is a two-edged sword that can cut through reams of confusion, but also can cut off future potential options if not carefully probed or tested. American Express Travel Services thinks so highly of active listening by its customer representatives that it hired outside professionals in the behavioral sciences to train its leaders. It wants its people to hear what is being said, to be able to communicate it back, and then to "set expectations about what the conclusion of the call is going to be" for the customer. They are taught to listen for "nuances, and then go beyond the obvious" (Wiersema, 1996. pp. 131–32). "Customer satisfaction depends on meeting your customers' requirements. But you can't meet customer needs if you don't listen to them" (Cannie, 1994, pp. 77, 82–84).

Effective listening begins with controlling two sets of variables: the physical and the psychological setting or situation. For the physical setting, you remove barriers between you and the customer; respect their own personal space by not getting to close; and control incoming stimuli such as phones or other customer intrusions to maintain a quiet and interruption-free setting. And finally, as noted previously, a handshake or comforting pat can help facilitate the interaction exchange in a positive manner. In the psychological mode of interaction, use all forms of message communication by making eye contact, gesturing, using nonverbal prompts such as nodding the head or raising the hands or palms open in supplication, and use verbal prompts such as "ok" and "ah-hum."

The service provider should develop OLAF skills (observe – listen – ask – feel) (Carr, 1990, p. 102). Watch the body language of a person, and listen. Get information and feel their situation. In responding to Carr's (1990, p. 102) question about what was the most important response in dealing with an unhappy customer, a ten-year veteran American Airline flight attendant said, "listen." A frontline staff member represents an invaluable source of information about what the customer likes and dislikes about your service. Encourage the service provider to be open and probe details about positive and negative service practices. And, equally important, it is also necessary to determine what you are not doing that the customer would like you to do (Cannie and Caplin, 1991, p. 203).

In enumerating various ways to listen to customers, Bell and Zemke (1992, pp. 39–40) cite face-to-face contact, such as managers and secret shoppers mingling among customers, and also frontline contacts, who are in immediate contact with the demands of the customer. Being out in front with the customer is a natural place for people to meet in the marketplace, be it a resort, plane, park, casino, or hotel. The optimum situation is for the service provider "to be a good listener. Don't impose your beliefs or preferences on your customers." Furthermore, "get down in the trenches; have personal one-to-one encounters with your customers every single day" (Harris, 1991, p. 20). Listening to the customer requires an attentive ear and a willingness to attend to another's needs. Techniques in effective listening include judging the "content of what they (customers) are saying" and not how. Do not "jump to make judgments." Make "eye contact and listen" for meaning, "resist distractions and interruptions," and "seek clarification" when the customer is done convening their needs and expectations to you (Timm, 1998, p. 30). In understanding customer expectations, Petite (1989, pp. 98–99) states "you need to know how to ask questions and listen to responses," and you also need to monitor the changing needs of customers through "constant communication and dialogue." Reichheld (2001, pp. 153, 160) returns communication to its roots: communion "which denotes an intense, two-way exchange … Real communication has to do with careful listening, observation, and dialogue, and is founded on truth." The good listener asks questions about what the individuals are communicating. "They adopt deliberate summarizing … reference points … and invite expanding" of the other person's point of views in an open manner (Duck, 1991, p. 44).

In summary, "Listening is the supreme act of courtesy. Listening is at least fifty percent of effective communication" (Petite, 1989, pp. 115, 117). As key to its effectiveness, face-to-face listening means "responding through body language." "Listening is the highest form of persuasion" by raising the customer's self image (Willingham, 1992, p. 63). "Employees should listen when a customer speaks instead of busying herself or himself with paperwork or even making an offhand remark to another employee or customer. Listening is complimenting" (Tschohl and Franzmeier, 1991, p. 194). Get feedback to modify, maintain the status quo, change, and reinforce a service element. "Make it easy for the customer to comment, ask for comments, and never ignore" a comment (Carr, 1990, pp. 137, 146). "When a customer provides honest comments, he's doing you a favor … and that's how he looks at it." Give him a reason to do you the favor (Carr, 1990, p. 146). Communicating and listening is the final commandment that helps in understanding what motivates customers in fulfilling their requests (Yeh *et al.*, 2000, p. 256).

Communication linking

Communication includes the symbols in memory and how they are perceived and used by the self. This "include(s) the expression of the face, attitude, gesture, the tones of voice, words" that Cooley (1998, p. 100) has credited as part of the interaction process. The treatment of language and gestures in explicit dialogue is not a matter of a set course of action. The symbolic representations of language contain both denotative and connotative dimensions of meaning that are expansive, especially when we get beyond the denotative and descriptive sphere. "From such ambiguity, a feature probably more common than rare in everyday life, there arises the give and take" (Davis, 1982, p. 118). The give-and-take of interaction is an attempt to ferret out what the customer truly desires. Information and communication obtained about a prospective tourist destination is not used solely to make a buying decision. Various kinds of communication, such as advertisements, are intended to communicate, shape, mold, persuade, and help a potential customer reach a decision (Peck and Wiggins, 2006).

The primary form of communication that intensifies a customer's awareness is word-of-mouth (Moutinho, 1987). As a result, a customer forms an "image of a destination or service" as a function of their "level of awareness in relation to the product," their "beliefs and attitudes developed about the product," and finally their "expectations implying the benefits expected to be derived from the tourist product." Word-of-mouth communication carries strength as an information source because it is perceived as having no ulterior motive (Zeithaml *et al.*, 1993). What you hear from other people, especially opinion-leaders and influential persons in a circle of contacts, can spell out the difference in making decisions about a service. Communication problems, either verbal or symbolic through expressions, cause what Timm (1998, p. 25) terms the customer "turnoffs." Some of these interpersonal failures are not greeting or recognizing the customer, defusing inaccurate information, ignoring the customer by dealing with other employees or interrupting phone calls, a rude and condescending attitude, pressure sale tactics, slovenly appearance, or saying anything that causes the customer discomfort.

"Love of the frontline and learning how to pay attention to such 'soft' issues as customer perception, listening, time and customization" are driving forces behind service performance (Peters, 1991, p. 5). "The key to building a relationship and sustaining communicative behavior is in the way in which each participant adjusts to each other," not internecine action (Botschen, 2000, p. 281). If the encounter is "supportive," "then firms can ensure positive and consistent personal encounters by giving care and attention to the sensory input received by the customer." A manager and service provider can exercise "considerable control" over the interaction process "by paying close attention to the dominant senses of sight and hearing" (Botschen, 2000, p. 283).

Marketing communications can link the customer and service provider with a shared vision when the messages establish mutually acceptable goals (Horovitz and Panak, 1994), and the closer you can get the customer to a company's service provider, the better the result. Advertising's internal or "secondary audience" is the company's employees (Gilly and Wolfinbarger, 1998). This is why more and more advertising features employees: it shows customers the importance of service through people. It also demonstrates to employees how important their role is in the service. Employees are expected to live by two principles in striving for professional dedication to service – listen and communicate (Wiersema, 1996).

While positive interactions have been stressed, mistakes are also actions that unfortunately can destroy the connective link. Morgan (1999, pp. 155–56) reports ten common mistakes that employees make with customers. (1) Taking the customer for granted and ignoring those polite "niceties" like good morning and other courtesies in language communication. (2) Using jargon and expecting the customer to understand the lingo. (3) Speaking so fast that the customer has to ask the employee to repeat, or so low they can't be heard. (4) Giving short clipped answers instead of an adequate explanation. (5) Not being proactive when a problem arises. (6) Not appearing to care about the customer if they have a complaint. (7) Being preoccupied with other tasks and talking to other service providers while the customer waits. (8) Interrupting the customer and not listening to what they are saying. (9) Making judgments about the customer on the basis of their appearance, dress, manner, or language skills. (10) Arguing with the customer. Since communication is so central to the service process, Bly (1993, pp. 107–49) enumerates several tips for effective communication to improve performance in the service process. These include listening to the customer more than talking, and then asking questions and intently listening to the answers; being enthusiastic, positive, sincere and genuine; being available for instant access; and responding promptly to customers' requests.

Box 7.5 Considering culture: speech tempo

Acceptable norms regarding the speed of spoken language vary around the globe. Most Chinese, for example, have been reported to speak more slowly than most Americans. What factors fuel these differences in cultural acceptable speed variations? One theory suggests that the tempo of spoken language is positively correlated with a country's level of industrialization. An alternative explanation posits that languages that are spoken slowly transmit more information per syllable than others.

Communication skills and the predisposition to interact are essential requirements for a service provider. Although listening skills are essential to the service provider role, they cannot be so reserved as to be unwilling to communicate. A personality scale by McCroskey and Richmond (1987) appears to be a valid instrument in measuring willingness to communicate. Based on supporting evidence that individuals possess varying behavioral tendencies to communicate more or less across communication situations, their scale measures such a disposition. The willingness-to-communicate scale includes items related to four communication contexts – public speaking, talking in meetings, talking in small groups, and talking in dyads; and three types of receiver: strangers, acquaintances, and friends. Since encounters are initially between strangers, the reliability for measuring this interaction was the highest. Such techniques and others like it may be helpful screening devices in selecting frontline staff. An "enlargement" effect has occurred in modern society where men view themselves as part of a global entity. "The man of today inclines to look for a common nature everywhere and to demand that the whole shall be brought under the sway of common principles of kindness and justice" (Cooley, 1998, p. 109). Pity the poor service provider who oversteps these bounds and is interpreted as violating a customer's rights. Care must be taken and a prompt response made to any misinterpretation, to see that justice is done.

The interactive processes indicated in this chapter are central in an exchange between service provider and tourist customer. They need to be facilitated in a positive manner to achieve satisfactory and loyal customer judgments and attitudes.

8 Going beyond satisfaction to loyalty

This chapter goes beyond just attempting to ensure customer satisfaction, and sets a higher mark of achieving a more complete state of customer loyalty. Customers are not intrinsically loyal, but need to be won over in today's saturated competitive landscape. Consequently, we focus on exceeding customer expectations and achieving customer delight. The chapter explains that customer delight entails leaving customers with a positive surprise. Related topics, such as return-on-quality theory, add depth to the discussion. Return-on-quality theory contends that firms must gauge the projected financial returns from investing in a service quality improvement so that they can weigh the potentials of various quality initiatives against each other. In other words, firms must possess an understanding of which service-related amenities customers value the most and what truly drives their loyalty.

Satisfying and exceeding customer expectations for service

Providers and satisfaction

Service is experience, developing memories and recollections of joy. "Recent theories that have been subjected to rigorous empirical evaluations propose that customers' perceptions of service quality will predict their satisfaction and, ultimately, their intentions to return" (Ford, 1998, p. 99). Research also supports the notion that customers use multiple comparison standards for the evaluation of service quality and satisfaction (Ekinci, 2003). Inefficient, careless, thoughtless service by noninvolved service providers creates a situation of disenfranchised tourist customers. "Customer satisfaction is the name of the game"; "you do it through a focus on customer care" (Brown, 1999, p. 23). Any encounter can be critical in driving customer satisfaction and loyalty (Zeithaml and Bitner, 2000). Superior service will keep customers loyal while "sustained" service adds a "whole new dimension" (Connellan and Zemke, 1993, p. 11). The more customers are satisfied, "the longer they stay and thus higher the retention rate. A retention of 80 percent means that, on average, customers remain loyal for five years whereas one of 90 percent pushes the average loyalty up to ten years" (Buchanan and Gilles, 1990, pp. 248–49).

Toward achieving those goals, Petite (1989, p. 39) is of the opinion you "can't teach attitudes, but you can create environments where care and concern for people in general – employees and customers – are intrinsic corporate values." Psychologically, however, attitudes are nothing more than the flip side of that same valued coin. They can be learned and implemented through behavioral action "By far the most important way you can help keep customers loyal and break down barriers to customer loyalty is through your own behavior: the goals you set, how well you communicate your commitment, how you spend your time, what behaviors you model and reward, what messages you send, and what resources you commit" (Cannie, 1994, p. 104).

Successful companies approach acquisition of customer knowledge and customer satisfaction with passion. Moreover, they understand the critical role of the human element in transactions (Brown, 1995). Multiple attributes affect tourists' perception of satisfaction about their situation. Kozak (2003, p. 237) finds in the various situations examined and among the different cultural groups participating in the survey "that hospitality and customer care, level of prices, and accommodation services were the top three core competencies." Caring for the tourist as a host seems almost a given, but there are resorts that unfortunately overlook the importance of the social interaction between tourist and service provider. We maintain from our observations that frontline personnel are a crucial attribute leading to customer satisfaction and delight that adds to valuation. To demonstrate, a restaurant investigated by Newton (1992, p. 270) places its customers on the level of guests, as they would be treated in their own home. That is certainly a very high standard to hold up, but one worthy of recognition and value.

"Your customer contact people are the heart of your attempt to satisfy your customer. You need to regard them with the same respect and give them the same support that a successful commander gives his frontline troops" (Carr, 1990, p. 58). Satisfied employees yield satisfied customers (Scheuing, 1999). For a company to become commitment-based, everyone must buy into the philosophy (Lowenstein, 1997). Customer loyalty needs to be part of every employee's work role to ensure the culture of the company. Despite the individual provider being placed at a time and duration disadvantage in a brief encounter, they are in a position to bolster respect for their organization. All the service elements taken together "can dispose a customer to develop a sort of brand loyalty, to feel positive about an organization – an airline, hotel, or fast food restaurant" (Gutek, 1995, p. 157). Evidently, first and last impressions alone will not create or sustain customer loyalty (Heskett *et al.*, 1990). It takes service elements that build service loyalty by going beyond customer satisfaction. In a quality control study reported by Edvardsson *et al.* (1994, p. 124), service satisfaction included not only the needs of the customer, but also the staff's response in meeting those needs. When the frontline staff captures a customer for keeps "make sure you make a proper fuss about it so others know this is the way to go" (Furlong, 1993, p. 90).

"Satisfied employees are both a cause and consequence of customer satisfaction" (Day, 1999, p. 14). One of the owners of the River Café told Lewin and Regine (2000, p. 149) "respect for everyone who works here. If you involve everyone equally, you get a culture of commitment, a strong work ethic, everyone working together, everyone *wanting* to work together, and having fun doing it. If you treat people well, create good working conditions, encourage their growth through experience, engage in constant dialogue, a powerful commitment emerges. That way, everybody benefits." Bhote (1996, p. 41) singles out factors that are seen as instrumental in stimulating customer loyalty, among them creating empowered employees who actually run and are responsible for day-to-day operations on the frontline. Provider empowerment is the best approach in building loyalty (Bowen and Lawler, 1992, p. 149). Empowerment has also has been shown to aid in improving service delivery and in deriving new service offerings. Firms therefore not only should strive to achieve psychological empowerment of individual employees, but should go beyond that to create an organization-wide empowerment climate (Seibert *et al.*, 2004).

For an employee to be truly empowered, you need to "create a workforce to understand your vision, values and strategies as well as what customer focus means" (Weinzimer, 1998, p. 97). Trust is very important in a company–employee relationship. Labor-intensive service companies that do not build trust-based relationships with their employees often have difficulty fostering trust with customers as well. Excessive turnover may result among employees, but even worse are those employees who "stay on the job physically but quit emotionally" (Berry, 1999, p. 133). This lack of physiological activity at work is sometimes referred to as presenteeism (Cascio, 2006). Thus it is how the company treats the employee with respect and dignity that matters. The loyal customer breeds a loyal employee. It is basically simple cash flow. Specifically, when a firm is spending less to acquire new customers, it has more funds available to pay employees (Griffin, 1995). Morale increases while productivity also increases, and commitment becomes a service provider value.

Exceeding expectations

"A more proactive approach to loyalty management is to start from the earliest stages of customer development and devise ways to nurture and enhance loyalty throughout the customer's history with your company" (Griffin, 1995, p. 27). Getting to understand customer satisfaction as the first step to customer loyalty is not so matter of fact. "The key to customer satisfaction is almost never a matter of exceeding expectations, but typically a test of whether we can even find out, understand, and meet the customer's definition of minimum acceptable competence in those fleeting moments of truth when we, and they, find out how good we really are" (Schaaf, 1995, p. 23). To earn customer loyalty, Timm (1998, p. 29) feels that any service company must (1) "reduce turnoffs" to value, their delivery system, and their service providers, and then (2) exceed customer expectations. To accomplish this, an imbalance is created in the service that goes beyond the norm and provides a premium. In that sense, loyalists are customers who are completely satisfied (5 on a scale of 1 to 5) and keep returning to the company. Loyalists constitute a company's bedrock. There is a perfect fit between their needs and the company's offerings. "Within the loyalist group are those whose experiences so exceed their expectations that they become missionaries or apostles for the company" (Bhote, 1996, p. 28).

To reach a loyalty standard, exceeding customers' expectations sometimes entails the element of surprise, and the best opportunity … is during the service process. The company surprises customers with details that are part of the service process, and involves them with more than what they anticipated. It is also the "extra effort" customers receive from a company (Berry, 1995, pp. 89–92). In order to surprise the customer, it is often the total service package of attributes that impresses, not just one incident. "Great service companies 'major in minors.' They use details to be different and to signal to customers that the company is special" (Berry, 1995, pp. 90, 92). Another tactic to produce a surprise effect emanates from extra effort in service "by going to extra ordinary lengths to please." Such a firm does more than just meet and satisfy its customers' expectations; it 'wows' its customers and cultivates deeply felt loyalties (Berry, 1995). As a customer, "we want to be wowed, not merely satisfied." Heil *et al.* (1997, pp. 71–85) suggest that in achieving this objective the customer can be entertained, educated, or informed, or the service experience can be made special or cheap. These extra unexpected add-ons will most likely pull the customer to a higher level of delight and excitement. To consistently wow customers, firms must align customer expectations and firm goals. In other words, "knock your socks off" service must be based on reliable and valid customer feedback data (Connellan and Zemke, 1993). "Stop and look at where customers form impressions about your business. Look at the service your customers are receiving and challenge yourself and your team to make changes to get to the level of 'Wow' service" (Fritz, 1999, p. 14). "Wow" is an expression that simply means customers are saying the service is exceptional. It is important to reach that juncture, to "make your service even better than your customers expect. That way, they are sure to notice it, react to it with commendations of it to friends and relatives, and to want more of it" (Tschohl and Franzmeier, 1991, p. 177). When a service program reaches beyond just satisfying a customer and delights them, they are wowed because "customers have not expected or anticipated [those services] which trill them and raise the loyalty quotient" (Bhote, 1996, p. 9). "Delight the customer" and if you succeed, "top companies have come to realize that creating a memorable experience at every customer interaction is one of the most effective strategies for increasing customer share" (Yeh *et al.*, 2000, p. 54). The service/quality challenge for the service provider and service delivery system is to meet or exceed this customer's expectations while not hindering the service encounter for other customers.

On top of that, customer delight entails leaving customers with a positive surprise (Berman, 2005). Each service is a unique event, never to be repeated exactly (Collier, 1994, p. 38). When expected features are present, the customer is simply satisfied; when they are absent, the customer is dissatisfied. But when exciting features exist and the customer was unaware of their possibility, the customer is delighted and very satisfied, although they are not dissatisfied if these are not present. Extra service is essential for customer loyalty.

Zeithaml *et al.* (1993) hypothesize three different levels of customer expectation to include desired service that the customer wants, adequate service that the customer will accept, and predicted service that the customer thinks is likely to occur. The researchers gathered data from focus groups representing business, nonbusiness consumer groups, product service companies and pure service nonproduct companies. The difference between what a customer desires in service performance is a zone of tolerance between what should and can be at the desired end of the service spectrum, as opposed to what may be appropriate at an acceptable level of service performance. The researchers found a number of antecedent factors affecting these service expectations. Customers responsible to another party (such as wife or friend) hold the provider as in a sense accountable for that service performance and add pressure to obtain a desired level. Extraneous factors such as insufficient competition; the level of effort to which the customer is willing to commit to the service process; and exceptional situational factors that may affect service performance, such as bad weather, a labor strike, or sickness, all play a role in accepting adequate service.

The declaration of loyalty by the customer is expressed through high satisfaction sentiments (Diller, 2000). Nevertheless, a very important distinction needs to be made between loyalty and satisfaction – it is easy to confuse the behavioral function of both these concepts in describing the transaction process. They must not be treated as interchangeable concepts (Diller, 2000). While satisfaction and loyalty are connected, each also depends on extraneous intervening processes. Diller (2000, p. 38) goes on to say that there are motivational and demotivational factors at work in this decision process. In evaluating customers' judgments, the positive correlation with satisfaction with meeting their expectations or exceeding them, and the relational strength of their willingness to continue to do business with the company and to recommend it to others is very significant. And finally, relationship closeness and emotional strength are also important where "the greater the frequency of experiencing positive, as compared with negative" (Barnes, 2000, pp. 96–98) emotions, the greater the closeness of the relationship. Such results translate into increased frequency of business with those customers who perceive a close relationship. In evaluating customer loyalty, the "I like" and "I am satisfied" expressions are too weak emotionally to discriminate between service practices; we need instead to use adjectives such as "love" and "hate" to get at the more powerful feelings of the customer (Bell and Zemke, 1992, p. 27).

In the hospitality service sector of travel and tourism, consumption patterns can be monitored through a guest database system of information, and communication links to the customer (Magnini *et al.*, 2003). This gives the hotel operator a reliable look at the market segment they are aiming to retain as loyal customers. Yesawich (1991) reviews the process of gaining a loyal following by recognizing repeat and frequent guest patronage and rewarding that pattern of usage, and engaging those patrons in an ongoing dialogue on how to maintain and improve service within that price and quality range. These patrons will be predisposed to return and hopefully will also refer the service to fellow travelers.

Building a loyal following is simply smart economics. It is the equivalent of a savings bank of customer patronage. Famulla (1999) points out that it costs approximately five times more to create a new customer than it does to retain an existing one. Among the loyal customer base, the same research shows that service-related issues are responsible for nearly 70 percent of defections. That is an extraordinarily high percentage. The breakdown is due to weak and poor service, costing the firm revenue and maybe, in time, its existence.

Educating the public through advertising and awareness of the services being offered, as well as their limitations, is essential for molding loyal customers. Filipczak (1991) cites Professor Leonard L. Berry as saying that shaping expectations is one of the most important aspects of keeping customers loyal. If they know and fully appreciate what is being offered, and receive what was promised, the groundwork for a loyal customer has been laid. In his book *Discovering the Soul of Service*, Berry (1999) quotes a CEO of a major company who refers to what he calls the Loyalty Chain that is built on "respect" for the service provider working for the company. If that employee is treated with dignity and "enthralled," that link in the chain is joined to a customer, who ends up being treated in turn with equal dignity by the employee.

As a core value of a company, respect for both customer and employee consists of trust, sensitivity, and listening (Berry, 1999). As interpersonal expressions in the exchange process, the customer's expectations are also molded by the messenger, not just the message. Bly (1993, pp. 82–83, 87) suggests there are two easy steps to delivering superior customer satisfaction. (1) "[C]reate an expectation on the client's part that is realistic, yet one you can not only meet but actually exceed. (2) Consistently exceed expectations and deliver more than promised in a way that delivers revenue to you via increased client retention and repeat business." Very simply, in expediting these steps "you can create an extraordinarily high level of pleasure and satisfaction in your clients rendering them exceedingly small and simple favors." Give the customer or client more than their fair share, but just a "little" more than what they expect to receive. Overdoing it can undermine your credibility, and the customer will assume that you are low-balling them. Customizing the service, being responsive, and adding information to the services offered increases the chances of exceeding normal expectations and delighting the customer, who will become a patron (Peters, 1991, p. 5). "Remember, 100 percent customer satisfaction is your goal. So you can reach beyond to that level of loyalty. The only way you can rightfully say you are providing customer satisfaction is to ask the customer how you are doing and how you might improve" (Cannie, 1994, p. 5). "By setting 100 percent customer satisfaction as your goal, and by doing things right the first time, on time and every time, you improve productivity" (Cannie, 1994, p. 76).

Customer satisfaction–dissatisfaction

"No business or organization can succeed without building customer satisfaction and loyalty. Likewise, no person can make a good living without meeting the needs of customers" (Timm, 1998, p. 2). "A satisfaction plan cannot impose satisfaction. It cannot persuade a customer that he is satisfied; neither can it take the dictatorial approach that says, 'You will be satisfied.' Satisfaction cannot be legislated, only conferred" (Hanan and Karp, 1989, p. 44). You have to strive mutually with your customers to achieve a goal of total satisfaction in services and programs that are acceptable to them. Satisfaction will be determined by the value of the difference between what the customer receives and what she or he pays to receive (Hanan and Karp, 1989). In tourism, it means not only money for food, lodging, transportation, and entertainment, but also the preplanning involvement, the nonwork time forfeited during the trip, and foregone alternative activities. The total impact of these behaviors is not insignificant when added into the social costs of engaging in a trip. "The stronger your commitment to customer satisfaction compared to your competition, the greater your competitive edge" (Carr, 1990, p. 163). Customer satisfaction leads to customer loyalty; yet one survey (Bhote, 1996, p. 21) showed that 62 percent of companies did not consider customer satisfaction a top priority that would lead them to the potential of having loyal followers in the marketplace. This lack of focus is apparent in the satisfaction ratings contained in the University of Michigan's American Customer Satisfaction Index (ACSI) (Blumenthal, 2005).

The Marriott Corporation "found that each percentage-point increase in the customer satisfaction measure-of intent-to return was worth some fifty million in revenues" (Connellan and Zemke, 1993, p. 3). The vast majority of customers served do not generate the profit that is gained from the core market (Hanan and Karp, 1989, p. 5). Non-core customers should not be ignored or allowed to become dissatisfied. "What it does mean is that corporate policy should not enforce their total satisfaction" (ibid., p. 5). A customer identified as moderately satisfied in a customer satisfaction program represents potential for the firm. "If current customers are the most productive source of additional or repeat business, lost customers probably represent the second best" since they are more familiar and never totally reject a service (Vavra, 1992, pp. 167, 207).

When dealing with customers' perceptions of evaluation, companies are concerned with customer satisfaction rather than loyalty (Gitomer, 2002). Blattberg *et al.* (2001, pp. 71–75) point out that customer satisfaction is not enough to generate loyalty and retention. The authors cite empirical evidence of companies that scored well in the Baldridge competition on satisfaction but did not increase their following. Satisfaction is part of the equation, but so are value, loyalty incentives, and available service or product suitability for meeting and exceeding expectations, ease of acquisition, and the service given to the customer. "Empowered customers look askance at the way businesses undervalue their long-term loyalty. Due to downsizing, temporary and part-time staffing practices, and sometimes downright silly cost-cutting efforts, these customers may no longer be developing the kinds of personal relationships with the people in an organization that once cemented loyalty" (Schaaf, 1995, p. 290). By providing undivided attention, the service provider raises the status of the customer in their own eyes. The provider can take certain steps to ensure an effective exchange, especially when a problem occurs with a service element.

Dissatisfaction is a reality of doing business in the service sector. But it is not based on customers' quick judgments when loyalty is at stake. Customer loyalty is believed to be built over time, but Ford (1998, p. 110) quotes research that claims loyalty lags behind satisfaction, so that a single experience of dissatisfaction with a company is not likely to change the customer's loyalty. In other words, a history of successful transactions often builds a psychological buffer in the consumer's mind (Hess *et al.*, 2003). If a service provider does not provide the basic core of what is expected by the customer, then the customer will respond negatively and punish the service provider (Meyer and Blumelhuber, 2000, p. 116).

In many circumstances, a complaining customer whose problem is solved becomes more loyal than a customer with no problem. This, we believe, is because, until the customer has a problem, "service and quality" are merely advertising slogans. More specifically, summarized by Magnini *et al.* (2007), paradoxical increases in satisfaction can occur after a service failure and recovery situation for three theory-based reasons. First, according to the expectancy disconfirmation paradigm, an excellent redress effort can trigger a positive disconfirmation of customer expectations. Second, in accordance with script theory, a service failure is a deviation from a customer's mental script, and therefore spawns heightened awareness – allowing the firm a chance to wow the customer. Finally, in tandem with Morgan and Hunt's (1994) commitment and trust theory of relationship marketing, a superb service recovery has a direct impact on the trust the customer has in the firm. While these theoretical anchorings of the recovery paradox appear robust, it is prudent to note that research conducted by Oh (2003) finds that paradoxical post-failure satisfaction increases are difficult to achieve in particular situations, such as scenarios involving meetings and convention services.

In an analysis of more than a 100 companies, profits could improve from "25 percent to 85 percent by reducing customer defections by just 5 percent" (Berry, 1999). Work by Harvard professors Heskett *et al.* (1997) is even more telling about how profit is linked to service satisfaction and loyalty. The most fundamental lesson to be learned is that "customers cannot be satisfied until after they are not dissatisfied. Your first service priority should be to eliminate all the opportunities for dissatisfying customers, because they are what cause customers to leave. Then you can invest in satisfying and delighting them" (Donnelly, 1992, p. 84). Given poor service, "service companies can spend as much as 35 percent or more of their operating costs redoing things that weren't done right in the first place" (Harris, 1991, p. 51). Poor service quality can be absolutely devastating to future customer response and loyalty. "All the wonderful service in the world can result in nothing real, zero input, and no profit, if a vision is missing of what the customer needs" (Goodman, 1999, p. 19).

Creating value and quality for the customer

Management responsibility

"We must be able to create more value 'up there' by management than 'down there' at the frontlines. Who do you suppose we're creating that value for?" (Schaaf, 1995, p. 69). Such a business strategy and system ignores the customer and the frontline provider, who collectively are not included in formulating a service design. That is an error that can be corrected by flipping the traditional top-down organizational system on its head. As a result, the head of customer services and the service provider would be on the same level, to more cooperatively formulate a plan agreeable to all parties in the social organization. "If we look at a business sideways instead of up and down, the basic challenge becomes visible: balancing competing interests" (Schaaf, 1995, p. 72). A chief of British Airways said that a corporation is more than good intentions and fine ideas. It is the "values which drive the company and the belief the company has in itself and what it can achieve" (Newton, 1992, p. 269). An effective service strategy understands and incorporates customer value drivers (Berry, 1995). Very simply, customers receive more value than the costs they may incur in a transaction. A service strategy embodies "the company's belief system" and pushes "the organization to perform beyond industry norms." "When management stands behind its values, they resonate in behavior throughout the organization, and when there is life in corporate values, a strong and meaningful culture results" (Weinzimer, 1998, p. 29). This is accomplished through a set of advertised value sets, in company policy, and through management behavior. This is the role of management. It is critical, however, for firms to realize that when they define a set of values, they need to ensure the company's policies and procedures support it (Weinzimer, 1998). For instance, Ritz-Carlton uses the measure of having each associate carry a copy of its corporate values in their pocket (Michelli, 2008). Those organizations that customers value most in seeking service demonstrate their commitment to quality service through their customers' bill of rights (Brown, 1995).

Satisfaction is not enough to establish a lasting relationship with a customer (Morgan *et al.*, 2000, pp. 78, 81). It also takes trust and commitment. Both values are positive and point to a positive relationship with the provider. Trust presumes confidence, commitment and attachment (Morgan and Hunt, 1994). A service situation must nurture "fair play, honesty, communication, and awareness of relationship partners." When the social content of relationships is strong, trust and loyalty are built, and attachment reinforces the desire to remain a part of a service providers' relationship. Unlike a one-time transaction with a customer, companies should vigorously strive to build customer relationships, since they are the "link to the future – tomorrow's customers, tomorrow's employees, tomorrow's partners" (Berry, 1999, pp. 124, 148). But if expectations are dashed, then customers find alternatives. When true relationships are established, however, customers also can expect the company to become more knowledgeable and skilled in serving them over time.

A series of customer–company encounters should facilitate more customizing of the service to customers' specifications. The providers in a company get better at what they are doing as a result of experiencing a bond with the customer (Rust *et al.*, 2004a,b). Interpersonal trust is an important factor in maintaining and nurturing a loyalty relationship. Griffin (1995, pp. 83–87) suggests attracting a new customer by using an honest universal message in your company advertisements. Next, "Consistently and consciously put the customer's interests ahead of your own," then "use only honest facts and figures to back up claims," and finally, "promise only what you can deliver." The key interactive process for building trust is listening to what the customer is saying/not saying, how it is being said and articulated with gestures, and taking mental notes of the impression and message being conveyed. It is not easy to just listen and not talk; it is even harder to listen with an open mind. Griffin (1995, p. 912) also suggests listening to a customer as if they were a "visitor from another planet." That posture helps neutralize any preconceived expectations. Listen for "negative evidence" and also listen for "ideas," not focusing on plain facts, because the fullness of an ideal is an explanation for a person's action or inaction, facts, values, and judgments. Suspending judgment of what a customer is conveying verbally and nonverbally takes discipline, and to figure out what a customer truly wants, that will satisfy him/her to build loyalty, is often mystifying. In responding, the service provider must have an old-country doctor's bedside manner to get at the essence of identifying a need or solving a problem. Asking pointed questions, probing into the substance of a case, and doing so with "feeling and emotions are usually far more persuasive than intellect ... Probe customers to find out what is creating loyalty and what the company can do to increase and extend it." Such interaction is a delicate balancing act between reason and the heart, but so is being human, whether you're a customer or service provider. The secret of companies possessing outstanding customer relations programs which foster loyalty "rests first in creating effective employees" (Griffin, 1995, pp. 98, 113, 146). Recognizing the importance of frontline workers through training and empowerment cements the bonds between customer, company, and service provider.

Value attributes

Customers' value drivers evolve continually (Weinzimer, 1998). Recognizing the customer as a real person is a special value. "Customers buy value, which is made up of many elements. For almost everyone, almost all the time, being treated as a person creates value. The reverse is also true: being treated perfunctorily or impersonally almost always decreases value" (Carr, 1990, p. 61). Delivering world-class service requires a powerful, exciting vision that moves people to act in concert to delight the customer. This vision must be based on a set of values such as honesty, trustworthiness, innovation, openness, flexibility, and a proactive service program centered upon customers' value drivers (Scheuing, 1999). Giving value for the customer to be satisfied takes different forms. Willingham (1992, pp. 75–76) list the following for consideration: to be entertained, to receive pleasure, to enjoy peace of mind, to receive recognition, to economize, to impress others, to obtain better health, to promote social relations, to gratify self, to prevent future losses, or to acquire. When accomplished at a high level of satisfaction and with expectations exceeded, the result is loyalty. Griffin (1995, pp. 209–10) also indicates that a company wishing to institute a successful customer loyalty program needs to follow the eight steps listed in Box 8.1.

Box 8.1 Successful customer loyalty program

- Calculate retention rates using appropriate company indicators for the situation.
- All employees must be aware of the importance of customer loyalty.
- Build performance and compensation into loyalty goals and objectives.
- Review loyalty rates on a monthly basis for continuity and effects of market demand.
- Involve employees in the development and running of the loyalty programs.
- Use marketing and customer care service rewards in cultivating loyalty.
- Identify the biggest customer loyalty "breakers" in the company.
- Continue to change and improve what creates service loyalty in your company.

Ford (1999, pp. 241–47) also proposes some basic strategies for fostering customer loyalty. (1) Perceive and see your service from the customer's eyes and perspective. (2) Make the customer's encounter with the company a delight or redefine the customer's expectations of great service. (3) Build partnerships like a marriage by personalizing and customizing the service delivery system for the customer. (4) Get back to basics by supporting the essential points of contact though listening skills and handling customer exchanges, especially criticism. (5) Hire and train the best employees possible. (6) Act like you mean it, and lead to inspire great service.

Bringing satisfaction to customers includes knowing and offering what they value. In dealing with what customers value, Reidenbach *et al.* (1999, p. 141) promote the design and use of a value map to (1) identify key customer interfaces; (2) identify back-room activities related to these critical customer interfaces; (3) identify information system requirements; (4) identify related management-reporting systems; (5) determine the flows among system levels; (6) assess the need and opportunity for changing the system; (7) implement the changes; (8) monitor the results. This map helps keep service providers on track and in tune with the needs of their customers. On the other hand, Cannie and Caplin (1991, pp. 142–43) report on those needs and values that directly influence a customer's decision to continue use of a service. (1) Customers want to be treated with dignity and respect. (2) Customers want your service to meet their expectations, in which case, loyalty results. (3) Customers want to feel successful in dealing with a service. (4) Customers want help with their problems. (5) Customers want to be treated as individuals with unique needs. (6) Customers want you to be observant of their primary public role as a senior, middle-aged adult, adolescent, etc. (7) Customers want you to respect their time. (8) Customers want someone on their side. (9) Customers want information. (10) Customers must realize tangible benefits from using your service. These fundamentals of customer participation must be recognized and acted upon by all roles in the service organization. Identifying the right kind of customer needs and values attracts users to a service, and ultimately leads to their loyalty.

A service performance occurs in real time, with real feelings and perceptions resulting concerning what is valued. Excellence and innovation in service are found in companies that deliver consistently high customer output through their frontline staff. The hotel is not just clean, it is immaculate, and there is nothing "ho-hum" about the service, since staff are willing to try new approaches that may just increase customer benefit. Dealing with customers with "joy, respect, and integrity" is a big part of the social interaction encounter that brings "satisfaction and pleasure" to those taking part in the service exchange (Weinzimer, 1998, p. 5). The customer does not have to second-guess or continually question what they may be receiving. The customer can trust what they are getting as the genuine article. To make such values authentic and customer loyalty the goal, stable leadership at the management level is an absolute must. Finally, members if the company work together to produce a satisfactory result, and they reach out to the community to share in their good fortune. The customer service value matrix depends on how effectively a firm operates in perceiving the expectations, needs, and wants of the customer, preparing the frontline workforce to understand and create value, and finally providing customer service with superior output.

In the service exchange, "every time a customer has an experience that confirms the value of the purchase – and the value of the total transaction with you – his expectations rise that you will provide him value in the future" (Carr, 1990, p. 66). In defining customer value, the "successful organizations were more likely to define it as 'exceeding customer expectations', while less successful businesses were satisfied with 'meeting customer expectations.' Clearly, it's the businesses willing to 'go the extra mile' that are rewarded with satisfied, loyal customers" (Brown, 1995, p. 278). The past experience of the customer is an important variable in affecting their level of service expectation. The more time customers spend in situations, the more they are able to compare value (Zeithaml *et al.*, 1993). Customer loyalty ensues when a company has delivered superior value through superior service. Firms can use customer service to drive value, to combat negative price differentials, and to defend against competitors' size advantage (Lowenstein, 1997). "Creating value through labor-intensive service operations" require(s) much human input over time that is characterized as "daunting." (Berry, 1999, p. 5); this is precisely why the role of the service provider is so important in the loyalty equation.

Quality and price

"The perspective taken here is that customers are not intrinsically loyal. The reason for this conclusion is that studies investigating the correlates of loyalty generally find that loyal or repeat-buying segments do so because of price, service, or quality. In other words, they are loyal to the relative benefits of the product in a cognitive loyalty sense," which is the weakest of the loyalty dispositions held by individuals (Oliver, 1997, p. 397). We suspect that if the human interpersonal ingratiate was factored into a customer's judgment and attitudes about a service, the strength of that attachment might be greater. The doorman at a Chicago Hotel, for example, welcomed a patron with a greeting: "Welcome back to Chicago." That customer was thrilled to hear that kind of greeting in the 34-degree weather, because it was warm and sincere, and she "felt like she was back home." Even better yet, hospitality firms are advised to train employees and managers in mnemonic techniques so that they can enhance their ability to remember the faces and names of regular customers (Magnini and Honeycutt, 2005). There is no underestimating the power of empathy in a service mode that becomes more a family than just a business connection.

Okun's (2002, p. D1) review of an owners' guide to restaurant service protocol points out that greeting the customer promptly and explaining options for the customer makes for a good connection and service quality. The following underlying common characteristics of quality service are taken from successful companies. They include the service providers' friendliness, quality people, committed management to service, and adequate staffing (Tschohl and Franzmeier, 1991, pp. 167–69). These characteristics are people-related, service provider-based, and management-linked in an interactive service system. Customer-perceived quality is hinged on two service attributes according to Armistead and Clark (1994, pp. 142–45). "Quality assurance" relates to instilling customer confidence; "quality improvement" is an optimistic attitude in the organization that is not willing to accept that certain problems will be always present. Supporting a proactive approach to problem solving asserts that there are permanent solutions to problems. Maintaining quality in a service system helps to support employee morale, since employees can then take pride in the level of service they are offering, Positive service contacts, because they are based on a quality program, make the interaction between service provider and customer easier to fulfill. Quality goals also involve employees to offer newer ways to accomplish service goals. In this way, the service provider takes a personal position and stake in a service delivery system. Ritz-Carlton, for example, goes the extra mile in generating associate "buy-in" to quality improvement initiatives. Each Ritz-Carlton property has a T-3 team, composed of managers and associates from all functional areas, who collectively derive strategies for solving and implementing action plans to improve the property's three biggest quality deficits (Michelli, 2008).

Bettencourt (1997, pp. 398–99) finds that the "relationship between satisfaction and loyalty behaviors is mediated by customer commitment." In achieving customer commitment, fulfilling "customer expectations and needs appears most affective" in assuring a high level of perceived service quality. According to Liswood (1987), retention marketing leads to earned loyalty needs. This kind of marketing has to be concerned with the quality and type of customer interaction in the service situation. Whether received directly through interpersonal exchanges or indirectly by telephone, computer, or customer surveys and focus groups, this marketing information means being able to keep current customers happy and satisfied. In a study that modeled post-consumption satisfaction, Voss and Parasuraman (1995, p. 36) tested a service quality model in a manipulated low- and high-end hotel. Employee quality was found to be an important common factor in the service quality model. Results from the analyses revealed that if a firm is providing a high level of service, it would do well to elevate customers' reference quality rather than deteriorate it. The results further suggested that high service quality provides a differential advantage only if consumers' reference quality is also high. Firms offering a low level of service, on the other hand, will benefit from deflating customers' reference quality standards of expectation. Since the standards are not high among customers, then the firm can outperform by exceeding expectations and delighting the customer in these lower service situations.

In defining service quality, Collier (1994, pp. 165–68) focuses on whether customers' specifications were satisfied, whether the customer received fair value for the price, whether the quality of service was fit for use, and whether the service personnel were up to the task. Monetary cost or price is one type of burden; nonmonetary costs, such as incompetence, slowness, or inconvenience, are another kind that compromise service quality (Berry, 1999). In considering price as a key variable in the service equation, there are at least three types of customer. There is the price-sensitive customer, who focuses on the comparative price of a service and will change providers if the price exceeds that of comparable competitors. Then there is the price–quality customer, who balances price against quality in a balanced trade-off accounting for 50 percent of the market. Finally, there is the time- and quality-sensitive customer, who will pay a premium to conserve time and increase efficiency, performance, and quality (Blumberg, 1991, p. 84).

Price becomes part of understanding the value of the service performance. For example, if you pay a thousand dollars for a one-way ticket to fly to Los Angeles, you expect that an airline would provide more than a seat. Service systems are about how value is delivered to the customer through a company's policies, procedures, and processes that are defined by the customer as being of high or low quality value. Value is a combination of customer service quality and price (Collier, 1994, pp. 7, 32). In a tourist situation, what the customer gets in a service encounter is a cultural experience involving lodging, food, transportation, recreation/entertainment, and a functional experience in how the service was delivered by the organization and persons working for the travel enterprise. "One of the biggest mistakes managers make is assuming that value and price mean the same thing to customers" (Berry, 1999, pp. 12, 16, 20–21). Price is part of the value received, but only the monetary part. Value also includes the benefits the customer receives from the service. Managers can be so focused on the goods and service price they are providing that they forget that values and beliefs forge a bond with the customer, which stands for something. Given that customer expectation, Albrecht (1992, pp. 112–14) clearly identifies certain levels of perceived customer values used in judging a service. First is the *basic*, where the essentials that would be common in every situation are present. Next is the *expected*, or what the customer has come to take for granted. Following these is the *desired*, or what would be nice and would be appreciated if the service experience included them. Finally there is the *unanticipated* or *surprise* factor – something exceptional that reaches beyond the expected. "Customers are loyal because they get the best value, not because a company does the best job in promoting its product or service" (Reichheld, 1994, p. 245). All service companies must stay on top of the changing value needs of their customers. "When customers find the quality of the core product and the relationship benefit compare favorably with the price they pay, they will perceive the product to be of superior value than other brands" (Liljander, 2000, p. 171).

Loyalty goal and profit consequence

Loyalty

It goes without saying that customer loyalty is a must. "Unlike satisfaction, loyalty has both attitudinal and behavioral components i.e. making repeated purchases, purchasing across service lines, referring others, and resisting the pull of competitors" (Baloglu, 2001). It is important to treat each transaction as significant, directed, and tailored as much as possible to that particular customer. Flexibility and adaptability to the needs of customers is essential in a loyalty-based marketing system. "Customer loyalty can be defined and measured in terms of the amount and the quality of transactions between parties" Diller (2000, p. 30). In that sense, "one of the greatest benefits of customer service is customer loyalty. This is true because most business is repeat business," but that service not only can maintain loyalty, but can help restore it is a double bonus (Tschohl and Franzmeier, 1991, pp. 18, 20). The quest for customer loyalty builds on knowledge of the customer's wishes. "Guessing isn't good enough," neither is one annual survey to "keep the data fresh" (Schaaf, 1995, p. 121). When asking a customer who just left a five-star resort in Arizona what they did to deserve that kind of accolade, the reply was simple but profound, "attention to detail." "(If) it's in the details ... that's [where] some of the most valuable insights will be found" (Schaaf, 1995, p. 121). Perhaps few hospitality firms understand attention to detail better than Ritz-Carlton, whose associates each carry "preference pads" to record guests' preferences that will later be recorded in the company's guest database (Michelli, 2008).

There are limits to be put on any service practice. A Hyatt spokesperson, calling for the use of judgment when formulating a service strategy, said in a speech to the American Hotel and Motel Association: "it means that when you serve a Bloody Mary, you don't have to serve a vegetable garden on top of it. Hyatt Hotels, as much as any company, was responsible for growing that vegetable garden" (Schaaf, 1995, p. 221). The alternative is first to find out and determine whether your guests want the garden and are willing to pay for it. Any quality initiative should be viewed as a financial investment in the sense that the quality initiative that is projected to produce the most return on investment (in terms of customer satisfaction) is the one that should be implemented (Rust *et al.*, 2004). Again, it is worth repeating that "customers appreciate being asked and listened to, and tend to reward close-loop communication with loyalty" (Scheuing, 1999, p. 30). A successful loyalty program is "not static ... it must constantly be updated, improved, and adjusted as conditions and people change" (Griffin, 1995, p. 228). Brand loyalty depends on three factors: "customer satisfaction," "the customer's perceived reliability of the service," and the "effective two way communication between the customers and the company" (Vavra, 1992, p. 64). Yoon and Uysal (2005) confirm that destination loyalty has relationships not only with motivation, but also with satisfaction. If tourists as customers are satisfied with their travel experiences, they are more likely to recommend them to other people. Satisfaction directly affects loyalty in a positive direction. Their study also indicates that satisfaction is determined to be a mediating construct between motivation and destination loyalty.

As a customer becomes familiar with various services, they begin to trust their outcomes. "Trust is a logical outgrowth of principles and ethics. It takes time to build. It is a step-by-step iterative process, but it is enduring in terms of the loyalty that it engenders on both sides" (Bhote, 1996, p. 45). If the customer does not trust the service provider, then the organization also becomes suspect. Both reputations are seen to be important for maintaining loyalty. If there is little trust, the customer will not fully disclose their expectations or wishes, and may be just be marking time to find themselves a better provider. "Loyalty is more than a customer's long relationship with a particular company ... it is a feeling of affinity or attachment to a firm's products or services" (Day, 1999, pp. 146–47). Loyalty produces positive results and outcomes for the service provider; the biggest and most obvious is that "the customer who is trusted and accommodated comes back for more. We are attracted to those who show an interest in serving us well" (Broydrick, 1994, p. 48).

Having once developed a loyal client advocate, there is then the opportunity to multiply that relationship through word-of-mouth testimonials and support, which is a powerful and inexpensive way for expanding client/customer expansion. Customer loyalty is driven by "overall satisfaction and commitment of the customer to repeat purchases, willingness to recommend, and resistance to switch to competitors" (Timm, 1998, p. 15).

The role of loyalty in corporate profit analyses cannot now be denied. It has not always been the case, however, that service quality and profitability were thought to be related, but "since the early 1990s, the relationship has been persuasively established" (Rust *et al.*, 2000, p. 188). Customer satisfaction guarantees a "source of profits" (Hanan and Karp, 1989, p. 22). Clear linkages are reported between satisfaction, loyalty, and profitability, noted as the main outcome of customer involvement and commitment (Zeithaml and Bitner, 2000, p. 80). Understanding service profit hinges on a customer's perceived level of satisfaction and whether they achieve loyalty status. As an effect, loyalty ensures that a company has delivered superior value through repeated use of the company's tourist and travel services. As a cause, revenues and market share grow, while sustainable growth attracts more highly productive employees. Loyalty also produces customer savings through the retention of customers and shareholders, who act more like partners to stabilize a company. Rust *et al.* (2000, p. 189) cite studies showing that by improving service satisfaction, and satisfaction at the attribute and process level, profitability increases (Bolton and Drew, 1991; Rust *et al.*, 1994, 1995; Zeithaml *et al.*, 1996). Not all customer segments, however, contribute equally to a company's profit; the pyramid must still be recognized and the most important customer segment cared after. As Hanan and Karp (1989, p. 22) indicate, the business mission is to create and grow the maximum number of satisfied customers for the company in the most cost-effective manner, thereby maximizing profits. Oliver (1997, p. 408) concurs that the ultimate test of the effect of long-term satisfaction is loyalty-generated profit. Maximizing customer satisfaction is crucial for a sustained business activity.

9   Where do we go from here?

Preview

Following a brief recap of content, this chapter takes a look at future directions in frontline provider research. In doing so, it explains, for example, how emotional intelligence screening can be used to enhance employee-selection processes. Since highly emotionally intelligent individuals possess an enhanced ability to manage their emotions, and handle interpersonal relationships better than those with lower levels of emotional intelligence, gauging this attribute in the selection of frontline service providers is vital. After discussing directions in selection, technologies such as data- and text-mining are used to demonstrate emerging technologies on the customer information front. Emerging data- and text-mining technologies can uncover nonobvious patterns in data and text files that can provide insight into how to serve the customer better. The chapter concludes with coverage of trends in employee motivational strategies and in identifying sustainable competitive advantages.

Recap: building a service encounter strategy

While not a panacea for success, we contend that internalizing and implementing the information contained in this book will offer service firms a formidable advantage over their competitors. The first two chapters define encounter theory, the theoretical model of social relationships upon which much later inquiry is premised. In doing so, these opening pages describe the importance of social situations and identify the observable attributes that aid in describing the intersubjective set. Along these lines, distinctions are enumerated between interactive encounters and relational service situations, and the power of emotions and motivations in the encounter situation is addressed.

Chapters 3 and 4 explain the critical need to properly understand the wants and motivations of disparate customer segments, and role of the service manager in accommodating those wants and motivations from a social interaction perspective. A management visioning process is outlined, and the reliance of the process and outcomes on frontline interactions is stressed.

Thus, according to this logic, information generated at the frontline must be used to formulate strategies, which must be communicated clearly to frontline actors to avoid role ambiguity and its negative correlates.

Chapters 5 and 6 describe the positioning of the service provider role, and means by which to appeal to the customer and provider roles through various communication channels. These discussions stress the strong bidirectional association between employee and customer satisfaction. Stated differently, frontline providers who perceive high levels of distributive, procedural, and interactional justice are more prone to deliver service that leaves customers with mirroring justice perceptions.

Next, Chapter 7 describes in detail the verbal communication skills most likely to result in customer rapport and ultimate satisfaction. Nonverbal communication is also discussed at length in this section. Since most human communication is a result of nonverbal cues, this content is quintessential for service providers to understand and practice. The chapter concludes by addressing how various combinations of verbal and nonverbal habits can be used to illustrate to customers that they are being listened to during frontline interactions.

Chapter 8 extends beyond previous discussions by providing direction on how to achieve customer delight and customer loyalty. It is also indicated that it is possible for firms to invest too much time and effort in service quality, therefore they must weigh service quality initiatives against each other to assess their potential returns. This process mandates that firms have an understanding of which service-related amenities customers value the most. And this final chapter offers a discussion of emerging areas of interest in frontline interactions:

Future directions in recruiting and selecting frontline personnel

Not everyone is well-suited to be a frontline customer service provider. As discussed, customer contact personnel must possess the proper combination of traits. Thus, evidently, a firm's ability to provide customers with superior service at the frontline is contingent upon having top-rate employee recruiting and selection programs. In terms of recruiting, we posit that the hospitality and tourism firms that have a well-liked and distinct brand personality in the marketplace will have the best ability to recruit top personnel. In other words, individuals desire to identify psychologically with a potential employer. Therefore it may be wise for firms to conduct research to determine external constituents' perceptions of their brand personality. Sentence completion and word-association techniques are often useful in eliciting brand personality perceptions (for example, "people visit firm x because ... "). Firms can use the results from these research initiatives to change, reinforce, or develop their brand's personality in their integrated marketing communications. Again, since talented service providers are few and far between, possessing a distinct and appealing brand personality should aid recruitment. We extend this logic to propose that, just as consumers seek self-concept congruity between themselves and their purchases, they often also seek this same self-concept congruity between themselves and the brand at which they are employed. Thus it is critical for service providers to be in possession of up-to-date knowledge of constituencies' perceptions regarding their brand's personalities and identities.

Also in terms of recruitment, we predict that nontraditional means of attracting staff will become even more critical in future years as competition in the industry continues to escalate. Nontraditional types of recruiting come in many forms. For one, service managers are advised always to be on the lookout for exceptional providers in other service settings and drop them a business card if appropriate. Likewise, service managers should seek talent from nontypical sources, such as from the pool of retirees who are often eager for extra income and socialization. Of course, service managers must remain aware that their best recruiting mechanism is happy employees. Creatively designed incentive programs that encourage employees to recruit other qualified individuals to the firm should therefore be in place.

Next, in terms of selection, as the horizon continues to become saturated with tourism companies, those firms that have well-structured and highly refined selection procedures will have a distinct advantage over those that do not. Behavioral interviewing methods are a must. Asking applicants situational questions that are difficult to respond to with pre-scripted answers is extremely useful in gauging communication ability and service-related attitudes. There is an art to properly administering behavioral interviewing; hence firms are advised to mandate interviewer training. Trained behavioral interviewers can become well-versed in crafting interview questions that require the respondent to provide (1) a situation, (2) an action, and (3) results (SAR) in all responses. Along these lines, not only managers but also other frontline staff members can be trained as interviewers in order to enhance the firm's ability to judge the suitability of an applicant from multiple perspectives.

Also with regard to selection, we propose that all firms should consider some sort of emotional intelligence screening of frontline applicants. This is recommended because handling the stress of the frontline requires that providers have the ability to manage their own emotions and recognize the emotions of others. Firms could develop their own emotional intelligence survey items, or better yet, adopt an emotional intelligence scale from extant literature. There are a number of existing scales that demonstrate high reliability and validity and can be applied appropriately to the selection process of frontline providers in tourism settings (e.g. Schutte *et al.*, 1998).

Emerging ways of arming the frontline with customer information

With the proliferation of modern database technology, many firms are likely drowning in customer data. Yet we predict that those firms that are able to implement successful data-mining programs will have a distinct advantage over their competitors. To reiterate from a previous chapter, data-mining entails the use of software to detect useful and nonobvious trends in data. For example, the "association" task of data-mining software can find connections between records in a database; the "forecasting" task can predict future values of continuous data variables; and the "deviation detection" task can identify data anomalies. With the implementation of an effective data-mining program, it is possible for frontline associates to be better prepared to accommodate customers upon their arrival. For instance, mined information could indicate to frontline staff which customer segments are most likely to request particular amenities.

While it is not yet commonly used, in future years arming frontline providers with the proper information will likely entail conducting sentiment analysis with text-mining software. Text-mining can be described as the use of software to extract patterns from natural language text. A promising application of text-mining technology for hospitality and tourism firms is in the analysis of open-ended comments on customer comment cards and customer surveys. Currently, open-ended responses are likely read by a select group of individuals within a firm, but then what happens to the information? It is unlikely that firms currently have mechanisms in place to determine if a written comment is an anomaly, or if it has sufficient validity. With text-mining technology, the comments can be analyzed in order to detect patterns or trends in customer sentiments regarding various facets of a firm's offerings. In another application of text-mining technology, firms can analyze the comments written in internet blogs about their offerings and performance.

Since blogging is rapidly becoming a common consumer activity, this text-mining application can provide firms with the ability to analyze a blog's content. Travel and tourism is one of the most popular topics across all internet blogs, so opportunities to mine these narratives for insights in how to best serve consumers on the frontline are ripe. As with information resulting from data-mining initiatives, presuming that the mined information is shared with frontline providers, enhanced customer service could result.

The combined use of data-mining and text-mining technologies would likely provide insight into some interesting consumer behavior trends. One trend that we foresee is that, in the unstable world in which we reside, the safety and security concerns of travelers will remain at the forefront. For instance, many of the staff members of the Trident-Oberoi and Taj Mahal Hotels in Mumbai were hailed as heroes following the November 2008 terrorist attacks at their properties. We also propose that detailed analysis of consumer data will continue to unravel more cross-cultural consumer behavior differences. For example, perceptions of justice and fairness following a service failure and recovery likely vary by culture. The use of data- and text-mining technologies can be used to substantiate these positions. In a nutshell, firms should consider employing these emerging data- and text-mining technologies to extract fine-grained customer information.

Text-mined and data-mined information can also yield deeper insights into consumer responses to various frontline service initiatives. For example, it seems possible that certain expected service attributes do not lead to significant increases in satisfaction if present, but might cause dissatisfaction if not available. Conversely, other unexpected service attributes may not trigger dissatisfaction if not present, but catapult satisfaction to higher levels if offered. Thus text- and data-mining programs can provide this consumer-centric knowledge to frontline providers. Since all investments in service quality initiatives do not have equal returns, this information can be used to compare the potential returns of those being utilized or considered for adoption.

An additional technological method for arming frontline associates with useful customer information is also emerging within the industry; in our assessment, the Ritz-Carlton Corporation has paved the way. As mentioned in Chapter 8, at Ritz-Carlton frontline employees carry "preference pads" on which they manually record guests' habits that they observe. These transcriptions are then given to line managers, who enter the information into the company's guest information system (named Mystique). Information about a guest in Mystique may include the individual's preferred pillow type or even his/her preferred name (e.g. James vs. Jim). For privacy and control purposes, only authorized individuals within the company have access to the Mystique system. Nevertheless, in each of the hotel's departments, pre-shift meetings are held and the appropriate Mystique information about arriving guests is disseminated among the frontline staff. Such activities result in top-rate personalized service. While this system as implemented by Ritz-Carlton appears very straightforward, such systems are not commonplace in the industry. Thus we propose that both hospitality and tourism providers should develop comparable customer preference systems tailored to the specifics of their operations. Since emotions in service settings are known to be contagious, we posit that such systems will ultimately result in bolstered customer and employee satisfaction ratings.

New insights into making things easier at the frontline

As discussed at several points in this book, a customer's satisfaction judgment is a result of a mental comparison between an actual experience and expectations. That is, if the actual experience exceeds expectations, then the customer is left satisfied. Therefore we postulate that a competitive advantage will be gained by the firm that knows best how to shape customer expectations in its integrated marketing communications. Components of integrated marketing communications can include items such advertisements, website design and content, and public relations initiatives. If expectations are set too low, then individuals might be unwilling to try a provider; conversely, communications that exaggerate offerings artificially inflate expectations. Striking the correct balance requires the appropriate blend of customer-focused and competitor-focused research. Firms that can achieve this balance will alleviate strain on the frontline staff because customers will arrive with properly founded and well-formulated expectations.

While the notion of blueprinting a servicescape has been present in the academic literature for nearly two decades, to the best of our knowledge, it has failed to gain critical mass in practice. A proper service blueprint should plot: (1) the areas where customers can flow; (2) the areas where customers cannot go, but which they can see; and (3) the back-of-house areas restricted to employees. We argue that taking the time to plot a detailed service blueprint accurately can yield several valuable benefits. First, a service blueprint can show a frontline associate how his/her role ties in to the rest of the service offering. Second, blueprinting can illuminate inefficiencies in systems that are designed to service customers. Third, through blueprinting, firms can identify additional ways to serve customers at various contact points. While blueprinting is not a guarantee for success in the service world, we argue that the benefits are sizable and far outweigh the costs. Since poor service and low morale at the frontline are often the result of inefficient service systems, those firms that actively blueprint their servicescape should have an advantage over those that do not.

In addition to blueprinting, it is our observation that the qualitative research technique known as photo-elicitation is under-utilized in the industry. The photo-elicitation research technique can be described as an in-depth interview that is guided by a photograph(s). It is our position that if a service manager were to snap photos of frontline associates while working (with their permission), they could then use the photos to conduct some insightful photo-elicitation sessions to determine what aspects of the frontline need to be improved. In the photo-elicitation session, for example, the manager would sit down with the associate who appears in the photo and could ask him/her to view the photo and recollect what she/he was thinking at the time when the photo was taken. This is a useful research technique because the photo will likely elicit far more thoughts than an in-depth interview with no photo present. Moreover, unlike traditional interviews, photo-elicitation sessions are not influenced by the researcher's questioning style or sequence. Another benefit inherent in the technique is that the service manager does not specify the salient attributes being studied; thus the frontline provider may comment on job facets not previously considered by the manager. Lastly, in comparison with other interviewing methods, in photo-elicitation the subjects are often more at ease because attention is focused on the photo as opposed to being on the subjects. Based on these streams of logic, we contend that service firms should consider applying the use of photo-elicitation to draw out what improvements need to be made at customer-contact points. And just as these sessions can be held with associates, they can also be held with customers – potentially providing some unique perspectives.

We also take the position that the proper atmospheric variables can make life easier at the frontline. We believe future research will continue to reveal the large role that atmospheric cues play in employee and consumer psychology. The proper use of music, for example, can relax customers and employees alike, creating better frames of mind in which to interact. Olfactory cues can achieve similar results; firms should consider the use of ambient scents at the frontline. The same can be said for the sense of touch. Touching various textures can create hedonic pleasure for both customers and employees. Likewise, visual cues also play a large role in human psychology. A visually clean and uncluttered servicescape has mood-enhancing effects for employees and guests. Thus we urge service providers to consider all the human senses when designing their physical offerings, as we predict that research has merely begun to scratch the surface in this area. The testing of combinations and congruencies between various facets in the ambient environment may also have potential in providing employees and customers with enhanced servicescapes in which to interact.

In a hospitality and tourism context, new technologies that can be used on the frontline are perhaps evolving more rapidly now than ever before. For example, point-of-sale computer systems are quickly becoming more efficient; GPS devices have many potential applications in tourism settings; and wireless internet devices can be of service to both employees and customers in diverse tourism locations. This rapid technological advancement puts service providers at risk of being left technologically behind competitors. Hospitality and tourism providers of today (and in the future) must possess the expertise to sift through the ever-increasing tsunami of emerging technological devices and to identify the ones that have the best return on investment in terms of frontline efficiencies leading to enhanced employee and customer satisfaction. Just as important, however, is that firms must be aware that technological adoptions can backfire (for example through reduced efficiency and satisfaction) without proper implementation, training, and employee buy-in. Those firms that can make and implement the wisest technologically related decisions will have an advantage in frontline interactions.

Motivating the modern frontline workforce

As discussed throughout this book, there is no denying that role ambiguity, role conflict, and lack of psychological empowerment are key deflators of employee motivation in the service sector. Moving forward, further examination of the interplay between these three constructs may prove useful in enhancing our understanding of frontline interactions. Under what conditions, for example, does empowerment have positive or negative relationships with role ambiguity and role conflict? Evidently, empowerment can yield a number of positive outcomes at the frontline because it expedites problem resolution and facilitates employees' ownership of tasks. In part for these reasons, Taco Bell outlets have recently begun to stress the importance of empowerment among their frontline staff. Nevertheless, there is still sizable room for research to be conducted regarding the antecedents, consequences and correlates of empowerment. For instance, does one type of managerial leadership style lend itself better to employees' acceptance of decisional authority than competing leadership styles? Even the effects of a worker's cultural norms on his/her comfort with empowerment have yet to be fully examined.

Regarding culture, one thing unique to today's frontline hospitality tourism workforce is the ethnic diversity that characterizes it. For example, in the USA, the vast majority of frontline hospitality workers are from ethnic minorities. Likewise, in another example, ethnic diversity abounds in the European workforce with the common migration of workers from Eastern to Western European countries. A key to future success in competing on the tourism frontline is to know how best to manage and harness this ethnic diversity.

In response to this ethnic diversity, firms should adjust their training starting points. While requiring additional training for some ethnic groups as opposed to others would likely open up a legal nightmare, what firms could do is offer daily ten-minute training sessions on a variety of topics. Frontline staff could be invited to join the session if they feel that they can benefit from it, or if their performance evaluations identify weaknesses in the given areas. Since ethnically diverse workers come from myriad backgrounds, such training opportunities would be useful in homogenizing the appropriate service standards.

Those entrusted with managing a diverse set of frontline employees must also understand that interest in various forms of motivation can vary by culture. Evidently, for both morale and legal purposes, all of a firm's employees should be treated the same, but an understanding of the correlation between certain ethnicities and motivators can be useful in a firm's decision-making. For example, if a hospitality property's staff is primarily Hispanic, management should consider hiring enough workers to rotate Sundays off, since many Hispanic cultures places great value on not working on Sunday. Along the same lines, we predict that those firms that best understand cultural differences in communication will have an advantage in coming years. For instance, some cultures have low-context, explicit verbal communication styles (e.g. the Swiss) and others have high-context, implicit communication patterns (e.g. the Japanese) (see Box 5.3). An understanding of both motivational and communication patterns is needed to manage diverse workers most effectively.

Lastly, in order to enhance cohesiveness among frontline staff, those in charge must use training opportunities to reduce any ethnocentric attitudes that may exist among them. For a frontline provider to think that his/her own culture knows best how to do things can only lead to conflict and lack of teamwork on the job. Similarly, a manager will unconsciously use his/her own cultural values and experiences as a basis for decisions – this is known as a "self-reference criterion." Such a reliance on one's own cultural background in decision-making can be demotivating to a multicultural work team; thus education and cultural training must be used to minimize the influence of self-reference criteria.

Staying one step ahead on the frontline

As we all know, a service offering cannot readily be patented. Providers in the field must therefore continually seek and implement new ways of beating their competitors at the customer frontline. It is our position, for example, that the first firm that offers face recognition and name recall training for its frontline employees will have a sizable advantage over the last firm to offer such training. The same can be said for any customer service innovation – the first firm that implements it spurs customer delight because the customer is pleasantly surprised, but the last firm to implement it is simply providing something that is commonly expected. Since services cannot be patented, the best service innovations typically eventually evolve from unique innovations to basic and expected offerings. For instance, as technological advances cause customer–provider co-production of the service experience to become more commonplace, those firms that develop innovative techniques to serve both the customers who embrace the technology and those who resist the technology will have a competitive advantage over competitors who are slower to take such actions.

Therefore, after reading and digesting the content of this book, we beckon hospitality and tourism providers to (1) scan and stay on a par with competitors' offerings; (2) find and implement novel ideas that can WOW customers at the frontline; (3) select the new ideas that promise the greatest return on investment; (4) choose the service innovations that will likely have the greatest response lag among competitors; and (5) above all else, deliver the fundamentals consistently at the frontline. While this may seem to be a tall order, we remind you of the words of Walt Disney: "If you dream it, you can do it. Always remember that this whole thing was started with a dream and a mouse." Good luck.

Bibliography

Ahlert, H. (2000) 'Enterprise management: integrating corporate and customer information', in T. Hennig-Thurau and U. Hansen (eds), *Relationship Marketing*. New York: Springer.

Ahuvia, A. (2005) 'Beyond the extended self: loved objects and consumers' identity narratives', *Journal of Consumer Research*, 32(1): 171–84.

Albrecht, K. (1992) *The Only Thing That Matters*. New York: Harper Business.

Albrecht, S. L., Chadwick, B. A. and Jacobson, C. K. (1987) *Social Psychology*. Englewood Cliffs, NJ: Prentice Hall.

Alea, P. V. and Chekouras, R. (1999) 'The care and handling of the mature market', in R. Zemke and J. A. Woods (eds), *Best Practices in Customer Service*. Amherst, MA: HRD Press.

Alexander, C. N. and Lauderdale, P. (1977) 'Situated identities and social influence', *Sociometry*, 40(3): 225–33.

Allen, C. T., McQuarrie, E. F. and Barr, T. F. (1998) *Implementing the Marketing Concept One Employee at a Time: Pinpointing Beliefs about Customer Focus as a Lever for Organizational Renewal*, Report No. 98-125. Cambridge, MA: Marketing Science Institute.

Altinay, L., Altinay, E. and Gannon, J. (2008) 'Exploring the relationship between the human resource management practices and growth in small service firms', *The Services Industries Journal*, 28(7): 919–37.

Amaldoss, W. and Jain, S. (2008) 'Trading up: a strategic analysis of reference group effects', *Marketing Science*, 27(5): 932–42.

Amenumey, E. K. and Lockwood, A. (2008) 'Psychological climate and psychological empowerment: an exploration in a luxury UK hotel group', *Tourism and Hospitality Research*, 8(4): 265–81.

Andaleeb, S. S. and Conway, C. (2006) 'Customer satisfaction in the restaurant industry: an examination of the transaction-specific model', *Journal of Services Marketing*, 20(1): 3–11.

Anderson, E. W. and Fornell, C. (2000) 'Foundations of the American customer satisfaction index', *Total Quality Management*, 11(7): 869–81.

Anderson, K. and Zemke, R. (1991) *Delivering Knock Your Socks Off Service*. New York: AMACOM.

Anderson, K. (1999) 'Standards for service: from countability to accountability', in R. Zemke and J. A. Woods (eds), *Best Practices in Customer Service*. Amherst, MA: HRD Press.

Andrews, C. (2008) 'Use behavioral interviewing to hire right the first time', *Hotel and Motel Management*, 223(20): 18.

Armistead, C. G. and Clark, G. (1994) *Outstanding Customer Service*. New York: Irwin.

Arthur, M. M. (2003) 'Share price reactions to work-family initiatives: an institutional perspective', *Academy of Management Journal*, 46(4): 497–505.

Ashforth, B. E. and Humphrey, R. H. (1993) 'Emotional labor in service roles: the influence of identity', *Academy of Management Review*, 18(1): 88–115.

Axtell, R. E. (1991) *Gestures*. New York: John Wiley & Sons.

Babin, B. J. and Boles, J. S. (1998) 'Employee behavior in a service environment: a model and test of potential differences between men and women', *Journal of Marketing*, 62 (April): 77–91.

Babin, B. J., Boles, J. S. and Robin, D. P. (2000) 'Representing the perceived ethical work climate among marketing employees', *Journal of the Academy of Marketing Science*, 28(3): 345–58.

Baldasare, P. M. and Mittal, V. (1997) 'Strategies to manage customer relationships', *Marketing News*, 31(11): 6.

Baker, K. G., Hozier, G. C. Jr and Rogers, R. D. (1994) 'Marketing research theory and methodology and the tourism industry: a nontechnical discussion', *Journal of Travel Research*, 34(3): 3–7.

Baker, W. and Sinkula, J. (1999) 'The synergistic effect of market orientation and learning orientation on organizational performance', *Journal of the Academy of Marketing Science*, 27(4): 411–27.

Bakker, A. B., Demerouti, E., De Boer, E. and Schaufeli, W. B. (2003) 'Job demands and job resources as predictors of absence duration and absence frequency', *Journal of Vocational Behavior*, 62(2): 341–56.

Baloglu, S. (2001) 'An investigation of a loyalty typology and the multidestination loyalty of international travelers', *Tourism Analysis*, 6(1): 41–52.

Barnes, J. (1994) 'The role of internal marketing: if the staff won't buy it, why should the customer?', *Irish Marketing Review – Dublin*, 5: 55–64.

Barnes, J. G. (2000) 'Closeness in customer relationships: examining the payback from getting closer to the customer', in T. Hennig-Thurau and U. Hansen (eds), *Relationship Marketing*. New York: Springer.

Bateson, J. (2002) 'Consumer performance and quality in services', *Managing Service Quality*, 12(4): 206–9.

Batson, D. C. (1995) 'Prosocial motivation: why do we help others?' in A. Tesser (ed.), *Advanced Social Psychology*. New York: McGraw-Hill.

Bell, R. A. (1987) 'Social involvement', in J. C. McCroskey and J. A. Daly (eds), *Personality and Interpersonal Communication*. Newbury Park, CA: Sage.

Bell, C. R. and Zemke, R. (1992) *Managing Knock Your Socks Off Service*. New York: AMACOM.

Bendapudi, N. and Leone, R. (2003) 'Psychological implications of customer participation in co-production', *Journal of Marketing*, 67(1): 14–28.

Bennis, W. (1979) 'Emotional expressions in interpersonal relationships', in W. Bennis, J. Van Maanen, E. H. Schein and F. I. Steele (eds), *Essays in Interpersonal Dynamics*. Homewood, IL: Dorsey Press.

Berman, B. (2005) 'How to delight customers', *California Management Review*, 48(1): 129–51.

Berry, L. L. (1983) 'Relationship marketing', in A. Payne, C. Martin, M. Clark and H. Peck (eds), *Relationship Marketing for the Competitive Advantage* (1998 edn). Oxford: Butterworth-Heinemann.

—— (1995) *On Great Service*. New York: The Free Press.

—— (1999) *Discovering the Soul of Service*. New York: The Free Press.

—— (2000) 'Cultivating service brand equity', *Journal of the Academy of Marketing Science*, 28(1): 128–37.

Berry, L. L., Zeithaml, V. A. and Parasuraman, A. (1990) 'Five imperatives for improving service quality', *Sloan Management Review*, 31(4): 29–38.

Bettencourt, L. A. (1997) 'Customer voluntary performance: customers as partners in service delivery', *Journal of Retailing*, 73(3): 383–406.

Bhote, K. R. (1996) *Beyond Customer Satisfaction to Customer Loyalty*. New York: AMA Membership Publications Division.

Biddle, B. J. and Thomas, E. J. (1966) 'Basic concepts for classifying the phenomena of role', in B. J. Biddle and E. J. Thomas (eds), *Role Theory*. New York: John Wiley & Sons.

Bitner, M. J. and Hubbert, A. R. (1994) 'Overall satisfaction versus quality: the customer's voice', in R. T. Rust and R. L. Oliver (eds), *Service Quality*. Thousand Oaks, CA: Sage.

Bjarnadottir, A. (1998) 'Individual performance in customer service roles', *Dissertation Abstracts International*, 58(10-B): 5680.

Blackwell, R. D. (1997) *From Mind to Market*. New York: Harper Business.

Blanchard, K. H. (1989) 'The role of a manager', *Journal for Quality & Participation*, (September): 8–12.

Blanchard, K. and Bowles, S. (1998) *Gung Ho*. New York: William Morrow and Company.

Blattberg, R. C., Getz, G. and Thomas, J. S. (2001) *Customer Equity*. Boston, MA: Harvard Business School Press.

Blumberg, D. F. (1991) *Managing Service as a Strategic Profit Center*. New York: McGraw-Hill.

Blumenthal, R. (2005) 'Failing to meet great expectations', *Barrons*, 85(4): 13.

Bly, R. W. (1993) *Keeping Clients Satisfied*. Englewood Cliffs, NJ: Prentice Hall.

Bolton, R. N. and Drew, J. (1991) 'A longitudinal analysis of the impact of service changes on customer attitudes', *Journal of Marketing*, 55: 1–8.

Bonn, M. A., Joseph-Mathews, S. M., Dai, M., Hayes, S. and Cave, J. (2007) 'Heritage/culture attraction atmospherics: creating the right environment for the heritage/cultural visitor', *Journal of Travel Research*, 45 (February): 345–54.

Botschen, G. (2000) 'Internationalization of encounter-based relationship strategies', in T. Hennig-Thurau and U. Hansen (eds), *Relationship Marketing*. New York: Springer.

Boulding, W., Kalra, A., Staelin, R. and Zeithaml, V. (1993) 'A dynamic process model of service quality: from expectations to behavioral intentions', *Journal of Marketing Research*, 30(1): 7–27.

Bowen, D. E. and Lawler, E. E. (1992) 'The empowerment of service workers: what, why, how, and when', in A. Payne, C. Martin, M. Clark and H. Peck (eds), *Relationship Marketing for the Competitive Advantage* (1998 edn). Oxford: Butterworth-Heinemann.

Bower, B. (1992) 'False impressions', *Science News*, 141 (March 28): 200–203.

Brantley, R. L. (1988) 'Customer service representatives play pivotal roles', *Savings Institutions*, 109(9): 98–99.

Briton, N. J. and Hall, J. A. (1995) 'Beliefs about female and male nonverbal communication', *Sex Roles*, 32(1–2): 79–90.

Brock, F. (2002) 'Catering to the elderly can pay off', *The New York Times*, (February 3): BU 11.

Brown, A. (1989) *Customer Care Management*. Oxford: Heinemann Professional.

Brown, S. (1996) 'Enhancing profit', *Executive Excellence*. 13(8): 9.

Brown, S. A. (1995) *What Customers Value Most*. Toronto, Canada: John Wiley & Sons.

—— (1999) *Strategic Customer Care*. Toronto, Canada: John Wiley & Sons.

Brownell, E. O. (2000) 'Magical words create customer satisfaction and loyalty'. *Manage*, 51(3): 10.

Broydrick, S. C. (1994) *How May I Help You?* New York: Irwin.

Buchanan, R. and Gilles, C. (1990) 'Value managed relationships: the key to customer retention and profitability', in A. Payne, C. Martin, M. Clark and H. Peck (eds), *Relationship Marketing and Competitive Advantage* (1998 edn). Oxford: Butterworth-Heinemann.

Burton, D. (2002) 'Consumer education and service quality: conceptual issues and practical implications'. *Journal of Services Marketing*, 16(2): 125–243.

Buttle, F. (1996) 'Relationship marketing', in F. Buttle (ed.) *Relationship Marketing*. London: Paul Chapman Publishing.

Callero, P. L. (1992) 'The meaning of self-in-role: a modified measure of role-identity'. *Social Forces*, 71(2): 485–501.

Canary, D. J. and Cody, H. J. (1994) *Interpersonal Communication*. New York: St Martin's Press.

Cannie, J. K. (1994) *Turning Lost Customers Into Gold*. New York: AMACOM.

Cannie, J. K. and Caplin, D. (1991) *Keeping Customers for Life*. New York: AMACOM.

Cant, M. (1992) 'Quality – the client advantage'. *Facilities*, 10(3), 5–7.

Carr, C. (1990) *Front-Line Customer Service*. New York: John Wiley & Sons.

Cascio, W. F. (2006) 'The economic impact of employee behaviors on organizational performance', *California Management Review*, 48(4): 41–59.

Chakrapani, C. (1998) *How to Measure Service Quality & Customer Satisfaction*. Chicago: American Marketing Association.

Chebat, C. and Kollias, P. (2000) 'The impact of empowerment on customer contact employees' roles in service organizations', *Journal of Service Research*, 3(1), 66–81.

Chernish, W. (2001) 'Empowering service personnel to deliver quality service', in J. Kandampully, C. Mok and B. Sparks (eds), *Service Quality Management in Hospitality, Tourism and Leisure*. Binghamton, NY: Haworth Hospitality Press.

Choi, S. and Mattila, A. S. (2008) 'Perceived controllability and service expectations: influences on customer reactions following service failures', *Journal of Business Research*, 61(1): 24–30.

Ciaramicoli, A. P. and Ketcham, K. (2000) *The Power of Empathy*. New York: Penguin.

Clark, B. (1989) 'Agents need products/services for older clients', *National Underwriter*, 93(40): 11, 14–15, 26–27.

Clark, R., Hartline, M. and Jones, K. (2009) 'The effects of leadership style on hotel employees' commitment to service quality', *Cornell Hospitality Quarterly*, 50(2): 209–31.

Clarke, S. O. (1992) 'A survey for their thoughts. *Small Business Reports*, 17(10), 11–15.

Claycomb, C., Lengnick-Hall, C. A. and Inks, L. W. (2001) 'The customer as a productive resource: a pilot study and strategic implications', *Journal of Business Strategies*, 18(1): 47–69.

Clutterbuck, D. (1989) 'Counsel of care', *Marketing*, (May): 32–33.

Cohen, E. (1974) 'Who is a tourist? a conceptual clarification', *Sociological Review*, 22(4): 527–55.

—— (1972) 'Toward a sociology of international tourism', *Social Research*, 39: 163–82.

—— (1984) 'The sociology of tourism: approaches, problems and findings', *Annual Review of Sociology*, 10: 373–92.

Collier, D. A. (1994) *The Service/ Quality Solution*. New York: Irwin.

Connellan, T. K. and Zemke, R. (1993) *Sustaining Knock Your Socks Off Service*. New York: AMACOM.

Conrad, D. (2001) 'I am your employee', *Casino Executive*, 7(2): 36.

Cooley, C. H. (1998) *On Self and Social Organization*; edited and with an introduction by H.-J. Schubert. Chicago: University of Chicago Press.

Court, A. (2005) 'Hotels try to make your stay personal', *USA Today*, October 25, d13.

Crane, V. M. (1991) 'Satisfaction rests on employees unseen by your customers', *Marketing News*, 25(3): 12.

Crompton, J. L. and MacKay, K. J. (1988) 'Users' perceptions of the relative importance of service quality dimensions in selected public recreation programs', *Leisure Sciences*, 11: 367–75.

Crotts, J., Ford, R., Heung, V. and Ngai, E. (2009) 'Organizational alignment and hospitality firm performance', *International Journal of Culture, Tourism and Hospitality Research*, 3(1): 3–12.

Czepiel, J. A. (1990) 'Service encounters and service relationships: implications for research', *Journal of Business Research*, 20(1): 13–21.

Dann, G. (1996) *The Language of Tourism: A Sociolinguistic Perspective*, Wallingford, UK: CABI.

Davis, F. (1982) 'On the "symbolic" in symbolic interaction', *Symbolic Interaction*, 5(1): 111–26.

Day, G. S. (1999) *The Market Driven Organization*. New York: The Free Press.

DeFrancesco, J. (1990) 'Public relations checklist', *Small Business Reports*, 15(1): 20–23.

Deighton, J. (1994) 'Managing services when the service is a performance', in R. T. Rust and R. L. Oliver (eds), *Service Quality*. Thousand Oaks, CA: Sage.

Denalli, J. (1989) 'Dealing with angry customers', *American Salesman*, 34(5):16–19.

Desatnick, R. L. (1987) *Managing to Keep the Customer*. San Francisco, CA: Jossey-Bass.

DeWitt, T. and Martin, D. (2009) 'Writing a credible form letter: implications for hospitality and tourism service recovery strategy', *International Journal of Culture, Tourism and Hospitality Research*, 3(4): 361–68.

DiBenedetto, B. (2001) 'Lord of the manner', *Casino Executive*, 7(3): 14.

Diller, H. (2000) 'Customer loyalty: Fata Morgana or realistic goal? Managing relationships with customers', in T. Hennig-Thurau and U. Hansen (eds), *Relationship Marketing*. New York: Springer.

Dittmar, H. (1996) 'The social psychology of economic and consumer behavior', in G. R. Semin and K. Fiedler (eds), *Applied Social Psychology*. London: Sage.

Dolnicar, S. and Leisch, F. (2003) 'Winter tourist segments in Austria: identifying stable vacation styles using bagged cluster techniques', *Journal of Travel Research*, 41(1): 281–92.

Dong, B., Evans, K. R. and Zou, S. (2008) 'The effects of customer participation in co-created service recovery', *Journal of the Academy of Marketing Science*, 36(1): 123–37.

Donnelly, J. H. (1992) *Close to the Customer*. Homewood, IL: Business One Irwin.

Drought, S. and McLaughlin, B. (1995) 'Enabling the front line: Investing in people, building value', *Compensation & Benefits Management*, 11(3): 65–70.

Drucker, P. (1977) *People and Performance: The Best of Peter Drucker on Management*, New York: Harper's College Press.

Du, R. Y. and Kamakura, W. A. (2006) 'Household lifecycles and lifestyles in the United States', *Journal of Marketing Research*, 43(1): 121–32.

Duck, S. (1991) *Understanding Relationships*. New York: The Guilford Press.

Dull, S. (2000) 'How much are customer relationship management capabilities really worth? What every CEO should know', in S. Walls, D. L. Zahay and C. Place (eds), *Managing Customer Relationships*, Report No. 00-107. Cambridge, MA: Marketing Science Institute.

Edvardsson, B., Thomasson, B. and Ovretveit, J. (1994) *Quality of Service*. London: McGraw-Hill.

Ekinci, Y. (2003) 'Which comparison should be used for service quality and customer satisfaction?' *Journal of Quality Assurance in Hospitality & Tourism*, 4(3/4): 61–75.

Emling, S. (2002) 'Frequent fliers traveling light', *The Atlanta Journal – Constitution*, (January 30): A1, 12.

Endler, N. S. (1988) 'Interactionism revisited: a discussion of on the role of situations in personality research', in S. G. Cole and R. G. Demaree (eds), *Applications of Interactionist Psychology*. Hillsdale, NJ: Lawrence Erlbaum Associates.

Evans, K. R., Stan, S. and Murray, L. (2008) 'The customer socialization paradox: the mixed effects of communicating customer role expectations', *Journal of Services Marketing*, 22(3): 213–23.

Everhart, D. E., Shucard, J. L., Quatrin, T. and Shucard, D. (2001) 'Sex-related differences in event-related potentials, face recognition, and facial affect processing in prebuteral children', *Neuropsychology*, 15(3): 329–41.

Famulla, R. (1999) 'Centering on service', *Banking Strategies*, 75(6): 98–106.

Farr, R. M., (1996) *The Roots of Modern Social Psychology*. Oxford: Blackwell.

Feyereisen, P. and de Lannoy, J. D. (1991) *Gestures and Speech: Psychological Investigations*, Cambridge: Cambridge University Press.

Filipczak, B. (1991) 'Customer education (some assembly required)', *Training*, 28(12): 31–35.

Fisk, R. P., Brown, S. W. and Bitner, M. J. (1993) 'Tracking the evolution of the services marketing literature', *Journal of Retailing*, 69(1): 61–104.

Fisk, R. P., Grove, S. J. and John, J. (2004) *Interactive Services Marketing* (2nd edn). Boston, MA: Houghton Mifflin.

Fitzgibbon, M. (1988) Support your customer service. *Management World*, 17(1), 7–8.

Ford, W. S. Z. (1998) *Communicating with Customers*. Cresskill, NJ: Hampton Press.

Fournier, S., Dobscha, S. and Mick, D. G. (1998) 'Preventing the premature death of relationship marketing', *Harvard Business Review*, 76(1): 42–44.

Fritz, J. (1999) 'Traveling the highway to "wow!" service', in R. Zemke and J. A. Woods (eds), *Best Practices in Customer Service*. Amherst, MA: HRD Press.

Furlong, C. B. (1993) *Marketing for Keeps*. New York: John Wiley & Sons.

Furnham, A. (2002) 'Happy staff is not the full answer: management style can be reflected in customer service – but the relationship is complex', *The Financial Times*. (February 5): 16.

—— (1999) *Body Language at Work*. Channel Islands: The Guernsey Press.

Garrett, J. (2001) 'The human side of brand: why Audi hires workers with the same traits as its luxury cars', *Gallup Management Journal*, (Summer): 4–5.

Gebhardt, G. F., Carpenter, G. S. and Sherry, J. F. (2006) 'Creating and market orientation: a longitudinal, multiform, grounded analysis of cultural transformation', *Journal of Marketing*, 70(4): 37–55.

Geddes, L. (1993) *Through the Customers' Eyes*. New York: AMACOM.

George, R. (2000) Legendary customer service at the Ritz-Carlton. Management Symposium Emory Hospital, November 10, Training Seminar.

Gergen, K. J. (1994) *Realities and Relationships*. Cambridge, MA: Harvard University Press.

Gilbert, D. (1996) 'Airlines', in F. Buttle (ed.), *Relationship Marketing*. London: Paul Chapman.

Gilly, M. C. and Wolfinbarger, M. (1998) 'Advertising's internal audience', *Journal of Marketing*, 62(1): 69–88.

Gilpin, S. C. (1996) 'Hospitality'. in F. Buttle (ed.), *Relationship Marketing*. London: Paul Chapman.

Gitomer, J. (2000) 'Great customer service begins with employees'. *Atlanta Business Chronicle*, (April 21–27): 3B.

—— (2002) 'What's wrong with (your) customer service?' *Atlanta Business Chronicle* (October 4–10): 2B.

Goffman, E. (1966 'Presentation biases'. in B. J. Biddle and E. J. Thomas (eds), *Role Theory*. New York: John Wiley & Sons.

Goodman, J. (1999) 'Quantifying the impact of great customer service on profitability'. in R. Zemke and J. A. Woods (eds), *Best Practices in Customer Service*. Amherst, MA: HRD Press.

Goodman, J. and Yanovsky, M. (1997) 'Treating employees as customers: estimating the bottom line impact of employee dissatisfaction and setting rational priorities'. *Customer Relationship Management*, (September): 22–25.

Goodwin, C. (1998) 'Privacy as a dimension of service experience', in Sherry, J. F. (ed.), *ServiceScapes*. Chicago: NTC Business Books.

Gonos, G. (1977) 'Situation vs. frame: the interactionist and the structuralist analyses of everyday life', paper presented at American Sociological Association meeting, Chicago, September.

Grayson, K. (1998) 'Customer responses to emotional labor in discrete and relational service exchange', *International Journal of Service Industry Management*, 9: 126–54.

Gremler, D. D., Gwinner, K. P. and Brown, S. W. (2001) 'Generating positive word-of-mouth communication through customer-employee relationships', *International Journal of Service Industry Management*, 12(1): 44–59.

Griffin, J. (1995) *Customer Loyalty*. New York: Lexington Books.

Griffin, R. (1994) 'Critical success factors of lodging yield management systems', doctoral dissertation, Virginia Polytechnic Institute and State University.

Grove, S. J. and Fisk, R. P. (1997) 'The impact of other customers on service experiences: a critical incident examination of getting along', *Journal of Retailing*, 73(1): 63–85.

Gruber, K. J. (1980) 'Sex-typing of leisure activities: a current appraisal', *Psychological Reports*, 46: 259–65.

Guerin, B. (1994) *Analyzing Social Behavior: Behavior Analysis and the Social Sciences*. Reno, NV: Context Press.

Gupta, S. and Vajic, M. (2000) 'The contextual and dialectical nature of experiences'. in J. A. Fitzsimmons and M. J. Fitzsimmons (eds), *New Service Development*. Thousand Oaks, CA: Sage.

Gutek, B. A. (1995) *The Dynamics of Service*. San Francisco, CA: Jossey-Bass.

—— (1999) 'The social psychology of service interactions'. *Journal of Social Issues*. 55(3): 603–17.

Gwinner. K. P., Gremler, D. D. and Bitner, M. J. (1998) Relational benefits in services industries: the customer's perspective'. *Journal of the Academy of Marketing Science*. 26(2): 101–14.

Hall, E. J. (1993) 'Smiling, deferring. and flirting: doing gender by giving good service', *Work and Occupations*, 20(4): 452–71.

Hallberg, G. (1995) *All Consumers Are Not Created Equal*. New York: John Wiley & Sons.

Hallett, J. J. (1990) 'Retailing in the 1990's: love your customers or lose them', *Retail Control*, 58(2): 8–13.

Hanan, M. and Karp, P. (1989) *Customer Satisfaction*. New York: AMACOM.

Harris, R. L. (1991) *The Customer Is King*. Milwaukee, WI: ASQC Quality Press.

Hartley, J. (1999) 'Cooling the customer with heat'. in R. Zemke and J. A. Woods (eds). *Best Practices in Customer Service*. Amherst, MA: HRD Press.

Hartline, M.D. and Ferrell, O.C. (1993) *Service Quality Implementation: The Effects of Organizational Socialization and Managerial Actions on Customer-Contact Employee Behaviors*. Boston, MA: Marketing Science Institute.

—— (1996) 'The management of customer-contact service employees: an empirical investigation', *Journal of Marketing*, 60(4): 52–70.

Hays, J. M. and Hill, A. V. (2001) 'A longitudinal study of the effect of a service guarantee on service quality', *Production and Operations Management*, 10(4): 405–19.

Hays. J. M., Hill, A. V., Guers, S. E., John, G., Johnson, D. W. and Swanson, R. A. (2000) 'The impact of service guarantees on service quality at Radisson Hotel Worldwide', in J. A Fitzsimmons and. J. M. Fitzsimmons (eds), *Service Product Design*. Thousand Oaks, CA: Sage.

Healy, M. (1996) 'Max Weber's comeback: wearing topical hats', *People Management*, (January 11): 17.

Heil, G., Parker, T. and Stephens, D. C. (1997) *One Size Fits One*. New York: Van Nostrand Reinhold.

Heney, P. J. (2008) 'When free isn't really so free anymore', *Hotel and Motel Management*, 225(17): 6.

Hennig-Thurau, T., Gwinner, K. P. and Gremler, D. D. (2000) 'Why customers build relationships with companies-and why not', in T Hennig-Thurau and U. Hansen (eds), *Relationship Marketing*. New York: Springer.

Hennig-Thurau, T., Groth, M., Paul, M. and Gremier, D. D. (2006) 'Are all smiles created equal? How emotional contagion and emotional labor affect service relationships', *Journal of Marketing*. 70 (July): 58–73.

Hensel, J. S. (1990) 'Service quality improvement and control: a customer-based approach', *Journal of Business Research*, 20(1): 43–54.

Hess, R. L., Ganesan, S. and Klein, N. M. (2003) 'Service failure and recovery: the impact of relationship factors on customer satisfaction', *Journal of the Academy of Marketing Science*, 31(2): 127–45.

Heskett, J. L., Sasser, E. W. and Hart, C. W. L. (1990) *Service Breakthroughs: Changing Rules of the Game*. New York: Free Press.

Heskett, J. L., Sasser, E. W. and Schlesinger, L. A. (1997) *The Service Profit Chain*. New York: The Free Press.

Hilton, C. (1987) *Be My Guest*. New York: Prentice Hall.

Hinkin, T. R. and Tracey, J. B. (2000) 'The cost of turnover', *Cornell Hospitality Quarterly*, 41(2): 14–21.

Hintz, R. A. and Miller, D. E. (1995) Openings revisited: the foundations of social interaction. *Symbolic Interaction*, 18(3): 355–69.

Hochschild, A. R. (1983) *The Managed Heart: Commercialization of Human Feeling*. Berkeley: University of California Press.

Hodgson, J. D., Sano, Y. and Graham, J. L. (2000) *Doing Business with the New Japan*. Boulder, CO: Rowman & Littlefield.

Holm, O (1997) 'Ratings of empathic communication: does experience make a difference?' *Journal of Psychology*, 131(6): 680–81.

Horovitz, J. and Panak, M. J. (1994) *Total Customer Satisfaction*. London: *Financial Times* with Pitman Publishing.

Houston, M. B., Bettencourt, L. A. and Wenger, S. (1998) 'The relationship between waiting in a service queue and evaluations of service quality: a field theory perspective', *Psychology and Marketing*, 15(8): 735–53.

Iacobucci, D. (1998) 'Customer service interaction', in Sherry, J. F. (ed.), *ServiceScapes*. Chicago: NTC Business Books.

Ivins, M. (1999) 'From Texas, with love and peanuts', *New York Times*, March 14.

Jeschke, K., Schulze, H. S. and Bauersachs, J. (2000) 'Internal marketing and its consequences for complaint handling effectiveness', in T. Hennig-Thurau and U. Hansen (eds), *Relationship Marketing*. New York: Springer.

Jogaratnam, G. and Tse, E. (2006) 'Entrepreneurial orientation and the structuring of organizations: performance evidence from the Asian hotel industry', *International Journal of Contemporary Hospitality Management*, 18(6): 454–68.

Johnston, M. (2003) 'Frequent flier alert', *Money*, 5 December.

de Jong, J. P. and Den Hartog, D. N. (2007) 'How leaders influence employees' innovative behavior', *European Journal of Innovation Management*, 10(1): 41–64.

Joseph-Mathews, S. and Bonn, M. A. (2009) 'The service environment: functional or fun? Does it matter?' *International Journal of Culture, Tourism and Hospitality Research*, 3(3): 187–92.

Justice, M. (1984) 'Proper explanation of exclusion can reduce claims problems', *Rough Notes*, 127(4): 46–48.

Kaikati, A. M. and Kaikati, J. G. (2004) 'Stealth marketing: how to reach consumers surreptitiously', *California Management Review*, 46(4): 6–22.

Kandampully, J. A. (2007) *Services Management: The New Paradigm in Hospitality*. Upper Saddle River, NJ: Pearson–Prentice Hall.

Karande, K., Magnini, V. P. and Tam, L. (2007) 'Recovery voice and satisfaction after service failure: an experimental investigation into mediating and moderating factors', *Journal of Service Research*, 10(2): 187–203.

Karatepe, O. M. and Sokmen, A. (2006) 'The effects of work role and family role variables on psychological and behavioral outcomes of frontline employees', *Tourism Management*, 27(2): 255–68.

Karatepe, M., Yorganci, I. and Haktanir, M. (2009) 'Outcomes of Customer Verbal Aggression among Hotel Employees', *International Journal of Contemporary Hospitality Management*, 21(6): 713–33.

Kaydo, C. (2000) 'Start making sense', *Sales and Marketing Management*, 152(3): 88.

Kelley, S. W., Donnelly, J. H. Jr and Skinner, S. J. (1990) 'Customer participation in service production and delivery', *Journal of Retailing*, 66(3): 315–35.

Kelly, J. R. (1981) 'Leisure interaction and the social dialectic', *Social Forces*, 60(2): 304–22.

Kim, W. G., Han, J. S. and Lee, E. (2001) 'Effects of relationship marketing on repeat purchase and word of mouth', *Journal of Hospitality and Tourism Research*, 25(3): 272–88.

Kirca, A. H., Jayachandran, S. and Bearden, W. O. (2005) 'Market orientation: a meta-analytic review and assessment of its antecedents and impact on performance', *Journal of Marketing*, 69(2): 24–41.

Knutson, B. (2001) 'Service quality monitoring and feedback systems', in J. Kandampully, C. Mok and B. Sparks (eds), *Service Quality Management in Hospitality, Tourism and Leisure*. Binghamton, NY: Haworth Hospitality Press.

Kozak, M. (2003) 'Measuring tourist satisfaction with multiple destination attributes', *Tourism Analysis*, 7(3/4): 229–40.

Kyi, M. J. (1989) 'International customer service as a new competitive tool', *International Journal of Physical Distribution & Materials Management*, 19(10): 4–9.

Labone, M. (1996) 'The roaring silence in the sociology of leisure', *Social Alternatives*, 15: 30–32.

Labroo, A. A., Dhar, R. and Schwarz, N. (2008) 'Of frog wines and frowning watches: semantic priming, perceptual fluency, and brand evaluation', *Journal of Consumer Research*, 34 (April): 819–31.

Lamb, W. and Watson, E. (1979) *Body Code*. Princeton, NJ: Princeton Book Company.

Laws, E. (2004) *Improving Tourism and Hospitality Services*, Wallingford, UK: CABI Publishing.

Lee-Ross, D. (2001) 'Understanding the role of the service encounter in tourism, hospitality, and leisure services', in J. Kandampully, C. Mok and B. Sparks (eds), *Service Quality Management in Hospitality, Tourism and Leisure*. Binghamton, NY: Haworth Hospitality Press.

Lengnick-Hall, C. A. (1996) 'Customer contributions to quality: a different view of the customer-oriented firm', *Academy of Management Review*, 21(3): 791–824.

Levinson, R. E. (1988) 'Obsession – the magic ingredient (part 1)', *American Salesman*, 33(7): 26–30.

Lewin, R. and Regine, B. (2000) *The Soul at Work*. New York: Simon & Schuster.

Liljander, V. (2000) 'The importance of internal relationship marketing for external relationship success', in T. Hennig-Thurau and U. Hansen (eds), *Relationship Marketing*. New York: Springer.

Lim, T. S. (1994) 'Facework and interpersonal relationships', in Ting-Toomey, S. (ed.), *The Challenge of Facework*. Albany, NY: State University of New York Press.

Lin, C. (2002) 'Segmenting customer brand preference: demographic or psychographic', *Journal of Product and Brand Management*, 11(4/5): 249–68.

Liswood, L. A. (1987) 'Once you've got'em never let'em go', *Sales & Marketing Management*, 139(7): 73–77.
—— (1990) *Serving Them Right*. New York: Harper Business.
Littlejohn, S. W. (1983) *Theories of Human Communication*. Belmont, CA: Wadsworth Publishing Co.
Locander, W. B. (1989) 'Brokering marketing into total quality'. *Survey of Business*, 25(1): 31–35.
Lowenstein, M. W. (1997) *The Customer Loyalty Pyramid*. Westport, CT: Quorum Books.
Macaleer, T. S. (1995) *Specializing in Different Customer Types*, Report No. 1121-95-CH: 29–30. New York: The Conference Board. www.conference-board.org
Macaulay, S. and Cook, S. (1993) 'Managing and training for customer service'. *Management Development Review*, 6(6): 19–23.
Macdonald, C. L. and Sirianni, C. (1996) 'The service society and the changing experience of work'. in C. L. Macdonald and C. Sirianni (eds). *Working in the Service Society*. Philadelphia: Temple University Press.
Magnini, V. P. and Ford, J. B. (2004) 'Service Failure Recovery in China'. *International Journal of Contemporary Hospitality Management*, 16(5): 279–86.
Magnini, V. P. and Honeycutt, E. D. (2005) 'Face Recognition and Name Recall: Training Implications for the Hospitality Industry', *Cornell Hospitality Quarterly*, 46(1): 69–78.
Magnini, V. P. and Karande, K. (2010) 'An experimental investigation into the use of written smell references in ecotourism print advertisements', *Journal of Hospitality and Tourism Research* (in press).
Magnini, V. P., Honeycutt, E. D. and Hodge, S. K. (2003) 'Data mining for hotel firms: use and limitations', *Cornell Hospitality Quarterly*, 44(2): 94–106.
Magnini, V. P., Ford, J. B., Markowski, E. P. and Honeycutt, E. D. (2007) 'The service recovery paradox: justifiable theory or smoldering myth?' *Journal of Services Marketing*, 21(3): 213–25.
Maister, D. (1989) 'Marketing to existing clients', in A. Payne, C. Martin, M. Clark and H. Peck (eds), *Relationship Marketing for Competitive Advantage* (1998 edn). Oxford: Butterworth-Heinemann.
Malhotra, V. A. (1980) 'Power and communication: an outline of a critical symbolic interaction', paper presented at the ASA Annual Meeting, August.
Manstead, A. S. R. (1996) 'Situations, belongingness, attitudes, and culture: four lessons learned from social psychology', in C. McGarty and S. A. Haslam (eds), *The Message of Social Psychology*. Oxford: Blackwell.
—— (1998) 'De rol van affect bij de vorming en varandering van attitudes: The role of affect in attitude formation and attitude change', in G. Bartels, W. Nelissen and H. Ruelle (eds), *De transactionele overheid: Communicatie als instrument*. Amsterdam: Kluwer.
Marr, N. E. (1994) 'Do managers really know what service their customers require?' *International Journal of Physical Distribution & Logistics Management*, 24(4): 24–31.
Martin, J. (2002) 'Professionalism disappearing', *The Atlanta Journal – Constitution*, January 27, M2.
de Matos, C. A., Henrique, J. L. and Rossi, C. A. (2007) 'Service recovery paradox: a meta analysis', *Journal of Service Research*, 10(1): 60–77.
Mattila, A. S. (2004) 'The impact of service failures on customer loyalty', *International Journal of Services Industry Management*, 15(2): 134–49.

Mattila, A. S. and Ro, H. (2008) 'Customer satisfaction, service failure, and service recovery', in H. Oh and A. Pizam (eds), *Handbook of Hospitality and Marketing Management*. Amsterdam: Elsevier.

Maxham, J. (2001) 'Service recovery's influence on consumer satisfaction, positive word-of-mouth, and purchase intentions', *Journal of Business Research*, 54 (November): 11–24.

Maxham, J. and Netemeyer, R. (2002) 'A longitudinal study of complaining customers' evaluations of multiple service failures and recovery efforts', *Journal of Marketing*, 66 (October): 57–71.

—— (2003) 'Firms reap what they sow: the effects of shared values and perceived organizational justice on customers' evaluations of complaint handling', *Journal of Marketing*, 67(1): 46–62.

McColl-Kennedy, J. R., Daus, C. S. and Sparks, B. A. (2003) 'The role of gender in reactions to service failure and recovery', *Journal of Service Research*, 6(1): 66–82.

McCormick, A. E. and Kinloch, G. C. (1986) 'Interracial contact in the customer-clerk situation', *Journal of Social Psychology*, 126(4): 551–53.

McCroskey, J. C. and Richmond, V. P. (1987) 'Willingness to communicate', in J. C. McCroskey and J. A. Daly (eds), *Personality and Interpersonal Communication*. Newbury Park, CA: Sage.

McHugh, P. (1968) *'Defining the Situation*. New York: The Bobbs-Merrill Co.

McMullan, R. and Gilmore, R. (2008) 'Customer loyalty: an empirical study', *European Journal of Marketing*, 42(9/10): 1084–94.

Mead, G. H. (1934) *Mind, Self and Society*, Chicago: University of Chicago Press.

Meuter, M. L., Bitner, M. J., Ostrom, A. L. and Brown, S. W. (2005) 'Choosing among alternative service delivery modes: an investigation of customer trial of self-service technologies', *Journal of Marketing*, 69(2): 61–83.

Meyer, A. and Blumelhuber, C. (2000) 'Relationship marketing success through investments in services', in T. Hennig-Thurau and U. Hansen (eds), *Relationship Marketing*. New York: Springer.

Meyers, S. L. (2001) 'Loyal employers reap benefits', *The Atlanta Journal – Constitution*, November 29th, G1, 4.

Michel, S. (2001) 'Analyzing service failures and recoveries: a process approach', *International Journal of Service Industry Management*, 12(1): 20.

Michelli, J. (2008) *The New Gold Standard*. New York: McGraw-Hill.

Mohr, L. A. and Henson, S. W. (1996) 'Impact of employee gender and job congruency on customer satisfaction', *Journal of Consumer Psychology*, 5(2): 161–87.

Mook, J. R. (1996) 'Personality testing in today's workplace: avoiding the legal pit-falls', *Employee Relations*, 22(3): 66–88.

Morgan, R. L. (1999) 'Six tools for improving how you deliver service to customers', in R. Zemke and J. A. Woods (eds), *Best Practices in Customer Service*. Amherst, MA: HRD Press.

Morgan, R. M. and Hunt, S. D. (1994) 'The commitment and trust theory of relationship marketing', *Journal of Marketing*, 58(3): 20–39.

Morgan, R. M., Crutchfield, T. N. and Lacey, R. (2000) 'Patronage and loyalty strategies: understanding the behavioral and attitudinal outcomes of customer retention programs', in T. Hennig-Thurau and U. Hansen (eds), *Relationship Marketing*. New York: Springer.

Morisaki, S. and Gudykunst, W. D. (1994) 'Face in Japan and the United States', in S. Ting-Toomey (ed.), *The Challenge of Facework*. Albany, NY: State University of New York Press.

Moutinho, L. (1987) 'Consumer behaviour in tourism', *European Journal of Marketing*, 21(10): 5–44.

Mulford, M., Orbell, J., Shatto, C. and Stockard, J. (1998) 'Physical attractiveness, opportunity, and success in everyday exchange', *American Journal of Sociology*, 103(6): 1565–92.

Murphy, J. A. (1996) 'Retail banking', in F. Buttle (ed.), *Relationship Marketing*. London: Paul Chapman.

Myers, D. G. (2005) *Social Psychology* (8th edn). New York: McGraw-Hill.

Narcisse, S. and Harcourt, M. (2008) 'Employee fairness perceptions of performance appraisal: a Saint Lucian case study', *International Journal of Human Resource Management*, 19(6): 1152–69.

Naumann, E. (1995) *Creating Customer Value*. Cincinnati, OH: Thomason Executive Press.

Naylor, G. (2003) 'The complaining customer: a service provider's best friend?', *Journal of Consumer Satisfaction, Dissatisfaction and Complaining Behavior*, 16: 241–48.

Netemeyer, R. E., Maxham, J. G. and Pullig, C. (2005) 'Conflicts in the work–family interface: links to job stress, customer service employee performance, and customer purchase intent', *Journal of Marketing*, 69(2): 130–43.

Neumann, M. (1992) 'The trail through experience', in C. Ellis and M. G. Flaherty (eds), *Investigating Subjectivity*. Newbury Park, CA: Sage.

Newton, S (1992) 'Customer obsession', *Managing Service Quality*, 2(1): 269–74.

Nininen, O., Buhalis, D. and March, R. (2007) 'Customer empowerment in tourism through consumer centric marketing', *Qualitative Marketing Research: An International Journal*, 10(3): 1352–2752.

Noe, F. P. (1999) *Tourist Service Satisfaction*. Champaign, IL: Sagamore Publishing.

Noe, F. P. and Uysal, M. (2003) 'Social interaction linkages in the service satisfaction model', *Journal of Quality Assurance in Hospitality & Tourism*, 4(3/4): 23–35.

Noe, F. P., Uysal, M. and Jurowski, C. (1993) 'Effects of user and trip characteristics on responses to communication messages', in M. Uysal and D. Fesenmaier (eds), *Communication and Channel Systems in Tourism Marketing*. New York: Haworth Press.

Nucifora, A. (2000) Resolve customer problems like a fighter pilot. *Arrivals*, 3(30): 20.

Nunes, J. C. and Dreze, X. (2006) 'The endowed progress effect: how artificial advancement increases effort', *Journal of Consumer Research*, 32(4): 504–12.

Nygaard, A. and Dahlstrom, R. (2002) 'Role stress and effectiveness of horizontal alliances', *Journal of Marketing*, 66(2): 28–45.

Oh, H. (2003) 'Reexamining recovery paradox effects and impact of ranges of service failure and recovery', *Journal of Hospitality and Tourism Research*, 27(4): 402–18.

Okun, J. (2002) 'Great service makes a great meal', *The Buffalo News*, (August 14): D1 continued on D4.

Oliver, R. L. (1997) *Satisfaction: A Behavioral Perspective on the Consumer*. New York: Irwin/McGraw-Hill.

Oliver, R. L. and Burke, R. R. (1999) 'Expectation processes in satisfaction formation', *Journal of Service Research*, 1 (February): 196–214.

Panter, C. A. and Martin, C. L. (1991) 'Compatibility management: roles in service performers', *Journal of Services Marketing*, 5(2): 43–53.

Pease, A. and Pease, B. (2004) *The Definitive Book of Body Language.* New York: Bantam Dell.

Peccei, R. and Rosenthal, P. (2000) 'The antecedents of employee commitment to service: evidence from a UK service context', *International Journal of Human Resource Management,* 8(1): 66–86.

Peck, J. and Wiggins, J. (2006) 'It just feels good: customers' affective response to touch and influence on persuasion', *Journal of Marketing,* 70(4): 56–69.

Pelham, B. W. and Hetts, J. J. (1999) 'Implicit and explicit personal and social identity: toward a more complete understanding of the social self', in T. R. Tyler. R. M. Kramer and O. P. John (eds), *The Psychology of the Social Self.* Mahwah, NJ: Lawrence Erlbaum Associates.

Percy, T. (1998) 'On listening to customers', *Forbes,* 1 (September): 64.

Perris, G. and Scott, P. (1991) 'Building strategic customer relations', *Communications,* 28(10): 79–85.

Peter, J. P. and Olson, J. C. (2002) *Consumer Behavior and Marketing Strategy* (6th edn). New York: McGraw-Hill.

Peters, T. (1991) '20 ideas on service', *Executive Excellence,* 8(7): 3–5.

Petite, A. (1989) *The Manager's Guide to Service Excellence.* Toronto, Canada: Summerhill Press.

Piccoli, G. (2008) 'Information technology in hotel management', *Cornell Hospitality Quarterly,* 49(3): 282–96.

Pickard, J. (1993) 'The real meaning of empowerment', in A. Payne. C. Martin. M. Clark and H. Peck (eds), *Relationship Marketing for Competitive Advantage* (1998 edn). Oxford: Butterworth-Heinemann.

Pinar, M. and Rogers, J. D. (2000) 'Examining the impact of town and resort related factors on tourist satisfaction: a study in Bodrum, Turkey', *Tourism Analysis,* 4(2): 95–103.

Pinker, S. (2002) *The Blank Slate: The Modern Denial of Human Nature.* New York: Viking Penguin.

Plog, S. (2001) 'Why destinations rise and fall in popularity: an update of a Cornell Quarterly Classic', *Cornell Hospitality Quarterly,* 42 (June): 13–24.

Prelec, D. and Lowenstein, G. (1998) 'The red and the black: mental accounting of savings and debt', *Marketing Science,* 17 (Winter): 4–28.

Preston, P. (2005) 'Nonverbal communication: do we really say what we mean?' *Journal of Healthcare Management,* 50(2): 83–86.

Prus, R. (1996) *Symbolic Interaction and Ethnographic Research.* Albany, NY: State University of New York Press.

Raimondo, M. A., Miceli, G. and Costabile, G. (2008) 'How relationship age moderates loyalty formation: the increasing effect of relational equity on customer loyalty', *Journal of Service Research,* 11(2): 142–60.

Ramsey, R. P. and Sohi, R. S. (1997) 'Listening to your customers: the impact of perceived listening behavior on relationship outcomes', *Journal of the Academy of Marketing Science,* 25(2): 127–37.

Reich, R. (1998) 'The care and feeding of the rich', *The New York Times,* (April 5): WK15.

Reichheld, F. F. (1994) 'Loyalty and the renaissance of marketing', in A. Payne, C. Martin, M. Clark and H. Peck (eds), *Relationship Marketing for Competitive Advantage* (1998 edn). Oxford: Butterworth-Heinemann.

Reichheld, F. F. (2001) *Loyalty Rules.* Boston, MA: Harvard Business School Press.

Reidenbach, R. E., McClung, G. W. and Goeke, R. W. (1999) 'How to let customer value drive customer problem solving', in R. Zemke and J. A. Woods (eds), *Best Practices in Customer Service*. Amherst, MA: HRD Press.

Reynolds, K. L. and Harris, L. C. (2005) 'When service failure is not service failure: an exploration of the forms and motives of "illegitimate' customer complaining"', *Journal of Services Marketing*, 19(5), 321–35.

Ries, A. and Trout, J. (1994) *The 22 Immutable Laws of Marketing: Violate Them at Your Own Risk*. New York: Harper Business.

Roberts, C. (2001) 'Competitive advantages of service quality in hospitality, tourism, and leisure sciences', in J. Kandampully, C. Mok and B. Sparks (eds), *Service Quality Management in Hospitality, Tourism and Leisure*. Binghamton, NY: Haworth Hospitality Press.

Roscitt, R. (1990) 'Strategic service management'. *Journal of Business & Industrial Marketing*, 5(1): 27–40.

Rosenberger (2000) 'Relationship marketing from customer policy perspective', in T. Hennig-Thurau and U. Hansen (eds), *Relationship Marketing*. New York: Springer.

Rowley, G. and Purcell, K. (2001) 'As cooks go, she went': is labor churn inevitable?', *International Journal of Hospitality Management*, 20(2): 163–85.

Rust, R. T., Zahorik, A. J. and Keiningham, T. L. (1994) *Return on Quality Measuring the Financial Impact of Your Company's Quest for Quality*. Burr Ridge, IL: Irwin.

Rust, R. T., Zahonik, A. J. and Keiningham, T. L. (1995) 'Return on quality (ROQ): making service quality financially accountable', *Journal of Marketing*, 59 (April): 58–70.

Rust, R. T., Zeithaml, V. A. and Lemon, K. N. (2000) *Driving Customer Equity*. New York: The Free Press.

Rust, R. T., Moorman, C. and Dickson, P. R. (2002) 'Getting return on quality: revenue expansion, cost reduction, or both?' *Journal of Marketing*, 66(4): 7–24.

Rust, R. T., Lemon, K. N. and Zeithaml, V. A. (2004a) 'Return on marketing: using customer equity to focus marketing strategies', *Journal of Marketing*, 68(1): 109–27.

Rust, R. T., Zeithaml, V. A. and Lemon, K. N. (2004b) 'Customer-centered brand management', *Harvard Business Review*, 82(9): 110–18.

de Ruyter, K. and Wetzels, M. (2000) 'The impact of perceived listening behavior in voice-to-voice service encounters', *Journal of Service Research*, 2(3): 276–84.

Saks, A. M., Uggerslev, K. L. and Fassina, N. E. (2007) 'Socialization tactics and newcomer adjustment: a meta-analytic review and test of a model', *Journal of Vocational Behavior*, 70(3): 413–46.

Schaaf, D. (1995) *Keeping the Edge*. New York: Dutton.

Scheuing, D. E. (1999) 'Delighting your customers: creating world-class service', in R. Zemke and J. A. Woods (eds), *Best Practices in Customer Service*. Amherst, MA: HRD Press.

Schutte, N., Malouff, J., Hall, L., Haggerty, D., Cooper, J., Golden, C. and Dornheim, L. (1998) 'Development and validation of a measure of emotional intelligence', *Personality and Individual Differences*, 25: 167–77.

Seelig, B. J. and Rosof, L. S. (2001) 'Normal and pathological altruism', *Journal of the American Psychoanalytic Association*, 49(3): 933–59.

Seibert, S. E., Silver, S. R. and Randolph, W. A. (2004) 'Taking empowerment to the next level: a multiple-level model of empowerment, performance, and satisfaction', *Academy of Management Journal*, 47(3): 332–49.

Semin, G. R. (1997) 'The relevance of language for social psychology', in C. McGarty and S. A. Haslam (eds), *The Message of Social Psychology*. Cambridge, MA: Blackwell.

Sharma, A. and Lambert, D. M. (1990) 'Segmentation of markets based on customer service', *International Journal of Physical Distribution & Logistics Management*, 20(7): 19–27.

Sherif, M. and Sherif, C. W. (1969) *Social Psychology*. New York: Harper & Row.

Shoham, A. and Ruvio, A. (2008) 'Opinion leaders and followers: a replication and extension'. *Psychology and Marketing*, 25(3): 280–97.

Sirgy, M. J. and Su, C. (2000) 'Destination image, self-congruity, and travel behavior: Toward an integrated model', *Journal of Travel Research*, 38(4): 340–52.

Smith, A. K., Bolton, R. N. and Wagner, J. (1998) *A Model of Customer Satisfaction with Service Encounters Involving Failure and Recovery*, Report No. 98-100. Cambridge, MA: Marketing Science Institute.

Smith, E. R. and Mackie, D. M. (1997) 'Integrating the psychology and the social to understand human behavior', in C. McGarty and S. A. Haslam (eds), *The Message of Social Psychology*. Cambridge, MA: Blackwell.

Smith, S. (1999) 'How to create a plan to deliver great customer service', in R. Zemke and J. A. Woods (eds), *Best Practices in Customer Service*. Amherst, MA: HRD Press.

Smith, S. W. (1995) 'Perceptual processing of nonverbal-relational messages', in D. E. Hewes (ed.), *The Cognitive Bases of Interpersonal Communication*. Hillsdale, NJ: LEA Publishers.

Solomon, C. M. (1989) 'How does Disney do it?' *Personnel Journal*, 68(12): 50–57.

Solomon, M. R. (1998) 'Dressing for the part', in J. F. Sherry (ed.), *ServiceScapes*. Chicago: NTC Business Books.

Solomon, M. R., Surprenant, C., Czepiel, J. A. and Gutman, E. G. (1985) 'A role perspective on dyadic interactions: the service encounter', *Journal of Marketing*, 49(1): 99–111.

Sparks, B. (2001) 'Managing service failure through recovery', in J. Kandampully, C. Mok and B. Sparks (eds), *Service Quality Management in Hospitality, Tourism and Leisure*. Binghamton, NY: Haworth Hospitality Press.

Steele, F. I. (1979) 'The instrumental relationship', in W. Bennis, J. Van Maanen, E. H. Schein and F. I. Steele (eds), *Essays in Interpersonal Dynamics*. Homewood, IL: The Dorsey Press.

Steele, R. S. (1979) 'Psychoanalysis and hermeneutics', *International Review of Psycho-Analysis*, 6: 389–411.

Stryker, S. (1997) 'In the beginning there is society. Lessons from a sociological social psychology', in C. McGarty and S. A. Haslam (eds), *The Message of Social Psychology*. Cambridge, MA: Blackwell.

Sundaram, D. S. and Webster, C. (2000) 'The role of nonverbal communication in service encounters', *Journal of Services Marketing*, 14(5): 378–91.

Tansik, D. A. and Smith, W. L. (2000) 'Scripting the service encounter', in J. A. Fitzsimmons and M. J. Fitzsimmons (eds), *New Service Development*. Thousand Oaks, CA: Sage.

Tax, S. S., Brown, S. and Chandrashekaran, M. (1998) 'Customer evaluations of service complaint experiences: implications for relationship marketing', *Journal of Marketing*, 62(2): 60–76.

Tax, S. S., Colgate, M. and Bowen, D. E. (2006) 'How to prevent your customers from failing', *Sloan Management Review*, 47: 30–38.

Thelen, S., Mottner, S. and Berman, B. (2004) 'Data mining: on the trail to market gold', *Business Horizons*, 47(6): 25–32.

Thibaut, J. W. and Kelly, H. H. (1959) *The Social Psychology of Groups*. New York: Wiley & Sons.

Thomas, W. I. and Znaniecki, F. (1918) *The Polish Peasant in Europe and America: Monograph of an Immigrant Group*. Boston: Richard G. Badger/Gorham Press. www.archive.org/details/polishpeasantine01thomuoft

Timm, P. R. (1998) *Customer Service*. Upper Saddle River, NJ: Prentice Hall.

—— (2005) *Customer Service: Key to Career Success*. Upper Saddle River, NJ: Pearson-Prentice Hall.

Tisch, J. M. (2007) *Chocolates on the Pillow Aren't Enough: Reinventing the Customer Experience*. Hoboken, NJ: John Wiley & Sons.

Troyer, L. and Younts, C. W. (1997) 'Whose expectations matter? The relative power of first- and second-order expectations in determining social influence', *American Journal of Sociology*, 103(3): 692–732.

Tschohl, J. with Franzmeier, S. (1991) *Achieving Excellence through Customer Service*. Englewood Cliffs, NJ: Prentice Hall.

Turley, L. W. and Milliman, R. (2000) 'Atmospheric effects on shopping behavior: a review of the experimental evidence', *Journal of Business Research*, 49(2): 193–211.

Uysal, M. (1998) 'The determinants of tourism demand', in D. Ioannides and K. G. Debbage (eds), *The Economic Geography of the Tourist Industry*. London: Routledge.

—— (2006) 'Factors of satisfaction: a case study of Explore Park', in B. Prideux, G. Moscardo and E. Laws (eds), *Managing Tourism and Hospitality Services: Theory and International Applications*. Wallingford, UK: CABI.

Uysal, M. and Noe, P. F. (2002) 'Satisfaction in outdoor recreation and tourism settings', in E. Laws (ed), *Tourism Marketing: Quality and Service Management Perspectives*. London: Continuum.

Vandergriff, M. (1999) 'Building a picture of perfect service', in R. Zemke and J. A. Woods (eds), *Best Practices in Customer Service*. Amherst, MA: HRD Press.

Vargo, S. L. and Lusch, R. F. (2004) 'Evolving for a new dominant logic for marketing', *Journal of Marketing*, 68(1): 324–35.

Vavra, T. G. (1992) Aftermarketing. *How to Keep Customers for Life through Relationship Marketing*. Homewood, IL: Business One Irwin.

Venkatesan, R. and Kumar, V. (2004) 'A customer lifetime value framework for customer selection and retention', *Journal of Marketing*, 68(4): 106–25.

Vogel, V., Evanschitzky, H. and Ramaseshan, B. (2008) 'Customer equity drivers and future sales', *Journal of Marketing*, 72(4): 98–108.

Vogt, C. A., Fesenmaier, D. R. and MacKay, K. (1993) 'Functional and aesthetic information needs underlying the pleasure travel experience', *Journal of Travel & Tourism Marketing*, 2(2/3): 133–46.

Voss, G. B. and Parasuraman, A. (1995) *Prepurchase Preference and Postconsumption Satisfaction in a Service Exchange*, Report No. 95-113. Cambridge, MA: Marketing Science Institute.

Walker, J. L. (1995) 'Service encounter satisfaction: conceptualized', *Journal of Services Marketing*, 9(1): 5–14.

Wang, S. and Davis, L. (2008) 'Stemming the tide: dealing with the imbalance of customer relationship quality with the key contact employee versus the firm', *Journal of Services Marketing*. 22(7): 533–49.

Weinzimer, P. (1998) *Getting IT Right!* New York: John Wiley & Sons.

Wharton, A. S. (1996) 'Service with a smile: understanding the consequences of emotional labor', in C. L. Macdonald and C. Sirianni (eds), *Working in the Service Society.* Philadelphia: Temple University Press.

Wheeless, V. E. and Lashbrook, W. B. (1987) 'Style', in J. C. McCroskey and J. A. Daly (eds), *Personality and Interpersonal Communication.* Newbury Park, CA: Sage.

White, S. S. and Schneider, B. (1998) 'Climbing the commitment ladder: the impact on customer commitment of disconfirmation of service expectations', Report No. 98-108. Cambridge, MA: Marketing Science Institute.

Wiersema, F. (1996) *Customer Intimacy: Pick your Partners, Shape your Culture, Win Together.* Santa Monica, CA: Knowledge Exchange.

Wieseke, J., Ulrich, J., Christ, O. and Van Dick, R. (2007) 'Organizational identification as a determinant of customer orientation in service organizations', *Marketing Letters,* 18(4): 265–78.

Willingham, R. (1992) *Hey, I'M The Customer.* Englewood Cliffs, NJ: Prentice Hall.

Woods, J. A. (1999) 'Customer service value, and the systems view', in R. Zemke and J. A. Woods (eds), *Best Practices in Customer Service.* Amherst, MA: HRD Press.

Wyer, R. S., Swan, S. and Gruenfeld, D. H. (1995) 'Impression formation in informal conversations', *Social Cognition,* 13: 243.

Yeh, R., Pearlson, K. and Kosmetsky, G. (2000) *Zero Time.* New York: John Wiley & Sons.

Yesawich, P. C. (1991) 'The marketplace: getting to know you', *Lodging Hospitality,* 47(6): 64.

Yoo, J., Shin, S. and Yang, I. (2006) 'Key attributes of internal service recovery strategies as perceived by frontline food service employees', *International Journal of Hospitality Management,* 25(3): 496–509.

Yoon, Y. and Uysal, M. (2005) 'An examination of the effects of motivation and satisfaction on destination loyalty: a structural model', *Tourism Management,* 26: 45–56.

Yuksel, A., Kilinic, U. and Yuksel, F. (2006) 'Cross-national analysis of hotel customers' attitude toward complaining and their complaining behaviors', *Tourism Management,* 27(1): 11–24.

Zeithaml, V. A. and Bitner, M. J. (2000) *Services Marketing.* Boston, MA: Irwin McGraw-Hill.

Zeithaml, V. A., Parasuraman, A. and Berry, L. L. (1990) *Delivering Quality Service.* New York: The Free Press.

Zeithaml, V. A., Berry, L. L. and Parasurman, A. (1993) 'The nature and determinants of customer expectations of service', *Journal of the Academy of Marketing Science,* 21(1): 1–12.

Zeithaml, V. A., Berry, L. L. and Parasurman, A. (1996) 'The behavioral consequences of service quality', *Journal of Marketing,* 60(4): 31–46.

Zemke, R. (1999) 'Service recovery: turning oops! into opportunity', in R. Zemke and J. A. Woods (eds), *Best Practices in Customer Service.* Amherst, MA: HRD Press.

Zornitsky, J. (1995) *Frontline Facts,* Report No. 1121-95-CH: 13–15. New York: The Conference Board. www.conference-board.org

Zurcher, L. A. (1983) *Social Roles.* Beverly Hills, CA: Sage.

Index